Going To School

SUNY Series
Frontiers in Education

Philip G. Altbach, Editor
*In cooperation with the Graduate School of Education,
State University of New York at Buffalo*

The Frontiers in Education Series features and draws upon a range of disciplines and approaches in the analysis of educational issues and concerns, helping to reinterpret established fields of scholarship in education by encouraging the latest synthesis and research.

Books in the series include:

Going to School

The African-American Experience

Edited by
KOFI LOMOTEY

STATE UNIVERSITY OF NEW YORK PRESS

Published by
State University of New York Press, Albany

© 1990   State University of New York

For information, address State University of New York
Press, State University Plaza, Albany, N.Y., 12246

Library of Congress Cataloging-in-Publication Data

Going to school : the African-American experience / edited by Kofi
   Lomotey.
      p.   cm. — (SUNY series, frontiers in education)
   Includes bibliographical references.
   ISBN 0-7914-0317-3. — ISBN 0-7914-0318-1 (pbk.)
   1. Afro-Americans—Education.   2. Afro-American students—Social
conditions..   3. Academic achievement.   4. Achievement tests—United
States.   5. School improvement programs—United States—Case
studies.   I. Lomotey, Kofi.   II. Series.
LC2771.G65   1990
370'.089'96073—dc20   89-38816
                                                              CIP

10   9   8   7   6   5   4   3

Dedication

To my wife, Nahuja, and to my children, Shawnjua, Juba and Mbeja

To my mother, Eleanor Kelley, and to my sister, Saundra Kelley

Contents

Acknowledgments

Thanks go to Abdolramin Navehebrahum, Gage Blair, Valerie Cooley, and Junko Kanamura, four doctoral students in education at SUNY/ Buffalo: they were very helpful in the preparation of this volume.

I am appreciative of the comments of Gail Kelly, Mwalimu Shujaa, and David Nyberg on an earlier draft of the Introduction.

I am thankful to Sally Claydon; Carol Norris; Nancy Myers; and Pat Glinski for the typing of parts of the manuscript.

Finally, I acknowledge six men who, by their example and by their guidance, have, for many years, motivated me to strive to be, nay, demanded that I strive to be, the best that I can be: Hannibal Tirus Afrik, Mwalimu Shujaa, Alan Colón, Peter Harris, Arthur Brooks, and Yakubu Saaka.

About The Contributors

James R. Bliss is an Assistant Professor of educational administration at Rutgers—The State University of New Jersey. He received his Ph.D. degree from Cornell University. His research interests include topics in the administration and supervision of elementary and secondary schools.

Felix Boateng is the Director of the Black Education Program at Eastern Washington University in Cheney and Spokane, Washington. He also teaches courses in multicultural education in the University's Department of Education.

Margarida C. Carrasco completed her Ed.D. at Rutgers—The State University of New Jersey. She has extensive public school teaching experience in Portugal and in the United States.

James Comer is the Maurice Falk Professor of Child Psychiatry at the Yale Child Study Center. He is also the Associate Dean of the Yale School of Medicine.

Jacqueline Fleming, a Consulting Psychologist, is the author of the book, *Blacks in College,* and is an Adjunct Professor at Barnard College in New York City.

Janice Hale-Benson is an Associate Professor of Early Childhood Education at Cleveland State University and is the author of the book, *Black Children: Their Roots, Culture and Learning Styles.*

Norris Haynes is the Director of Research for the Yale Child Study Center School Development Program.

Asa G. Hilliard, III is the Fuller E. Callaway Professor of Urban Education at Georgia State University. He is an expert in the area of cultural bias in standardized tests.

Faustine C. Jones-Wilson is a Professor of Education at Howard University in Washington, DC, and is also the Editor-in-Chief of the *Journal of Negro Education.*

John U. Ogbu is a Professor of Anthropology at the University of California at Berkeley.

Booker Peek is an Associate Professor of Black Studies at Oberlin College in Oberlin, Ohio.

Joan Davis Ratteray is the President of the Institute of Independent Education, a nonprofit tax-exempt organization in Washington, DC, dedicated to providing technical assistance to independent schools, as well as research and dissemination on educational policies affecting the independent sector.

Mwalimu J. Shujaa is an Assistant Professor in the Educational Organization, Administration and Policy Department at SUNY/Buffalo and has done extensive work in the area of teacher culture and educational policy.

Barbara A. Sizemore is an Associate Professor and Chair in the Department of Black Community, Education, Research, and Development at the University of Pittsburgh and is the former Superintendent of Schools in Washington, DC.

About the Editor

Kofi Lomotey is an Assistant Professor of urban educational administration at SUNY/Buffalo. He is the author of *African-American Principals: School Leadership and Success* (Greenwood).

Preface

This volume, unlike previous literature on the topic, addresses a number of key issues related to the education of African-Americans. Moreover, the authors go beyond merely discussing these issues and suggest remedies in several areas related to improving the academic achievement of these students.

The volume presents a fresh dialogue, with new ideas, models, and theories, from compassionate, knowledgeable scholars who tackle critical topics and present clear, useful analyses and recommendations geared toward the formulation and implementation of practices and policies designed to improve the academic achievement of African-American students.

This volume will be valuable in a variety of classroom and organizational settings. It will be useful in the growing number of college courses focusing on urban schools where nearly one half of the students are African-American. Courses in teacher preparation can use the volume in their discussions on academic achievement. Black studies departments can use the book as a text when considering African-American education. National, state, and local organizations that focus partially or solely on the education of African-Americans will also find this text of value.

The contributors to *Going to School: The African-American Experience* tackle some very poignant and controversial issues related to the education of African-Americans—issues that have been masked as other less critical issues—and address them in ways that will contribute to a better understanding of the academic achievement of these students. This volume will be a valuable contribution to the dialogue around this critical issue and will serve as an impetus for increased efforts on various levels to achieve the goal of improving the achievement of African-American students.

Kofi Lomotey,
SUNY/Buffalo

Introduction

What is happening to African-American students in America's public schools? This is the pertinent, but often unanswered, question today. The question remains unanswered, in part, because it is rarely framed in that way. There is talk about the increasing cultural diversity in urban schools; indeed nearly 50 percent of urban students are African-American. There is talk about the increasing number of dropouts and about "at risk" students; African-American students fit into these categories in large numbers. There is talk about the inner-city students that the educational reform movement forgot; too often these students are African-American. The issue is invariably framed in terms of "at risk students," "inner-city students," and most recently, "the children of the underclass."

Much that has been written regarding the academic achievement of African-American students has come from institutions and individuals outside of the African-American community. It is the African-American "problem" as viewed by others. More often the thrust has not been toward improving the status of this group. The focus is all too often on the problem, with little discussion of a remedy.

Indeed, the status of African-American students is the most critical issue facing educators today. Will we rise to the challenge, as we approach the twenty-first century, and create an environment where African-Americans will be able to compete academically in America's public schools? We must. More is at stake than the life chances of African-Americans. The future of our entire country depends upon how well we educate African-Americans and other minorities in the years ahead.

The truth is that much is known about the condition of African-American education. Yet we find that little has changed in the achievement of these students since the introduction of standardized achievement tests in the early part of this century. Academic success continues to be an elusive goal for the large majority of African-American students on all levels—from elementary to higher education. Despite virtuous aims and copious oratory with regard to equal educational opportunity, America has frequently failed to educate African-American children effectively.

The underachievement of African-American students in public schools has been persistent, pervasive, and disproportionate. Since the introduction of standardized tests as measures of academic achievement, African-American students have always lagged behind their white peers. On average, by the sixth grade, African-American students trail their white peers by more than two years in reading, math, and writing skills as measured by standardized achievement tests.

One cannot identify a particular region of the country, a state, a city, or a school district that has been successful for any period of time in educating the majority of African-Americans in their charge. Indeed, one is hard pressed to identify episodic success or even a hopeful trend somewhere. The one exception is in the literature about effective schools which have identified some inner-city schools that have been successful in substantially raising the academic achievement of African-American students (Edmonds, 1979; Purkey and Smith, 1982). Even in these cases, because implementation has not been wide, the instances are few and far between.

If we look at statistics regading African-American success in high school, a similarly disturbing pattern emerges. In urban schools nationally, the African-American dropout rate is close to 50 percent (The Council of the Great City Schools, 1987). In California, the rate exceeds 40 percent (Wilson and Melendez, 1985). In New York City, the dropout rate for African-American males is more than 70 percent *(New York Times,* 1986). Additionally, one of every three African-American high school students is taking a general—non-academic and non-vocational—course of study (The Council of the Great City Schools, 1987).

In American schools, African-American students are *more likely* than other students to:

- be placed in special education
- be placed in vocational programs in high school

These students are *less likely* than other students to:

- be placed in gifted and talented programs
- be placed in academic tracks in high school
- receive adequate math, science, and social studies in high school
- have adequate access to computers

Moreover, these students show no awareness of a connection between their schooling and their later life.

Many explanations have been offered to account for these conditions. Generally, the theories fit into four categories: (1) cultural differences; (2) structural inequalities; (3) social deficit; and (4) genetic deficit. The first theory posits that the widescale failure of African-Americans in the educational system is due to a poor fit between the curriculum and the culture of the learners. The curriculum, culturally speaking, is irrelevant; the students cannot see themselves in the curriculum. Recent proponents of this line of reasoning include Hale-Benson (1986) and Wilson (1987).

The second theory, structural inequality, argues that there are systemic problems within institutions in America that foster inequalities. The schools, the theory argues, reproduce these inequalities, forcing specific groups to fit into particular categories in the society. Bowles and Gintis (1976), Suzuki (1977), and Ogbu (1978) are prominent in the literature arguing this position.

The social deficit theorists argue that the failure of African-American students to perform well is rooted in social conditions; African-American students do not do well in school because of inferior home environments and a low socioeconomic status. Coleman et al. (1965) and Jencks et al. (1972) are notable scholars in this area.

The much older genetic deficit theory is akin to what is referred to in the African-American community as "playing the dozens," or ridiculing someone's parents. Its basic premise is that a given African-American child cannot perform well intellectually because his or her parents could not perform well; the inability has been passed on due to racial genetic inferiority. Jensen (1969) and Shockley (1972) are two well-known scholars in this area.

Most scholars agree now that there are no significant differences in the intellectual capacities of different racial groups. Moreover, literature about effective schools has demonstrated that African-American students can overcome the effects of a poor home environment and do well in school (Edmonds, 1979; Willie, 1987). It seems that a complete understanding of the problem requires a synthesis of the former two models—cultural differences and structural inequalities—as it appears that they both offer some promising means of understanding the situation.

Surprisingly, most of the analyses heretofore have been from a pathological perspective—focusing on a variation from a sound and proper condition—rather than from an "adaptive vitality" perspective, which emphasizes the ability of African-Americans to survive and flourish in spite of barriers (Karenga, 1984). The problem has been "over-identified," as Edmonds argues when he says "we already know more than we need to [educate the children of the poor]" (1979, p. 23).

Whatever the perspective or focus of the previous literature, it has always been narrow and limited. Little has been presented that treats the cultural differences and structural inequalities models collectively. Ogbu (1978), a contributor to this volume, is among the few who have discussed these two models in juxtaposition.

This volume presents the views of a range of African-American educators on questions related to African-American academic achievement and explores the implications of limiting our consideration of African-American student success to academic achievement. Much of the information presented in this volume is new and represents findings from a wide range of research conducted by the contributors.

The political orientations and views here are diverse; they represent a wide spectrum of the debate within the African-American educational community. In the pages that follow, we also describe models that have been successful in improving the achievement of African-American students in various communities across the country.

Part One: Problem Identification

The concern in this volume is with the persistent, pervasive, and disproportionate underachievement of African-American students. The issue is given clarity in Part One; the authors put the problem in historical and political perspective. The interview with Booker Peek in Chapter 1 is included in order to gain insights into perspectives on the education of African-American students. Peek, a professor in Black Studies at Oberlin College, personifies the action-oriented academician. For nearly twenty years he has taken an active and personal role in improving the academic skills (and resultantly the life chances) of hundreds of African-Americans from pre-school through professional school in and around the Oberlin community. He discusses the concepts of political education and skills education and considers their significance in the success of African-American students and African-American people.

In emphasizing the role that politics plays in the classroom, Peek discusses how teachers and administrators, consciously and unconsciously, prepare African-American students to fail through imparting a political orientation that is alien to them. Here, the call is for teacher training programs to encourage potential teachers to be cognizant of the implications of not only the course material that they present but also of the context in which the material is presented. Skills education, Peek says, is important, but so is political education.

In Chapter 2, Faustine Jones-Wilson examines the condition of urban education, focusing on an analysis—from an Afrocentric perspective—of the various studies and reports of the current educational reform movement. She discusses the impact of these reports on the education of African-American students and urges African-American people to be ever vigilant for new information on African-American education. She stresses the effect that these developments can have on educational policy, particularly as it relates to the education of African-Americans.

Peek and Jones-Wilson emphasize the relationship between the education of African-Americans and the American political system, focusing on the role that politics has played and continues to play in education. From a policy perspective, their analyses suggest the need to extend beyond the educational setting (e.g., schools and school districts) into the political arena in an effort to facilitate meaningful long-standing improvements in the educational achievement of these African-American students.

Part Two: Factors Affecting Academic Achievement

In Part Two, the authors discuss factors that contribute to the present state of African-American education. Categories of factors include organizational, societal, and student. Organizational factors considered include organizational capacity and application of power (Bliss and Carrasco), the cultural relevance of the curriculum (Boateng), and the role of teachers (Shujaa). These foci seem quite appropriate; when students do not do well, it is the responsibility of the schools. Edmonds (1979) and others have shown that schools can overcome students' low socioeconomic status and effectively educate poor African-American students. Parents, community people, and educators must, as suggested in Part One, agitate the political system for educational change. The emphasis in the schools must be on changing the schools—not changing the students.

In Chapter 3, James Bliss and Margarida Carrasco highlight rarely considered factors which have an impact on efforts to improve the academic achievement of African-American and Hispanic students in urban schools. They report on a qualitative study of an urban school in a northeastern state. They describe how the school was unable to make state-mandated changes, in large part, because of organizational incapacity and inappropriately applied power.

Incorporating African-American culture into curriculum and instruction is important in order to facilitate learning for African-American children. With the current emphasis on Eurocentric values in curriculum and instruction (and the increasing shortage of African-American teachers), the African-American child is not likely to become a central focus of the curriculum in the near future. This is particularly disturbing given that, as stated earlier, African-American students represent nearly 50 percent of the student population in urban schools.

Students do better academically when they see themselves in the curriculum. February, Black History Month, is the only time African-American students have that opportunity. The contributions of Africans to world civilization need to be experienced by all students through the curriculum (Lomotey, 1989). The underrepresentation of African-American cultural values in the school curriculum will continue to perpetuate curricular and instructional inequalities that foster mediocre classroom experiences and exacerbate existing barriers to the attainment of academic success for African-American students.

Felix Boateng deals with this critical issue of relevant curriculum in Chapter 4. Boateng argues for the implementation of truly multi-cultural education programs. He believes that cultural differences among students can be accommodated within a school curriculum. In encouraging the development of these programs, Boateng examines some barriers to their creation. He then presents strategies needed to combat these obstacles.

In Chapter 5, Mwalimu Shujaa uses qualitative data from a study in which he was involved. He discusses the roles that teachers play in the implementation of educational change and their views of the implementation process. Shujaa emphasizes educational change in terms of the potential of recent reforms to improve the academic achievement of African-American students. The subset of the data that he draws from includes transcripts of interviews of African-American and white teachers in which they offer their perceptions of their roles in implementing reform policies that are intended to improve student achievement in predominantly African-American schools.

Educational institutions do not work in isolation from other institutions in society. Moreover, meaningful changes in the life chances of African-Americans cannot be made by focusing solely on the schools. Other institutions in the society, including social, political, and economic institutions, contribute to the underachievement of African-American children.

In Chapter 6, Norris Haynes and James Comer stress that institutions in society work in concert with each other to perpetuate inequalities. Moreover, they argue that in order to improve schools, you must improve society; in order to improve the status of African-American students, you must improve the status of African-Americans.

They consider some of the institutions that need to be reformed in order to effect meaningful educational improvements in the academic achievement of African-American students. Their discussion includes consideration of families; community-based organizations; businesses; local, state, and federal governments; and the mass media.

In Chapter 7, John Ogbu explains why African-American children do less well in school than other children. Ogbu discusses the effects that this persistent failure has on the upward mobility of African-Americans. He explores how African-American school performance is related to African-American perceptions of social and occupational opportunity structures as well as educational opportunity structure.

The focus of Ogbu is on the self-concept of students. We know that if students do not feel good about themselves, they will not do well. Ogbu argues that African-American students tend not to do well, in part, because their vision of their ultimate success in school, in society, and in the workplace is pessimistic. These students do not see success in their future and therefore are not inspired to excel.

The diversity of views expressed in this section emphasizes the complexity of the problem and argues that there are a multiplicity of factors to be considered and researched when seeking remedies for the underachievement of African-American students.

Part Three: Limitations of Academic Achievement Measures

Part Three deals with issues related to the use of standardized achievement tests. While this volume deals with the topic of academic achievement, much of the recent literature criticizes using such a limited criteria to evaluate schools. Educators and parents are not interested merely in developing students who can perform well on standardized achievement tests—although this may be one important outcome of schooling. We seek more from schools than just academic success. All educational institutions instill social and cultural values and beliefs in their students. These outcomes from schools are important also. Social responsibility, self-respect, respect for others, and comfort with one's own cultural background as well as with the backgrounds of others are of critical importance.

The poor construction and wrongful use of standardized tests are considered in Part Three. These tests, the authors argue, are a part of the arsenal used to maintain the current status of African-American educational progress.

Hilliard challenges the assumed legitimacy of using standardized achievement tests, including IQ tests. He argues that many are culturally biased and that most cannot withstand rigid tests of reliability and validity. While Hilliard does not argue for the elimination of standardized tests, he does stress the need for changes in their usage.

In Chapter 9, Jacqueline Fleming questions the widely held assumption that standardized achievement tests do not predict future success in higher education for African-American students as well as they do for white students. Fleming uses her research and the research of others to demonstrate that these tests do predict future college success for African-American students at predominantly African-American colleges as well as they predict future college success for white students at predominantly white colleges. She discusses the research, suggests possible explanations for her findings and offers recommendations that derive from the data.

The implications of this third section are many. First, both Hilliard and Fleming argue that tests are inappropriately constructed and utilized to diagnose and prescribe remedies for the underachievement of African-American students. The tests, they say, are co-conspirators in the perpetuation of the continued inferior educational status of African-American students. Increased efforts must be made to see that these tests are more appropriately constructed and to see that they are not used in a way that is, by design, harmful to African-American students.

Educators, from pre-school through higher education, need to acknowledge the numerous shortcomings of these tests, particularly as these shortcomings related to African-American students. In doing so, they need to make the necessary adjustments in classification, grouping, placement, and, in the case of higher education, acceptance procedures to compensate for the present inherent inequities in the tests.

Part Four: Programs That Work

Since the early 1970s there has been a significant body of research—the effective schools research—that looks at public elementary schools where African-American children have done well academically. The reader is inspired and given faith with the contributions in Part Four. The message is clear: African-American students can be effectively educated in large numbers.

In Chapter 10, Barbara Sizemore takes a look at one effective school in Pittsburgh and analyzes some of the characteristics that distinguish it. In Chapter 11, I report on a study which extends the research on principals in effective schools by focusing on African-American principals in three predominantly African-American effective elementary schools in California. Through vignettes, I discuss three qualities that these principals have in common.

There are well over 200 independent African-American elementary and secondary schools across the country. Since 1985, Joan Ratteray has studied these schools and worked with a large number of them. In Chapter 12, she describes these schools, relying on the results of a study she conducted with Mwalimu Shujaa. She examines the characteristics of the families of the children that attend these schools and raises and discusses several fundamental questions that need to be addressed in future research on these important institutions. Her queries include: Can the successes of these schools be adapted and replicated in other schools, and what are the long term effects of education in an independent school?

In Chapter 13, Janice Hale-Benson discusses the importance of an emphasis on the culture of African-American children in the instruction that they receive in school. She describes a model early childhood program, "Visions For Children," that focuses not only on academic achievement but also on other affective outcomes for African-American children. Hale-Benson also describes the methodology used to assess the effectiveness of the program.

The strength of this final section is clear in its message that African-American students can be effectively educated. Researchers should continue to seek out such models so that we can gain an even better understanding of the reasons for the successes of these public and private institutions.

Summary

Much is said in these pages. A threefold message is presented. First, the underachievement of African-American students is persistent, pervasive, and disproportionate; the severity of the problem has been well documented. Second, the reasons that this situation persists are varied; there is no simple explanation. Third, there are clear examples of environments that have, over long periods of time, been successful in educating large numbers of African-American students. These models can be replicated; the situation is not hopeless.

Finally, scholars interested in pursuing this topic have within these pages a number of appropriate directions in which to travel. Educators are provided with a number of suggestions geared toward improving their own individual educational arena for the African-American students in their charge. And for parents and community people we provide hope and information regarding the educability of all African-American children.

All of our children can learn. However, that eventuality will not be realized until politicians, educators, and the African-American community make it a priority.

Part One

Problem Identification

Editor's Note: Booker C. Peek is an Associate Professor of Black Studies at Oberlin College in Oberlin, Ohio. His training and expertise are in education. In 1975 when Oberlin closed its education program, he moved to Black Studies. Since Peek's arrival at Oberlin in 1970, he has been deeply committed to the education of all students—particularly African-American students—from preschool to professional school. He is personally responsible for the academic success of literally hundreds of students in Oberlin's public schools, its college, and in several undergraduate, graduate, and professional schools across the country. Year round, Peek runs tutorial programs for students of all ages—often in his own home or office and usually with his own funds.

This is how Booker Peek has chosen to live his life, and his family supports him wholeheartedly: his wife is a teacher at Oberlin High School; his oldest daughter is a physician; his son is a college graduate; and his youngest daughter is a college undergraduate. The bulk of the free time of each of the Peeks is spent studying or tutoring.

As a result of this all-encompassing commitment, Peek does *no* writing for scholarly publications, and he would have it no other way. Yet, by his genius and his practice, Peek has created an environment worthy of scholarly treatment. I pleaded with him to write for this volume; he respectfully declined. Still, I felt that it was important that what he had to say be shared with an audience larger than Oberlin. Therefore, I needed an alternative to a typical scholarly publication. What follows is the alternative: an interview. It is a tribute to a man who, in my mind, best exemplifies a lifelong commitment to the education of African-American people.

1　An Interview with Booker Peek

KOFI LOMOTEY

Lomotey: How long have you been at Oberlin College?

Peek: I'm in my eighteenth year; I came in September 1970.

Lomotey: From where did you come?

Peek: I came from the University of Florida where I was in Graduate School in the department of French. My residency at that time was in Gainesville, Florida.

Lomotey: Where had you attended school prior to that?

Peek: My undergraduate work was done at Florida A & M University, in Tallahassee, Florida, where I majored in French. Then I spent one and one-half years here at Oberlin College in a Masters of Arts teaching program. I was interested in high school teaching.

Lomotey: What is your title at Oberlin?

Peek: I am an associate professor of Black Studies.

Lomotey: Let me ask you a few general questions regarding the education of African-American people in America. How important do you believe education is to the future of African-Americans?

Peek: From my perspective it is essential. It is as essential as oxygen. I say from my own perspective because it is clear to me that depending upon what one views as the future of Black Americans, it may not be that important. I sense clearly that it is not that important to everybody. That is, we are going to have jobs, we are going to live, we are not going to be physically exterminated as the Jews were. If you are prepared to accept that kind definition of life where we exist as a people, purely, from my standpoint, clearly in an inferior position, you could say you could take education or leave it.

But if you think of the future of Blacks being at least as important as the future of white Americans, that is to say, they are not going to be in prison psychologically or in chains, then to that extent education has to be viewed as important as oxygen. There can't be any separation between the importance of education and oxygen.

Lomotey: How much of a problem in African-American education is attributable to the larger American social system?

Peek: Again, taking my definition of education to mean a quest for total liberation and what it would take to achieve it, I would say that the state of Black education is directly attributable to the social conditions in the society, starting with our enslavement—physical enslavement—and continuing up to now with our psychological enslavement where we don't quite have the same kinds of standards for our liberation or define it as do most other people; that's total and absolutely unquestionable liberation. In that sense, I would say the totality of Black education is affected by the social system.

Lomotey: Would you say there is a clear connection between the status of the education of African-Americans and our status in other realms of American society?

Peek: Absolutely. Now I'm taking the broader definition of education and by that I mean, what I define as a political education where people are aspiring to be totally free and liberated and have the same opportunity to maximize their potential as anybody else. To that extent then clearly our lack of education has contributed directly to our inability to prosper economically, and in other ways, as other groups have prospered. Absolutely. There is a direct correlation.

Lomotey: How important is it to focus on the culture of the learner in a school curriculum?

Peek: I would define it this way. You have skills education and you have political education. Political education, again, is a broad term I am using to apply to the culture, history, desire, and the aspirations of a child that have been shaped in great part by the parents, the grandparents, all of his or her environment. Political education is something that white society can't give Black Americans. In addition to political education I see a need to focus on skills education which encompasses reading, writing, arithmetic, and English or whatever the particular language might be—a mastery of materials that are tested by standardized tests—SATs. Those general skills are skills education. I see political education requiring skills education to be used as a tool in order to carry out whatever the political education might be. For Black Americans it has to be a total quest for liberation not only for ourselves but for all oppressed people throughout the world—particularly those in Africa. That's political education. So, I see a need for involving children with cultural education. That comes under political education and is the responsibility of parents and of family and anyone else who cares about the political development of the child. There is no way to eliminate that possibility; you will either be politically educated to represent and respond to your own needs and desires or you will be responding to the needs and desires of other people. You don't have an option there. You do have and option in respect to skills education. You may or may not get that. Skills education is something you have to work toward getting. Political education you are going to get one way or another. It may not be the political education you want, but you are going to get it in any event.

Lomotey: Some African-Americans have argued that you can't separate political education from skills education and their evidence is the fact that if you focus on the culture of a learner in the classroom, that learner is more likely to be successful in skill acquisition.

Peek: Right. I agree 100 percent with what you have just said. That's why I said skills education is a neutral phenomenon. It's like a gun or a jack or a can opener; it has no will of its own; it's just a tool. Political education is the feelings, emotions, the desires, the aspirations of the learner, of a person. It is his or her orientation to the world—what the world is about. That's why I said you cannot escape that. You are going to get it. What you get will depend upon the parents, your environment, the situation you are in, but you are going to get a political education.

It's the political education that one needs to have some tools for and the tools are the skills education, but the tools are neutral. That skills education may allow a person to live a life like Hitler or a life like Mother Theresa. There is nothing inherently good or bad about skills education except that skills education allows one to carry out his or her political education. There is an intermingling and interdependence of the two, but political education is vastly more important than skills education. Skills education is totally dependent upon political education. So to the extent that one needs to do whatever he or she must in order to acquire skills education, he or she ought to do that and obviously that decision comes because of the political education.

Why do you need the skills education in the first place? Because we have a certain need to solve certain kinds of problems in the world whether they be economic problems or religious problems or just a general quest for freedom. That need initially came because of a political education—

because you were born in a society where you necessarily have to take on certain characteristics of the family or the environment in which you live. In order to solve those larger problems, you need tools. One of those tools happens to be skills education.

Skills education is no big deal, if one is prepared to accept any kind of life. I would not suggest that there is something beautiful about skills education. It is no more beautiful than an automobile. If you want to get from one place to another, you need an automobile—or sometimes maybe an airplane or the bus or a bicycle; it's just a tool. Skills education is simply a tool that can be picked up or discarded as you may wish.

Political education is accessible to everybody. They must get it. So if one country has a political education that is aimed at the extermination of another country, that country won't have any power over the other country unless it gets skills education. If it gets skills education, it will build up a technological society and have tools necessary to carry out its diabolical, political education. The other country too has a political education, and presumably its political education would say it doesn't wish to be exterminated. So it's going to have to present something to counter the hostile country's political education. I can't simply say I have a political education which says I want to live forever, I want to be free but I don't have skills education. You have to apply skills education in order to carry out your political education.

I just want to stress that I would agree you don't separate the two. There is no way you really separate the two if you are serious about your political education because you are going to need skills education in order to carry out your political education.

Lomotey: What are your thoughts on the genetic inferiority theory of Milton Schwebel, Arthur Jensen, William Shockley and others?

Peek: Well, their view as I have understood it, is that Blacks are inherently inferior; we are an inherently inferior people. If that view is sustained, then it is justifiable and understandable that Blacks economically are impoverished, that Blacks intellectually will be impoverished, that Blacks will not be excelling in all the areas of importance that others are excelling in, and it would be, according to them, attributable to God—a genetic phenomenon. If you believe that, then you won't be alarmed at the discrepancy that we see in this country and throughout the world between Blacks and whites.

I believe they are sincere for the most part. I know in the case of Jensen, he has done a tremendous amount of work in trying to document and prove his viewpoints. I think to that extent he does a great job. I just totally reject most of his findings, not because I am alarmed by the fact that we may be an inherently inferior people. I reject it because of the evidence; it simply isn't there. What evidence there is is that Blacks have systematically been discriminated against historically and are still discriminated against today. That physical and psychological discrimination accounts far more for the discrepancy that I see existing in Black achievement than anything else. That is not to say that Blacks are not inherently inferior. I simply say the evidence is not there. That is not to say that Blacks perhaps are a superior race. The evidence simply isn't there. I simply say from my standpoint it is a neutral situation until we can equalize the conditions that are relevant to rearing children with the proper political education and skills education and give them the kinds of opportunities they deserve, we can't make the kinds of statements they are making or the projections or predictions they are making with respect to the inherent inferiority of anybody.

If you really wish to pursue that question, I think it's the proper thing to do. But, to simply look at the results today and to interpret those results and conclude that Blacks are inherently inferior is absolutely wrong. Especially if you are determining inferiority, as they often are, in terms of how Blacks perform on standardized tests.

The material that is on the SATs and GREs is accessible to all healthy normal children, Black or white. If they are given the opportunity from the earliest times to 18 years of age, they can excel in skills education. That means under my system all healthy normal children would be performing at or above the 600, 700, or 800 level on SATs. So, you can't use that standard today to judge who's inferior and who's superior; the discrepancies we see on that test are due primarily, if not wholly, to the environmental conditions that have occurred since we have been in this country.

Lomotey: How prevalent is the expression of the views of these in American public education?

Peek: I think they are not very prevalent in terms of people expressing those views outwardly. Fifty years ago they were very prevalently used. For the majority of Americans it was taken for granted that Blacks were inherently inferior, and no one made a big issue of that. Today, however, whites are much more sophisticated and much more reluctant to speak publicly about those kinds of views that Jensen or Shockley holds.

However, in terms of the reality—the actuality of those views existing— they exist. They exist regrettably in the minds of Black people. That is to say, we have accepted our low performance in skills education. We have accepted that low performance. So the evils that whites perpetrated initially have carried over into us today to the extent that we are participating in the conspiracy. We are participants in our own destruction because we, for the most part, accept those standards. So, you find many Black teachers and white teachers, you find many Black professors and white professors, none of whom are saying publicly that Blacks are inherently inferior of holding those views but totally accepting the level of performance of Blacks in the academic world of skills education. And as I've said earlier, if you fail in skills education, what you fail to do is to arrive at a position where your political education—how you view the world—has much meaning.

Lomotey: What do you see as the major barriers to academic success for African-American students in American elementary and secondary schools?

Peek: Again, speaking of academic success in terms of skills education, the basic barrier is that our political education is not what is should be. That is, in order for the skills education to take on meaning—to take on a significant form—the political education must change. For that to change we must start seeing it as abnormal that we do not perform in reading, writing, and arithmetic as well as the dominant culture. We must see that as abnormal. We have to see that a change must be undertaken regardless of the cost or the time. If we are unable to do that, we will remain in an inferior position. But if we are able to alter our political education, what would follow would be a strong desire to acquire skills education which is offered in school systems and in homes, and we would not accept the low-level performance which is typical for the majority of Black Americans. That would change virtually everything.

Political education is difficult to come by because of people like Jensen and Shockley and their predecessors who propagated the idea that Blacks were an inherently inferior race, and the result is, of course, that Blacks, to a great extent have accepted that though Blacks will be the first to speak publicly against it. I'm saying we have accepted it.

Lomotey: As far as you know, how prevalent is tracking in American public schools today?

Peek: In 1988 tracking is not done the way it was done 30 or 40 years ago where rigid IQ tests were given at an early age and children were put in a certain classroom for a certain situation and were kept there permanently. Still, however, a form of tracking exists at the high school level. Courses, although they are open to everyone, are far more accessible to students who have received a certain kind of skills education. So the result is that students will of their own volition choose to take or not to take chemistry or physics or biology or honors English or honors history, and so at the high school level we see a high degree of tracking in that courses are primarily accessible only to upper-middle-class white and Black students. But in terms of the system itself imposing a rigid form of tracking, such a system is less in vogue today than it was 20 or 30 years ago.

Lomotey: What are some of the reasons why the dropout rate of African-American students is so high?

Peek: Again, I think it's the political education of the family, of the teachers, and of the system itself. There is a kind of acceptance that we don't have to perform at the level that everyone else does—that the great problems of the world can be solved without Black participation. The American Constitution and America's sense of morality have to make schools and education accessible to Blacks, but we don't have to insist, nor do we feel, that Black excellence is necessary for the long-range security of this nation or the betterment of the world. Now, once that philosophy remains in place, then children are not taught properly. They are not taught by teachers who believe in them so they don't learn to read, and they don't learn to write because in school reading and writing and thinking critically are the tools that are offered, that's what is in vogue there. Students are turned off. It's boring; school gets boring—terribly boring. Reading and writing and thinking are activities that are extremely boring if you can't do them—if you don't have people who believe that you can do them and that you must do them. Children are looking for excitement. The excitement is there; there is dope. More importantly there is TV that is permeating the home at the earliest age of children. There they can find all the excitement that they want. So you have the infiltration of TV, the infiltration of drugs, the lack of teachers who are totally dedicated and believe that the security and the well-being of the world depends on the Black youth. You have all those factors converging on the schools, then you see there is a high dropout rate, illegitimacy—at a much higher rate in the Black community than it is perhaps in any other ethnic group. Numerically speaking there are more whites but percentage wise there are far more Blacks who have to drop out for reasons of pregnancy.

Lomotey: What is the importance of socioeconomic status or family background in the potential for academic success of African-Americans?

Peek: I think the economic and social background of the child is absolutely important for Blacks as it is for anyone else. That is to say, if the parents have had a superior education and are economically well off, they set the tone. For the most part, they have rejected the idea for themselves that their political education aspirations are any different from anybody else's and so they have high academic standards. They have them for themselves and so children born into those families acquire and benefit from the ethos existing there. They learn to read and write as a way of life. Their parents are likely to stress the value of education, the value of reading, the value of writing, the value of mathematics, the value of science to a much higher degree than parents who are on welfare. So there is no question that there is a very direct correlation between economic and social life of a family and the performance of the offspring. But I maintain that in spite of that, what I am excited about is that poor people can excel essentially as well as anybody else once we decide what they have to know. There aren't that many words above and beyond that list of words which children automatically learn in the society. It doesn't matter how poor you may be, or which environment you have been reared in, you acquire a certain standard, a certain English vocabulary, and I am saying, if you can build upon that, limited to roughly 3,000 to 5,000 words, suddenly in spite of your geographical location, you are able to read as well as anybody else. You have ideas and thoughts far beyond your immediate environment. So what I am saying is whether one is reared in an upper-middle-class home or not, once the parents understand and the school systems understand that that education can be supplemented by nearly 3,000 or 4,000 additional words, that child in that environment will suddenly have what would be considered an upper-middle-class education minus the social things that would go with that particular education. But as far as reading and writing are concerned, those skills can be acquired in a home where parents have not had the best education. Parents have to be taught that by the teachers— someone in the system. Parents who have been victimized are not going to know that. They are not going to know how close they are to providing their children with a first-rate education. They don't know. So if they don't know that, they are not going to be committed to doing whatever is necessary. So someone has to tell them this—maybe the government, maybe the teachers, maybe their friends—it doesn't matter. Someone has to show the people who have been oppressed, who can't read or write, and do not see the value in education that they might see. Someone has to intervene. Without that intervention though, the child is left helpless. That's why I maintain that the schools can play a big role; they do have the children there. But the schools are helpless because you have teachers who are products of this society with those views that Jensen has which suggest that it is abnormal for Black kids to perform at or above the 700 level to the extent that white students are. Until we come to expect that high level of performance, then no one will do very much.

Lomotey: You mention the federal government—what role do you think the federal government should play in improving the academic skills of African-American pre-collegiate students?

Peek: I think the role of the federal government can be to continue to support in the way that it does support public education and not syphon off funds to private schools in any way. I also think the federal government could join with the state government, which would join with the local governments, to share the information with the public about the accessibility of a superior education even for the poor if certain doable things were done. That is, one may not be reared or have been born in an upper-middle-class environment, but there are a small number of words and not that many ideas that one needs in order to have an upper-middle-class education in a certain sense. In a sense that is necessary to read and to write. The federal government can set the moral tone. The President could speak regularly about—not just about the importance of education, but specifics. Better than anyone else, the President can tell the American family, particularly the families tht are in the ghettos, the families where education is not valued the way it might. The President can give speeches regularly along with his various cabinet members on the specific things people can do.

If nothing more than parents asking their children when they come home to tell them about or discuss what went on in school everyday. For a child in the ghetto to sit and have to recount his or her activities in the day to an adult is a very challenging and rewarding experience. It requires that he or she remember; it requires that he or she be specific about the details of what happened. It is a far more mentally taxing thing to do than to simply allow the child to come home and watch MTV. Any adult at home can simply, however tired he or she may be, lie down and say to the child who is in first grade, or second grade or whatever grade, to tell him or her about school. That is a responsibility that the child would have to do everyday. The child would soon learn that the more he or she talked about things in the past, he or she would develop the capacity to do that. The first day may be difficult—hard to remember. After that, it would be a simple thing. The federal government should continue to support public schools the way it does and listen more to the National Educational Association of American Teachers.

If you are talking about what the federal government should do, in the context of Blacks, it would require a radical program. That is, it would attack this whole idea of the genetic inferiority of Blacks. Not in the sense that it is not true, but it is not true in the sense that if you use the SAT score or the regular means of measuring people's intelligence, that evidence that we have there simply shows or reflects the extent to which children have been discriminated against or have been oppressed. I think someone with a lot of power needs to convey that idea, and the President of the United States is best able to do that and that means that if we are not inherently inferior as judged by those tests, then what else accounts for the discrepancy? The discrepancy is attributable to the fact there is a racism that has been keeping Blacks in inferior positions, and making Blacks themselves feel inferior. Until we get rid of this sense of our own inferiority, little can be done. I'm simply saying if you were the President, if I were the President of this nation I would be speaking daily about the importance of education and obviously giving much more money to the system than we presently do. You've got to change the philosophy of the teachers and the parents. The philosophy of the parents cannot be changed unless it is done in the context of a total effort. That would have to start at the top with the President, the Congress, and the state. That's calling for something that is not going to happen very soon. It is not going to happen very soon that large numbers of people will find the Black intellectual performance that shamefully bad.

Lomotey: What role do you see African-American educators such as yourself playing in the improvement of the academic status of African-American students in pre-collegiate education?

Peek: Well, I have, myself, a very unique role. Most college professors wouldn't have the opportunity that I have. That is to say that I once was in the Education Department and all my work now in the Black Studies Department is focused directly on the public system in one way or another, working with children to achieve, what I call skills education. I work with college students who work with students. I, myself, work with elementary, junior high, and senior high school students on a daily basis.

If you are talking about the average professor, I think what the average professor can do in order to have an impact on pre-collegiate education is difficult to say. It would depend upon the town. In small towns like Oberlin, I would say college professors can have a very great impact. They can encourage more college students to take part in the education of children at the pre-collegiate levels. That's what they can do. Right now I am only reaching probably 200 students annually, hardly one-tenth of the students at Oberlin College. Clearly, in a small town like Oberlin, students could be encouraged to devote more time in pre-collegiate education— tutoring and working. If you are not careful, college students have the same biased views about Blacks and oppressed children as anybody else. So we need to have college students better educated. Who's going to do that? It can only come through the action of the faculty. A faculty would have to decide that that's needed. Again, you are talking about something that is a long way off. Faculties don't believe that they should do much about this genetic inferiority issue or that there is anything abnormal about the performance of Blacks in skills education, so they are not about to embark upon a sweeping program to get their students involved in larger numbers. In fact, the students are more likely to be tolerant of, less committed to, or believe in the idea of the inherent inferiority of Blacks than college professors.

I know what college professors should do. College professors should get exposed to Blacks and/or whites who are committed, believe that Blacks are not genetically inferior as evidenced by the criteria we have now, and develop ideas about what should be done in order to change the existing conditions. But, to ask professors to do that voluntarily is nonsense. They are not going to do that voluntarily.

I think the responsibility right now falls heavily on Blacks who are aware or whites who are aware. There are not that many whites who are aware, and don't believe there are that many Blacks who are aware, that the vast majority of Blacks do not say that they are inferior, but they believe it—they behave as if they are inferior. Far too many Blacks don't seem unduly alarmed about the performance of Blacks. Some of us have tried to say that these skills are upper-middle-class skills, and we ask who wants to learn these white skills. That's why I've said it's skills education, and it's somewhat neutral as to how you use skills.

So I don't think the solution is to dismiss reading, writing, and arithmetic as a solution to the problems. I find that too many Blacks have bought into that, instead of saying, "Yes, we are behind in terms of math skills as a race, and the reasons are that we have been discriminated against, we have been put in an inferior position, we have been mistreated, and here is the solution to the problem." We are not saying it loudly enough to the white establishment in my estimation, to the colleges, to the high school principal, to the board of educations, or to the school boards. We are simply, as Black intellectuals, not behaving as if there is something abnormal about our performance as a group and as if it is important that we change.

I would say, I think quite frankly, in many instances it is very liberal whites who have been perhaps more outraged than some conservative Blacks have been about the shameful performance of Blacks. I'm saying simply Blacks have to get outraged. I'm not talking about all Blacks; I'm talking about Black teachers for whom I have great sympathy. Then I'm saying Black professors. There is no excuse for Black professors—Black intellectuals—not to see the connection between Black freedom and liberation and skills education. I say if we look at how we behave, one would never know that there is that strong link. You never would know it.

Lomotey: Do you envision a day when African-American students will do as well academically as white students in American public schools?

Peek: Right now, looking at the SATs, at the 700 level which is the average of the students at Harvard, Yale, and most of these top schools in verbal skills, whites outperform Blacks roughly 100 to 150 to 1 in English skills and almost 200 to 1 in mathematics, while in the general population Blacks are outnumbered by only a 10 to 1 margin. I would say in terms of mastery of skills education—as I have defined it and as it is tested for on the SATs or GREs—that the day when Blacks will be performing on those kinds of tests in proportion to their numbers is far more removed from reality than the day when Black South Africans will reign supreme. Now I think that the reality of one man, one vote in South Africa is a long time away, but I would say that the thought that Blacks will be performing on tests and skills education at the level that whites are, proportionally speaking, that day is even more remote. When that occurs, the political education that we have as Blacks or any oppressed person would have will be complemented then by skills education. You can't keep people in an inferior position if they have skills education. You simply cannot do that.

Whites in South Africa, for example, can reign supreme, because even though they are numerically inferior, they are intellectually superior at this moment. If the Blacks ever acquire the intellectual skills that the whites have acquired, then there will be no way that the whites will maintain their power position. Whites know that; their political education tells them that in order for them to remain in power, they must prevent the Blacks, whatever their political education is, from getting skills education. In this country we are in the minority, so whites have done and will continue to do all that they can to prevent us from ever acquiring the skills education in large numbers. It is something that we have to fight for and aim for; otherwise, you would have to give up. Work toward that goal, but that goal is not going to come very soon.

Lomotey: Let me ask you a few questions about African-Americans in college. Is there a fundamental difference in the experience of African-American students at predominantly African-American and predominantly white colleges?

Peek: Yes, there is a fundamental difference. Absolutely. One difference is that at predominantly white institutions there is going to be a greater emphasis on skills education than that to which most Blacks have been exposed. That is the nature of these institutions. They are to further strengthen whites in skills education. Whites come to college with a variety of political educations, but the dominant one is that they want to be in power. See whites basically want to be in power. It is not about getting skills education to keep Blacks in an inferior position, because we don't pose a threat. We are not significant enough at this point to be posing a threat for them to be rushing to our skills education.

Skills education at predominantly white institutions is very important. It is very important in high schools, it is important in elementary schools, because the philosophy of white Americans is, almost without exception, that they want to be free people. That's the political philosophy. We have to get some tools, and those tools are skills education. So when Blacks come into a predominantly white institution, the first thing they are going to realize is that from an academic standpoint typically it is more challenging, typically it is more difficult than it would be at a predominantly Black institution. On the college boards, for example, the average Black is scoring around 350 on the SATs. Whites are scoring 100 points higher than Blacks, which means at any institution where the emphasis is on reading and writing and math skills (and that is what most colleges are all about) whites are in a vastly superior postition to that of Black students. So an immediate recognition is their much higher intellectual standards.

What happens is that the values of white Americans are vastly different. Blacks coming into an environment of a predominantly white institution suddenly realize that white people are very different in that they are aspiring to more; they want more power. They are hardly content and that phenomenon permeates or affects adversely all that white people are about. Blacks are not accustomed to wanting to be at the top or trying to be in a superior position. So at a predominantly white institution, you are clashing with the academic values, you are clashing with a philosophy, and that philosophy as Blacks would interpret it is anti-Black. It is an idea that they, whites, want to remain in control of everything, and suddenly Blacks have to give up all of their autonomy and that's something that typically would not happen at a Black institution. I say typically because, and I'll qualify that, because Black institutions are becoming increasingly under the control of whites. At most Black institutions, the faculty for the most part, is one-third to 50 percent white. So Blacks do meet a lot of white professors at predominantly Black institutions, but the saving grace though is—the redeeming feature is—that they are at least studying with Blacks who are no better prepared than they are and so the white professors then gear their standards for the particular college at which they work. So it is easier in that sense. There is no question in my mind that white people want to be free and their definition of freedom is very different from that of Black Americans; to be free Black Americans have realized, as have the South Africans, that skills educations is absolutely essential—so the standards in terms of skills education are very high.

Lomotey: What do the declining numbers of African-American students in higher education signify to you?

Peek: What that signifies is a desire, and perhaps success, on the part of whites to return to the Sixties era, the Fifties era, or before that time when there were very few Blacks going to college. In order to maintain the superiority of whites in all facets of our lives what is necessary is a dominance of whites in education. If they can dominate at the graduate level, then clearly you are not going to have as many Black scholars, Black doctors, Black lawyers. You are just not going to have the intellectual base necessary to bring about any significant changes. What that means in that fewer Blacks are getting into graduate schools, fewer Blacks are going to college, and in the long run fewer Blacks will finish high school. The dropout rate will be astonishingly high, and the net effect will be that the political education of white Americans is operating very effectively.

In order to maintain white power, whites have to have control of the quality and the amount of Black education. You understand that, Blacks have to understand that our political education must be that we must find a way to educate. We must insist at all levels that the thing we will never negotiate on or yield to is an acceptance of fewer Blacks being educated. I think, again, Blacks have not played a signigicant role. I think Black intellectuals, and of course there are exceptions, but as a rule, we have not said to white institutions, "We will not tolerate the low enrollments of Black students." We ought to do anything and everything necessary to bring to the public's attention that that is a form of extermination, a stronger form of extermination than any that white Americans could perpetuate upon us. This is so because if they are allowed to get away with that, then they will have done to us, they will be doing to us, precisely what Hitler did to the Jews—but worse because they will be intellectually exterminating us. If that occurs, then we are a dead people. Our race is doomed. What we ought to be saying, if that is true, is that we will not let that happen except over our dead bodies. We ought to be willing to pay any price and do anything in order to underscore that the last thing we will allow to happen is for little Black children not to get a first-rate education, or high school students not to get a first-rate education, and for colleges to close their doors, or universities to close their doors to Blacks. That we cannot accept, and we ought to put that in the context of what happened to the Jews. That is the modern day form of holocaust. It is no less than that. I think it is a more powerful tool.

If one were advising Hitler today, one would say, "Hitler, if you want to exterminate the Jews, what you need to do is control their education, stop them from getting an education, make them illiterate, and then pass out what is called SATs and let them all fail and say to the world, 'It's an open society and they just don't perform as well as anybody else.' " Because then no one will complain.

No one complains if whites can show Blacks' SAT scores are not as high and that's why they don't go to college or Blacks' GRE scores are not high enough and that's why they don't get into graduate school, and we say, "Oh, we are not qualified." That's absurd. We should say, "That's the sophisticated form of racism that Maddox didn't use or Hitler didn't use, but that's exactly what it is, no less." At that level, with respect to education, there can be no reason why we can't get an education.

It is not the same thing as saying that we must have as many Black pilots as we have white pilots regardless of qualification. It's not the same thing. you are talking about entry-level performances—opportunities at the entry level—there can be no barriers except over our dead bodies. That's how we put it. That's the kind of context you put that in.

I don't think Black intellectuals have reached that stage. We are appeased by white Americans. We have jobs, we have offices, we have secretaries, we have telephones. We have a lot of the things white Americans have, so we are not about to put it in that context. We just look at it as a phenomenon. We write about it, we discuss it, and we talk about it, but, as I've said at the very beginning of this conversation, we Blacks define our liberation in far narrower terms than many white define theirs.

Our political education is weak, so it follows that our skills education is weak. Given how we've decided to define our political education, we don't need as much education as whites, as a group. I think something needs to be changed radically. Why is it that they have a higher political philosophy than we? That is, they don't want to be in prison under any conditions. They don't, and they would destroy the entire world before they would allow the Soviet Union even to capture them. If the Russians were to say that they wanted to change our system from capitalism to communism, we would say no. You do it after we drop every atomic, every nuclear weapon we have. That's what we would unleash before we would do that. We are not going to give up our freedom. And I say Black people have nothing of the sort. We don't value freedom that way. I keep my job; I have to keep my office, and if they allow me to keep my office, my job, then basically I can live. I have my MTV and the basic material goods. Whites do not define their freedom in those terms (I'm generalizing, some whites do). But the nation doesn't when it comes to its freedom.

The easy answer is financial aid is not available the way it is for whites. That's what people usually say. I think there may be some truth to that. It would be difficult, for example, to show that at Oberlin College the institution is discriminating against Blacks financially. I don't think we could show that very easily. However, I think a lot of students feel a pinch. But I think what happens is that a few Black students who attend Oberlin College or any other institution, and as I said earlier, place a different emphasis on skills education. For those few, it is not valued to the degree that it is valued by some whites. Therefore, they and their parents have other priorities in life. They start questioning the cost of education. If the students are not getting their share of A's and they are not excelling at the skills education the way others are (that is, in effect they have more difficulty in college cutting it academically), they begin to question the amount of money they are spending, the amount of time they are investing in formal education.

My belief is that when the day comes that we say that our political education means nothing less than total liberation, we will pay any price and do anything to get the funds to go to college. I don't see that as the major problem. We would insist on getting professors who believe in us. When students have to pay all that money and don't get professors who believe in them, when they pay all of that money and they may not have friends who believe in them, teachers who believe in them, they don't have a society that believes in them, and they don't believe in themselves, then the value of skills education is diminished. It is as simple as that.

Now, I think that we can show that the federal government or the state government and many other agencies are not doing their part with respect to providing financial help. There is no question about that. I would certainly say that finance is a problem; there are some students who may not finish because of lack of finance. I don't think (certainly not at Oberlin College), that we could show that most institutions are discriminating against Blacks in terms of finance.

So, I think some of the problems that we are facing are more complex than simply saying the money isn't available. That's an easy answer and in some cases, certainly true. But I think the real issue is that we just do not value education in terms of our liberation the way or to the degree whites value it for theirs. We're able to buy as many TVs as whites but may not be willing to spend as much on education as they.

Now again, I am generalizing because there are Blacks who do value it to that extent and more. But I am saying, clearly for white Americans with power, education is absolutely essential. And I say with power because I want to make a distinction. This government doesn't really care whether 95 percent of the whites are well educated or not. So I am referring to whites desiring education in the context of a very small percent because what is needed in order for America to maintain its current position in the world, contrary to what many people believe, is the education of just a few.

I think the Reagan administration believes that; all levels of government, Democrat or Republican, believe that you can really maintain our current position with what we are doing now—educating the top 5 percent. You can get the armament or anything else you need. It's a bad policy, I think. I don't think people really believe when they say for us to maintain our status in the world that we have to educate everybody well. That's regrettable. I say that because if you are prepared to build enough nuclear weapons, you can have the kind of military might that we have and get it from the minds of a very few people. I think we need to educate everyone very well only because I believe we do not need to have our future always dependent upon our nuclear might. We need to educate everyone very well because it means we will get a different kind of government. We will view the world differently. We will be trying to find a way that we won't need to have armaments in order to defend ourselves against the rest of the world. That's where we would be heading.

But if one is prepared to say that he or she does not object to having military might and is willing to live with educating only one or two percent, then I am saying one can get from that one or two percent all of the intellect needed to have a highly sophisticated technology so as to protect the nation against other nations. The cost is that you are prepared to exterminate people.

So, I think that at the highest levels there is no doubt that our government doesn't feel that the security of the United States is in jeopardy because of the way it is educating the masses. It doesn't feel that way. To say that I felt that way would mean that it really cannot find a way to educate better. It can find a way to educate better. It doesn't need to. It doesn't want to. The survival of this nation is not dependent upon the quality of the education that Black people receive. Blacks have to understand that.

The present quality of life in this country is dependent upon the kind of education received by that one or two percent. So this nation is prepared to write off roughly 90 percent of whites and 15 percent of Blacks and many others. One or two percent of the nation receives a superior education. That's all it needs because it is willing to have a tremendous military might not based on numbers but based primarily on nuclear weapons. It can achieve that and that's what we've done.

2 The State of African-American Education

FAUSTINE C. JONES-WILSON

Introduction

Urban education is one segment of the larger educational structure in the United States. To consider the state of urban education is to focus on public schools in cities, and in some schools just outside those cities in the metropolitan areas surrounding them. Even though increasing numbers of African-American children are enrolled in private and parochial elementary schools, it still is true that the primary source of the education of African-American children is the public school.

African-American citizens must know what progress is being made, if any, toward making these schools institutions of quality that effectively impart information, skills, and values to these youngsters. Further, it is important that African-Americans know what issues exist with respect to public schooling, and what policies of proposed policies will affect curriculum, teaching, learning, evaluating, and financing with respect to public schools.

In this regard the African-American community must be aware of studies of schooling, recommendations for restructuring education, public perceptions and attitudes about the public schools. These studies, recommendations, and beliefs shape educational change and condition the public's willingness to support universal schooling at the taxpayers' expense.

For a number of years the reports on urban education have been troubling. In the early 1960s the dominant theme of educators was to educate the disadvantaged, a term whch became a euphemism for African-Americans and the poor (Passow, 1963a; 1963b; Daniel, 1964). The hopefulness in this outlook was replaced by the view that schools made

31

little or no difference. The report, *Equality of Educational Opportunity* by James S. Coleman (1966), was very influential in imparting this viewpoint. Arthur Jensen (1969), writing in the *Harvard Educational Review,* concluded that IQ differences accounted for what he called the failure of compensatory education, reviving the genetic deficit theory that had prevailed at the turn of the century in the United States. By 1972 a flood of social science literature proclaimed that the rate of return from educational expenditures was increasingly low, and probably not worth the price. Prominent in this literature were Christopher Jencks' *Inequality: A Reassessment of the Effect of Family and Schooling in America* (1972), and Daniel P. Moynihan and Frederick Mosteller's work, *On Equality of Educational Opportunity* (1972).

By the 1980s an air of pessimism pervaded the thinking even of those individuals and communities supportive of big-city schools and the children who attended them. "Passing the buck" for the ills of urban education became the norm rather than the exception. Negativism has been both cause and effect of doubts about the ability of urban public schools to succeed in educating African-American children and youth.

Demographic Background

Between 1970 and 1980 the African-American population increased 17.3 percent, from 22.6 million to 26.5 million (U.S. Bureau of the Census, 1982). It was distributed somewhat differently than the majority population, with African-Americans being concentrated in the South despite the post-war migrations. In 1980, 53 percent of African-Americans lived in the South, 38.5 percent lived in the North, and 8.5 percent were in the West. While African-Americans were about 12 percent of the national population, they were about 71 percent of the population of the District of Columbia, 35 percent of the total in Mississippi, more than 30 percent in South Carolina, and from 20 to 30 percent in Louisiana, Georgia, Alabama, Maryland, and North Carolina (U.S. Bureau of the Census, 1982). The public schools in these jurisdictions are heavily populated with African-American children, as are public elementary and secondary schools in most of the major cities in this nation.

In 1980, 58 percent of African-Americans lived in central cities, 23 percent lived outside central cities in metropolitan areas, and only 19 percent lived in nonmetropolitan areas (U.S. Bureau of the Census, 1982). African-Americans had a relatively young age structure, with a median age of 24.9 years compared to 30.0 for the total population and 31.1 for the white population. Thirty-one percent of African-Americans were in the school attendance years, between the ages of 5 and 19. Twenty-six percent were in the household-forming and prime childbearing years, ages 20-34, which suggests that they will produce more children in the decade of the 1980s and that these children will be candidates for public schooling in this decade and to the end of the century (U.S. Bureau of the Census, 1982).

African-Americans have used public schools to their advantage. Their educational attainment rates have climbed greatly in the last 30 years, from a 23 percent high school completion rate in 1950 to a 79 percent completion rate in 1978 (National Center for Education Statistics, 1980). This means that more young African-Americans are eligible to enter college or to enter the labor force in more desirable jobs that require at least a high school diploma for entry. It also means that the African-American to white high school completion gap has been narrowed, and that perceptions of the unworthiness of African-American attainment have been reduced.

High school dropout rates for African-Americans have also declined. In 1970, 44.4 percent of African-Americans 25 to 29 years old were high school dropouts. However, by 1980 only 22.6 percent in that age group dropped out of high school. These figures indicate that African-Americans are staying in school and using public school to their advantage. African-American-white differences, however, remain. Comparable figures for whites were 19.9 percent in 1970, and 12.7 percent in 1980 (National Center for Education Statistics, 1982).

These completion rates provide evidence that African-American youth have made progress with respect to educational attainment. The effect of the 1954-1955 *Brown* decisions, the passage and enforcement of civil rights and educational opportunity legislation in the 1960s, coupled with educational efforts of African-American parents and concerned civil rights leaders, along with the ability in the 1960s and early 1970s of mature African-American adults to work at gainful employment has meant that African-American youth finally had greater opportunity to stay in high school and to graduate. In essence, this is an explanation of increased educational attainment for African-American youth in urban schools in the last 29 years. Also, African-Americans have used public schools as a source of employment. Teaching has been a major profession for educated African-Americans.

However, the percentage of African-Americans in the teaching force is declining—from 8.1 percent of public school teachers in 1971 to 7.8 percent in 1981 (National Center for Education Statistics, 1982). Whites were 88.3 percent of public school teachers in 1971, but 91.6 percent in 1981. Of the recent Bachelor's Degree recipients newly qualified to teach in May, 1981, 8,400 were African-American (6.4 percent), but only 4,000 (5.0 percent) were teaching full time (National Education Center for Statistics, 1983). In 1980 only 3.9 percent of African-American males and 5.6 percent of African-American female college-bound high school seniors indicated that they intended to major in Education (National Center for Education Statistics, 1982). This means that there are smaller proportions of African-Americans in the teaching force, and that we are likely to have even smaller proportions in the future if these trends continue. While we would hope that the 4,400 newly qualified African-American teachers who are not teaching found meaningful employment in other occupations, the probability is that they are unemployed—given present unemployment rates of African-Americans and cutbacks in jobs.

The increased educational attainment that we have explored disguises the qualitative aspect of the education offered to African-American children and youth. The poor quality of education for African-Americans has been widely discussed, and thorough, eloquent explanations have been provided by Bernard C. Watson in *The State of Black America*'s issues in the early years of this decade (Watson, 1980, 1981, 1982). His analyses of that quality include terms such as "of grave concern" (1980), "unacceptable" (1981), and "a national scandal" (1982). However, Watson specified some signs of hope for public schools in his 1982 analysis. One of these was an increase in public confidence in the schools as evidenced by the responses of parents of public school children in the 1981 Gallup Education Survey.

The Year of the Studies

Nineteen hundred and eighty three was recorded in educational history as "the year of the studies of American schools." At least eight studies were issued in that year, reassessing education and seeking to improve all schools, including urban schools. Most of these studies urge a reassessment of the purpose of education, all of them cite weaknesses that exist in most schools. Some reports, notably *High School: A Report on Secondary Education in America* by Ernest L. Boyer (1983), point out that some high schools are offering excellent education, especially to those students that are college bound in the direction of the most prestigious higher education institutions.

Most of the reports give minimal attention to the issue of equity. They focus on improving education in general. In this sense, if their recommendations are implemented, the situation will be somewhat analogous to the National Defense Education Act, passed after "Sputnik," designed to improve all science and mathematics instruction in the nation, and the earlier G.I. Bill, passed after World War II, which provided educational assistance to all veterans. Many see clear advantages in having non-race-specific educational efforts today since so many Americans believe that African-Americans have had as much public help as they need or deserve and have benefited from general assistance programs along with all other citizens.

However, questions of power and control necessarily surface as reform measures are recommended. The clear danger to African-Americans is that we might be ignored in the quest for excellence and quality since so many power holders seem to believe us incapable of attaining the highest standards of mental performance. School reform and restoration must not be allowed to proceed without including urban sites.

The current alarm about the state of education is indeed ironic. African-American parents and community leaders have been pacesetters, in the forefront of calling for educational improvement. Throughout the 1950s, 1960s, and 1970s these African-Americans have agitated for better schools for their children. In too many communities theirs were voices crying out in the wilderness as they demonstrated, boycotted, picketed, sat-in, and sought community control of public schools in their neighborhoods as they pursued educational betterment. African-American parents permitted their children to be bused, "paired," and magnetized in an effort to gain equal educational opportunity for them. They supported the concept of educational parks, elected school board members, and selected superintendents in an effort to change and shape educational policy decisions. We wanted equal educational opportunity and excellence for our children. Instead of being granted that, we received castigation from the dominant group for what they called our special-interest efforts. Now there is reason for hope of educational improvement since excellence is becoming a white political movement with solid middle class and intellectual backing.

Probably the most publicized of the 1983 studies has been *A Nation at Risk: The Imperative for Educational Reform*, issued in April 1983 by the National Commission on Excellence in Education, which was appointed by Secretary of Education T.H. Bell (National Education Association, 1983). It concluded that a rising tide of mediocrity threatens our future, and its authors sought to generate reform of our educational system while renewing a national commitment to schools and colleges of high quality. The Commission believed that the support of the public is the most powerful tool for improving education, and our national task is to make a renewed commitment to education and to creating a learned society. All, regardless of race, class, or economic status, are to be included in developing their individual powers of mind and spirit.

A second significant study is *Educating Americans for the 21st Century: A Plan of Action for Improving Mathematics, Science and Technology Education for All American Elementary and Secondary Students so that their Achievement is the Best in the World by 1995* (National Science Board Commission on Precollege Education in Mathematics, Science and Technology, 1983). The National Science Board's 20 Commission members chose 1995 as a target date because it allows 12 years to complete one education cycle for a generation of school children. The report recommends heavy federal investment to improve mathematics, science, and technology education in elementary and secondary schools, along with retraining of teachers, establishment of exemplary schools and programs, increased time for academic subjects, increased requirements for high school graduation and for college admission, a national mechanism for measuring student achievement, rigorous standards for certifying teachers, and increased use of computers and other technology.

The third study was conducted by the Task Force on Education for Economic Growth, sponsored by the Education Commission of the States. It issued an action plan based on its conviction that education is the key to economic growth in our nation. Titled *Action for Excellence: A Comprehensive Plan to Improve Our Nation's Schools*, it highlights closer working relationships between business and the schools and urges continued federal funding for education, along with monies from all sources, and recommends that the federal government not "shrink suddenly from the issue of education as a national priority" (Education Commission of the States, 1983).

A fourth report is *Making the Grade: Report of the Twentieth Century Fund Task Force on Federal Elementary and Secondary Education Policy* (The Twentieth Century Fund, 1983). It found that elementary and secondary schools have been forced to depart from their primary functions and are in danger of losing sight of their fundamental purposes. The recommendations for improvement assume federal responsibility and funding for helping schools improve.

John Goodlad's eight-year study has emerged in *A Place Called School: Prospects for the Future* (1983). He specifies four conditions that affect current learning and that will have an enormous effect on the future of schooling. These are (1) a youth culture preoccupied with itself and composed of persons much less shaped by the traditional institutions of home, school, and church than was the case in the past; (2) the astonishing advance of technology in almost all aspects of life ("Television may be the closest thing we have to a common school. Can the schools have a future without technology?"); (3) the requirements of a large segment of the work place are obscure, and the best preparation for work is general education; this means de-emphasizing vocational education in schools; (4) the increasing need for a highly educated society. He concluded that *education* is what is most needed. Schooling is instrumental to the attainment of that end, but not sufficient, for "schools alone cannot teach what our young people require in a world most of us scarcely comprehend."

A sixth plan for schooling is Mortimer J. Adler's *Paideia Proposal* (1982), supplemented by *Paideia Problems and Possibilities* (1983). Adler holds that basic schooling must be general and liberal, and it must *not* be specialized or vocational. He has detailed three kinds of teaching and learning that are essential to his plan: (1) acquisition of organized knowledge in basic subject fields; (2) development of intellectual skills that remain with one for life in formed habits; (3) the enlargement of understanding, insight, and aesthetic appreciation.

He decried the prevalence of didactic teaching, accepts coaching as a necesary teaching style for the development of intellectual skills, and supports teaching by *asking* (the Socratic method), not by telling. Adler admits that it might take from 20 to 30 years to implement his Paideia Plan, but he is convinced that it must become universal.

The seventh study, *High School: a Report on Secondary Education in America*, was funded by the Carnegie Foundation for the Advancement of Teaching, and is a 30-month study of 15 public high schools that represent a cross-section of American public secondary education (Boyer, 1983). Boyer found that for 10 to 15 percent of students the American high school provides perhaps the finest education in the world. At the other end of the spectrum, perhaps 20 to 30 percent of students mark time in school or drop out; the academic experience is a failure. The majority of students attend schools where "pockets of excellence can be found but where there is little intellectual challenge." (pp. 38-39). He denies that there is a rising tide of mediocrity in public schools, but found that public education is beginning to improve.

An eighth study is *Academic Preparation for College: What Students Need to Know and Be Able to Do*, issued by the College Board (The College Board, 1983). This effort is also known as "Project Equality" and is part of a ten-year endeavor initiated in 1980 by the College Entrance Examination Board. The National Education Association's analysis of this publication is that it identifies the knowledge and skills needed by high school students if they are to perform successfully in college. The competencies are reading, writing, speaking and listening, mathematics, reasoning, studying, and computer competency. Those competencies must be linked with mastery of the subject matter in English, the arts, mathematics, science, social studies, and foreign language. An important recommendation is the development of writing skills in all courses.

These eight reports have made us "information rich" on the one hand and have constituted an information overload on the other. A panel of superintendents, associate superintendents, and school board members from public school districts of the Washington, DC, metropolitan area discussed these reports and their personal concern and experiences at a symposium cosponsored by the Howard University and George Washington University chapters of Phi Delta Kappa. In general these metro-area educational leaders felt that (1) Harold Howe II's overview of these studies is very good (Howe, 1983); (2) most school systems know what their problems are, and were working to solve them long before *A Nation at Risk* was issued; (3) we need to attract, train, and retain talented teachers for the nation's schools; (4) the recommendations are costly to implement, and no budgets for their implementation are forthcoming from any source. For example, to increase the school day and year and to raise teacher's salaries accordingly, while at the same time maintaining existing contractual agreements, would cost $47 million in one jurisdiction alone. Taxpayers already are in rebellion against school costs (Proposition 13 in California; TRIM in Prince Georges County, Maryland), states are hard-pressed for funds, and the federal government wants to reduce its commitment to public education. Who will bear the costs of implementation?

There are other reports and recommendations that deserve the attention of all persons concerned about urban education. R. Freeman Butts has taken a leadership role in promoting the revival of civic learning in teacher education programs. His goal is to prepare teachers so that they know the purpose of public education — to prepare citizens for responsible roles "in a political community governed by laws rather than by kinship, religion, or status" (Butts, 1982).

The Summer 1983 issue of *Daedalus* focuses on "The Arts and Humanities in America's Schools." Arts and humanities, it is held, merit attention in all America's schools and should not be shunted aside as policymakers worry about the basics and/or about mathematics, science, and computers for the students of our elementary and secondary schools.

The statistically oriented analyst or researcher will be looking for data that many of these studies fail to supply. These persons will benefit from publications of the National Center for Education Statistics. Useful tables and explanations are available in: (1) *The Condition of Education,* (2) *The Condition of Vocational Education,* (3) *Digest of Education Statistics,* (4) *Discipline, Order and Student Behavior in American High Schools,* (5) *High School and Beyond: A National Longitudinal Study for the 1980s* (National Center for Educational Statistics, 1980, 1982, 1983).

The Public's Attitudes Toward the Public Schools, 1983

Since 1969, the Gallup Poll annually has assessed public attitudes and opinions about the public schools, and the results have been published in *Phi Delta Kappan.* The September 1983 issue of that journal reports the results of the 15th Gallup Education Survey, which is defined as valuable to school officials in at least two ways: (1) to alert decision makers to overall public reaction to school policies and programs; and (2) to serve as a national benchmark against which local attitudes can be measured (Elam, 1983).

The value of this poll is that it tells us what the public is thinking about the system of schooling that they are paying for, as well as what parents think about the particular schools that their children attend.

Specifically, the poll tells African-American people: (a) whether white people continue to support public schools, and (b) where white people stand on those issues that affect our educational possibilities. For example, the poll asks about major problems confronting the public schools. In 1983, integration/busing were way down on the list of national concern (5 percent of the respondents cited them as major problems in 1983), but formerly they were named frequently as problems. Interestingly, only 1 percent of the respondents named government interference as a problem, while the present administration touts "government interference" as a major problem.

Although public expectations for the schools are high, their perception of the schools is that they are average or below in terms of quality. Nationally, only 19 percent of the public rated the schools A or B, 38 percent rated them C, 22 percent rated them D or F, and 21 percent did not know what grade to assign. Nonwhite respondents' ratings were somewhat higher than those of whites; 24 percent of nonwhites rated the schools as A or B, 32 percent rated tham C, 16 percent rated them D or Fail, and 30 percent did not know what rating to assign.

Local public schools received somewhat higher ratings than did public schools nationally, but a downward trend in ratings that began in 1974 continued. Adults with children in local public schools rated those schools higher than did adults with children in nonpublic schools or with no children in school.

Public schools populated by African-American children and youth are part of a national education picture that adults see as problematic. When questioned specifically about the problems faced by local schools, the top four problems named remain: (1) lack of discipline, (2) use of drugs, (3) poor curriculum/poor standards, and (4) lack of proper financial support. Only the third of these four problems is properly a public school *primary* responsibility for which the school may be held accountable and which it has the power to solve within its parameters.

It is important to note that the public understands the discipline problem, for it lays blame for the problem on: (1) lack of discipline in the home (72 percent), (2) lack of respect for law and authority throughout society (54 percent), (3) students who are constant troublemakers and often cannot be removed from schools (42 percent).

It is also important to recognize that while there is a national image that urban schools (populated mainly be African-American children) are full of problems—and in many instances this is true—their problems are for the most part the same problems being experienced by many or most schools in the nation today. Thus what some people would have us think of as urban problems (African-American problems) are school problems in general in this society. We might have more of the problems, i.e., to a greater degree, but our schools are not fundamentally different from other schools.

In the poll respondents favored promotion from grade to grade based on passing examinations and vetoed the idea of "social" promotion (75 percent). Two-thirds of all respondents believe that the work load given to elementary school children and high school youth in public schools is too light, and another survey of students indicated that the students themselves felt that they are not given enough homework.

Nonwhites favor extending the school year by one month and increasing the length of the school day by one hour, but whites reject these ideas. Most parents believe that their children are learning what they should be learning in terms of curricular content offered (74 percent).

In Gallup education polls over the years parents have said that education is essential to individual success and to the success of society as a whole. The public believes in the power of education. Now can schools fulfill their expectations? This is the question that remains to be answered through adequate funding, commitment to the public school's basic raison d'etre, and institution of changes necessary to meet goals.

Effective Schools Research

In most of the current educational literature it still is the norm to emphasize the gap between African-Americans and whites in achievement and/or to focus on the extent to which African-American students fall below national averages and norms. Much less publicized is the research that provides evidence that some urban schools are effective, and that more such schools could be successful if their fundamental characteristics were replicated and continued over time.

The work of George Weber (1971), Brookover and Lezotte (1979), Brookover et al. (1979), (1983), Edmonds (1979a, 1979b, 1979c), and others have received some attention. This body of research shows that in those effective public schools the following characteristics prevail: (1) strong administrative leadership; (2) a climate of high expectations where no children are permitted to fall below minimum levels of achievement; (3) an orderly but not rigid atmosphere, conducive to instruction; (4) a philosophy that makes it clear that pupil acquisition of basic academic skills is the first order of business, taking precedence over all other school activities; (5) the flexibility to allow school energy and resources to be diverted from other business in furtherance of the fundamental objectives; (6) systematic testing to monitor and evaluate pupil progress; (7) outreach to the community.

Joseph Featherstone focused on *Schools Where Children Learn* (1971) and *What Schools Can Do* (1976). Michael Rutter and his colleagues (1979) showed that schools can make a difference in helping students overcome the adverse effects of economic disadvantage and family adversity. In their three-year study of twelve secondary schools in inner London, a low-income area, the Rutter team found some schools that were demonstrably better than others at promoting academic and social success in their students. The area included a substantial minority of immigrants with the largest group composed of Black West Indians. Daniel Levine and Jere Brophy also described successful strategies for improving academic achievement in innercity schools in an article in *Phi Delta Kappan*, which featured a special section on urban education (Levine, 1982).

The federal programs that originated in the mid-1960s—Title I, Headstart, and the Elementary and Secondary Education Act—finally are being given credit for providing services that helped African-American students reverse earlier trends that saw them falling further behind in skills. In 1981 the National Assessment of Educational Progress reported that African-American youth improved either absolutely or relatively on almost all writing tasks given to 13- and 17-year olds and on one task given to 9-year olds. In 1983 data assembled by the National Assessment of Educational Progress and reported in *The Condition of Education* showed that 9-year-old African-American students performed significantly better in reading than their counterparts in 1971. Although the Black-nonblack gap remains, 9-year old African-American students made a larger gain in reading in this period than white students of the same age group (ten points as compared with three points) (National Center for Educational Statistics, 1983).

The evaluations of longitudinal studies reported in *Lasting Effects After Preschool* show that: (1) early education programs significantly reduced the number of children assigned to special education classes, (2) early education significantly reduced the number of children retained in grade, (3) early education significantly increased children's scores on fourth grade mathematics test, (4) low-income children who attended preschools surpassed their controls on the Stanford-Binet IQ test for up to 3 years after the program ended, (5) noncognitive measures such as children's being proud of themselves were improved, (6) no significant treatment/control differences were found in families' use of Title IV child welfare services (Lazar and Darlington, 1978).

Long-term gains for low-income children who attended the Perry

Preschool in Ypsilanti, Michigan, have been reported. The longitudinal study shows that these children, who attended the Perry Preschool beginning in the fall of 1962, were less likely to be enrolled in special education programs when they were in school, and were more likely to have graduated from high school, to have received some kind of postsecondary training, to have become economically self-sufficient, and to have avoided breaking the law by the time they reached age 19 (Schweinhart and Weikart, 1980).

One study has revealed the existence of three high-achieving African-American and poor elementary schools in Pittsburgh. The investigators, a team of Barbara A. Sizemore, Carlos A. Brossard, and Birney Harrigan, have labeled these schools "abashing anomalies" and found they were set in motion by these organizational factors: (1) the recruitment and selection of a moderately authoritarian principal who believed that African-American students could and would learn; (2) the willingness of the principal to risk being different; i.e., differing with the system's norm of low achievement for African-American poor schools; (3) the mobilization of consensus among school and community actors around high achievement as the highest priority goal; (4) the generation of a climate of high expectations for student achievement conducive to teaching and learning; (5) the choice of functional routines, scenarios, and processes for the achievement of this highest priority; (6) the willingness to disagree with superior officers around the choices of these routines and their implementation (Sizemore, Brossard, Harringan, 1983).

The school systems in such cities as Atlanta, Dallas, Houston, and Washington, DC, among others, seem to be improving as a result of special efforts. Some of these systems are headed by African-American superintendents who are putting forth special professional and personal efforts to encourage and assist institutional changes that would benefit African-American and poor children. Today there are approximately 100 African-American school superintendents. Floretta Dukes McKenzie reports that there is a pattern of rising achievement in the Washington, DC, school system (McKenzie, 1983).

In their research on the urban principal, Van Cleve Morris et al. found that "peripatetic" is a good word to describe the frenetic pace maintained by big-city public school principals (Morris et al., 1983). Although the roles played by various principals vary with the person, "creative insubordination" is employed by many of those who lead successful schools. Creative insubordination in this context means that the urban principal, on occasion, to protect the innercity, working rhythm, and morale of his school and teachers, deliberately ignores, misunderstands, or outright disobeys orders from superiors. The research shows that effective urban schools are characterized by strong administrative leaders who find creative ways to get around bureaucracies that stifle them. Prospective principals might not be innovative enough to figure out how to do this or might be afraid to try. But they could learn how to do it if they had administrative internships—a move recommended by Morris—that could follow an effective principal around from day to day to see how he or she manages "in spite of the system," yet does not get fired in the process (Morris, et al., 1983; Morris, Crowson, Porter-Gehrie, Hurwitz, 1984).

The reader must not take this survey treatment to mean that there are so many effective schools that African-Americans can be assured that their children will automatically receive an education of high quality. That would be a false reading of this overview. The most accurate summation is that some programs and some schools are working successfully in a sea of programs and schools that are mediocre or worse. Some urban school systems are improving slowly, but there is no "quick fix," there is no single solution, no one charismatic leader, no one reform that will transform urban education overnight.

Thoughtful analysts will want to read the entire April 1983 issue of *Educational Researcher*, which gives detailed information about what we know about effective schools, research for school improvement, and a critique of the effective schools research (1983). Questions about the effective school model are also raised by John H. Ralph and James Fennessey (1983).

Current Issues Affecting Urban Education

There are many unsolved issues that affect urban education today. Included are desegregation, the "back to basics movement," school finance, bilingualism, the handicapped, educational vouchers, tuition tax credits, merit pay for teachers, competency testing of teachers and students, effect of computers and technology, magnet schools as instruments of change, too many elective classes, and others. The most immediate and pressing concerns of urban educators are: (1) societal efforts to reverse direction; *i.e.*, the institution of policies and programs that reduce access to education or eliminate efforts to provide equal educational opportunity for underprivileged children; (2) merit pay for teachers; (3) competency testing of teachers; (4) competency testing of students; (5) the stiffening of graduation requirements; and (6) self-help efforts to improve the academic achievement of minority children. I will focus only on these six issues with full acknowledgement that the other issues remain great concerns in most urban areas.

Efforts to Reverse Direction

Meyer Weinberg's 1983 article, "Inner City Education: Reading the Writing on the Wall," provides a very good summary of gains made by minority students in public schools over the past decade. At its close, however, he sounds a warning that must become a flag for all concerned persons:

> Minority learning progress has been real. Efforts to reverse direction are also real and we must stop them in their tracks. It will take an enormous effort to consolidate and defend the fruits of the past decade (Weinberg, 1983).

He is no doubt referring to the efforts and activities that would "narrow the application of civil rights law in education and dismantle mechanisms for enforcing those laws," (Coleman, 1983) along with "crippling or effectively eliminating many programs designed to help those students 'most at risk'" (Hanrahan and Kosterlitz, 1983). I conceive these as efforts to undermine or eliminate public schools that are dedicated to the public purpose of providing schooling by the taxpayers for children and youth from ages 5 through high school—all the children of all the people, regardless of race, gender, ethnicity, handicap, or geographic region.

In 1981, then President Ronald Reagan was offered a blueprint for policy management in a conservative administration (Heatherly, 1981). The chapter on education addressed reshaping the federal role in education (Docksai, 1981). Those recommendations were taken seriously in 1981, 1982, and 1983, especially by the conservative officials who were in the Department of Education (Hanrahan and Kosterlitz, 1983). The Civil Rights Leadership Conference publication severely criticizes the civil rights division of the Justice Department and the Office of Civil Rights of the Department of Education (Coleman, 1983). The sum and substance of conservative efforts to change the federal role in education is to "shift from guaranteeing equal education opportunity to serving as a somewhat disinterested dispenser of dollars—albeit fewer of them," and those few through block grants to states and other such mechanism (Hanrahan and Kosterlitz, 1983). Programs to help the disadvantaged (read low-income, even moderate-income, urban African-Americans and Hispanics) are being downgraded and underfunded. The move to eliminate the Department of Education by converting it into a foundation is part of this general scheme, although we hear little about the conversion these days. Also, the reduction of information that flows from the government to the public is part of the plan to reverse the direction. In some cases the information is no longer gathered through research and study; in other cases the information is not released. The control of information by federal officials is not consistent with our democratic ethos.

Conservative support for tuition tax credits for parents for tuition paid to parochial and/or private schools would drain the treasury of funds and would support private education at the expense of public education. An N.E.A. policy paper, "Tuition Tax Credits," explores these credits as economic policy and as education policy following an overview and legislative history of the question (DiLorenzo, 1983). The data show that the general public does not support tuition tax credits.

In June 1983 the U.S. Supreme Court handed down the *Mueller v. Allen* decision, which upheld a Minnesota statute that permits deductions from state income tax for "taxpayers who incur expenses for tuition, books, and instructional materials and transportation in sending a child to public or private elementary or secondary school" (DiLorenzo, 1983). This is a tax *deduction*, not a tax credit or grant. However, even though it applies to public-school parents as well as private-school parents, it will be of greater benefit to parents whose children attend private schools. This decision adds a new dimension to the tax credit arguments and to a more general concern about the future of American schooling—especially public shooling (Kemerer, 1983).

The arguments for and against vouchers similarly reflect the concerns of African-Americans about the future of public schooling. Vouchers are likely to support private schools at public expense, further depressing public schooling and contributing to its demise. Bernard Watson has analyzed vouchers, choice, and private schools in *The State of Black America 1982* (Watson, 1982). Further discussion and analysis can be found in "Educational Vouchers: Regulating Their Efficiency and Effectiveness," in the November 1983 issue of *Educational Researcher* (Wise, Darling-Hammond, 1983).

Merit Pay for Teachers

Professional and lay literature is replete with articles that support or denounce the idea of merit pay for teachers as a way of improving the quality of education.

The cloudiness of the question, which has become a hot political issue, is reflected in its lack of precise definition. Merit pay means what it is defined to mean in various jurisdictions, although the general concept seems to be to reward teachers based on their classroom performance rather than on academic degrees, years of experience, and seniority in a particular system.

Unanswered questions abound: (1) who is an adequate judge of classroom performance; (2) what criteria will be used for judgment; (3) is "classroom performance" to be measured by variables that the teacher *can control*, such as thoroughness of preparation of lessons and interesting delivery of information, along with concern for all children — or is "classroom performance" to be measured by variables *outside* the teacher's control, such as the ability of children to understand what is being taught and to score high on their tests as a result; (4) will teachers of gifted and talented students be judged the same way as teachers of the average-ability or low-ability students; (5) will teachers of the educable mentally retarded or emotionally disabled be evaluated in the same ways as teachers of the "normal" students?

Merit pay plans have a possibility of being discriminatory against the minority-group teacher because a perception exists that most minority-group teachers are inferior to those of the dominant group. Current options for initiating merit plans also include many judgmental categories where discrimination can exist but would be hard to prove. As one example, the following qualifications have been cited as appropriate to establish "skill-level groupings" of teachers whose pay scales would be appropriate to the groupings: the amount of academic training of the teacher, the achievement of the student measured by the learning objectives of each class, the level of student discipline, the quality of teacher's relationship with parents, the teacher's relationship with peers, other factors considered important to individual school systems (Education Research Service, Inc., 1983). The last four of these categories could be utilized to discriminate against any teacher, and certainly can be used against minority teachers. The move toward merit pay is tricky and risky and should be monitored with care and caution.

Competency Testing for Teachers

Many states now require beginning teachers to pass the National Teachers Examination in addition to having an earned degree in the appropriate field and the stipulated teachers certification courses. There is a developing mood in the nation to have tougher standards for beginning practitioners.

In addition, there is some sentiment for the competency testing of in-service teachers in order to ensure that they have mastered the subject matter that they are employed to teach. This is a more controversial aspect of the competency testing push. Long-term teachers compare themselves to long-term physicians and lawyers, neither of whom is required to be retested periodically in order to practice their chosen profession. Neither are they retested based on the number of patients or cases they lose in a given year or so. Because the public is not satisfied with the quality of performance of students, teachers are blamed.

This issue can become a political football. While teachers must assume the responsibilities for which they are employed, they cannot be blamed for all the conditions and problems in and out of school over which they have no control but which affect the willingness and ability of students to master what is being taught in the nation's classrooms. The issue of competency testing for teachers must also be monitored with care and caution. This is still one more way of reducing the number of minority teachers under the guises of "excellence" and "accountability."

Competency Testing of Students

Minimum competency tests are used to measure a student's level of mastery of certain skills deemed important by his or her state. These are school skills—reading, writing, arithmetic—but might be called "life skills" as well, such as, reading a newspaper or keeping a bank account. In 1975, only a few states had enacted minimum competency laws; by 1978, 36 states had set some minimum standards, and now 39 states use minimum competency tests. Many school systems link these tests to yearly promotion and/or to high school graduation. African-American students are failing competency tests in larger proportions than are their white or Asian counterparts and, in some communities, their Hispanic peers. As a result, these youth will receive school attendance certificates, not high school diplomas, and will be unemployable unless remedial education and retesting are provided them.

The testing movement is a reality. While educators debate the pros and cons of the examinations, children are "slipping between the cracks." This means that African-American people need several simultaneous efforts: (1) monitoring the management and use of test results; (2) participating in construction of the tests to reduce bias of all kinds; (3) participating in planning for the implementation of testing, and for revising the testing plans, at local and state levels; (4) ensuring that there is compensatory instruction at the lower levels so that students are less likely to fail at the end of the high school experience; (5) remedial instruction and retesting for end of high school failures; (6) tutorial and other instruction so that African-American children learn test-taking skills, increase their vocabularies, learn to work speedily and accurately, and overcome their fear of test taking.

Test results can be used against teachers, as well. If students score poorly, it is said that teachers did not teach them well. Students and teachers have a vested interest in working together to ensure that students pass competency tests. Parents and citizens have an obligation to require of school systems adequate notification of performance standards and requirements, along with dates for implementation of these standards. Malpractice lawsuits have begun, and no doubt will increase if schools fail to meet standards established by minimum competency tests (Thomas, 1979).

African-American children, their parents, and organized groups need to understand that the current mood is to test us out of the educational and employment picures. The competition has increased for scarce places in education and in employment and the nation is turning against affirmative action in education and employment. The feeling is that people should merit education and employment opportunity, and merit is more than often determined by test scores.

While we as a group fail to score high on tests, the testing movement is growing and tests are being used as selecting and sorting devices — all in the name of merit to get the best qualified. African-Americans have sought a moratorium on testing, but instead of getting that, we are getting an escalation of the testing movement.

If more of us fail to receive high school diplomas because we are alleged to be incompetent, we will not be candidates for college. If we fail the National Teachers Exam, we will not be candidates for teaching positions. If we fail the Graduate Record Exam, the Medical School Exam, etc., we will not get into professional schools. If African-American graduates of law schools fail the bar exams, they cannot become practicing lawyers, etc.

We will indeed be remiss, in fact it will be unforgivable, if we who understand this fail to help the thousands of African-American children who, through ignorance and innocence, fall victim to test failure.

The Stiffening of Graduation Requirements

Competency testing is only one of the ways in which high schools are tightening requirements. Edward Fiske reported in the *New York Times* that at least 20 states have increased the number of academic courses necessary for a high school diploma and more than 15 other states are considering such steps. This has occurred just since 1980 (Fiske, 1983). English, mathematics, science, and computer courses are receiving priority. In Florida some schools have increased their day from six periods to seven. California has restored statewide graduation requirements that were abolished in 1969 (Kurtz, 1983). Many of these initiatives originated from public pressures within the states — from parents, political and business leaders — not from educators, education organizations, or the school studies.

Although some parents and groups argue that the additional require-ments are unfair, they are being instituted in the name of improving educational quality. It is clear that African-American students must meet these requirements and that, without motivation and the special attention of mature adults who care about them and minister to their intellectual needs, many of these students will fail. African-American students and their families must be made aware of current trends that could be inimical to them, and must be assisted so they can survive academically. More educated people will be needed in the future, not less educated people. The future of the ill-informed is not clear at this point, but the *situation* is very clear. There will be no need for ignorance and little tolerance for people who fail to contribute to the social order.

Neoconservatives are saying that the civil rights efforts and the quest for equality over the past 30 years have caused many of the problems existing in America today. Also it is held that the quest for equity in education has caused the problems in public education. Remember John Gardner's old question, "Can we be equal and excellent too?" The answer today seems to be "no," and the emphasis is on excellence, not on equality or equity. The real trend is to try to eliminate public schooling as a quality education option. Conservatives like to have private schools subsidized at public expense through vouchers, tuition tax credits, etc., and they have no interest in equal educational opportunity for African-Americans or the poor.

Self-help

In October 1983, middle-class, African-American parents and community leaders in Maryland's Montgomery County organized themselves around the goal of increasing the school achievement of their offspring, many of whom were not performing at the level expected by their families. Since these children and youth had been spared the hardships imposed by poverty and the limitations imposed by restricted life experiences, their parents knew that something was amiss with respect to racial/ethnic relationships, school effectiveness, and/or student initiative/effort. Only 34 percent of African-American youth passed the competency tests in Montgomery County. The parents and community leaders pledged to assume a responsible role in the quest to solve the school achievement problem; they did not pass the buck.

John Ogbu's research showed that, at school and in the community, African-American children in Stockton, California, diverted most of their efforts away from schoolwork and into nonacademic settings. Ogbu believes that "the poor school performance of African-American children is partly a result of not putting enough time, effort, and perseverance into their schoolwork." He reported that in interviews African-American children explained to him that one of the reasons that Chinese, Japanese, and some white children do well in school is that they spend more time and effort on schoolwork than do African-American students (Ogbu, 1983). Ogbu believes that because African-Americans realize that they face a job ceiling in the larger world, they develop a variety of coping mechanisms that do not enhance school success. Also, an antagonism and distrust has developed between African-Americans and the schools based on a history of segregated and inferior education. This makes it difficult for African-Americans to accept and follow school rules, he says.

Also important is the need for African-American teenagers to have information about contraception, pregnancy, and childbirth, including the economic and social costs of child-rearing. Of some 665,790 out-of-wedlock births in 1980, more than half (327,737) were to African-Americans as compared with 320,063 to whites. Self-help efforts must include reducing these out-of-wedlock births to African-American youth.

Teenage girls who give birth often do not complete high school, and thereby limit their own life chances and those of their young. Even if they do return to school, they are burdened with responsibilities of adulthood at a time when they should be relatively carefree and free to learn what is being taught in school. Instead, they must juggle school assignments with parental responsibilities — usually without sufficient funds to pay for child care or to participate in activities that would help them to grow and develop.

Changes in the African-American family have become a great concern in the African-American community. In 1980, half of the African-American families with children present were one-parent families, and most of these were headed by single women (Glick, 1981; Cummings, 1983). Many of these women are undereducated, underemployed, or unemployed, which means that their households suffer disproportionate social, economic, and environmental disadvantages compared with the majority population and compared with two-parent households in the African-American population. Race, social class, gender, lack of opportunity, job ceiling, insufficient education and skills, all interact to create ever-present and new crises for low-income, African-American families —especially those headed by women. African-American churches, community organizations, sororities, fraternities, and other groups must assist these families in the short run. In the long run, better schooling is needed, along with societal change that will show urban youth that they do have a chance for a meaningful future in this nation.

Conclusion

Urban education became the "whipping boy" for the nation's ills after 1954. When it became clear that the nation could not prevent public school desegregation forever, city schools and African-American youth were left behind as whites fled to the suburbs and to private or parochial schools. Overcrowding in the 1950s, caused by the baby boom, led to double shifts in urban schools and to social promotions as waves of the young were moved on to make space for the numbers behind them. Resistance to continued segregation and inferior education caused African-American parents and community leaders to take an activist role in changing school board composition, principals, and some teachers. This led to some parent-school hostility and antagonism.

The permissiveness of the 1960s led many youth to believe that they need not learn to read, write, or compute well. They were told that they could get necessary information from television, and that calculators would work their math problems. They hoped that they could talk their way through life, and even in the oral realm, the use of cultivated language was not taught or encouraged in too many schools. The Puritan-Protestant work ethic declined, and like many other Americans, some teachers and students exerted less effort than had their counterparts in the past.

At the same time, federal programs in education came into being. They were funded for short periods, and came and went in schools before anyone knew whether or not the innovations were workable. Neoconservative critics declared that the programs had failed by 1972, only seven years after they had been legislated, ignoring the fact that it takes time for children to learn and even more time when those children and their families have had generations of imposed handicaps and hardships that inhibit learning. The mental ability of African-Americans to learn academic materials was once again in question.

The economic hardships of the 1970s and the more conservative national leadership compounded the conditions cited above. By the end of 1980, all of these factors had created a social situation that was mind-boggling.

Urban schools can work, but we as a nation must rededicate ourselves to making them work. In 1983, four schools in the Washington, DC, metropolitan area received awards for excellence from the U.S. Department of Education: Brookland Elementary and Jefferson Junior High in Washington, DC, George Mason Junior High in Falls Church, Virginia, and T.C. Williams High School in Alexandria, Virginia. The awards were based on impressive student performance on standard achievement and minimum competency tests, low dropout rates, and high daily attendance rates (White, 1983). These are new beginnings, and it is our challenge to see that they are extended.

Part Two

Factors Affecting Academic Achievement

3 Changing an Urban School: Problems of Capacity and Power

JAMES R. BLISS
and
MAGARIDA C. CARRASCO

Introduction

Some people continue to believe that change is difficult to make happen because minority students and their families are variously inadequate (Edmonds, 1979, p. 21). Our data suggest instead it is because: (1) the capacity and power of school personnel largely determine the quality of instructional effort; and (2) the complex problems of urban schools are unlikely to be resolved by mandates in a tenure-dominated environment. Several prior studies anticipate this point of view (Fullan, 1985; Berman, 1986; Sarason, 1986; McDonnell and Elmore, 1987; McLaughlin, 1987). This study extends the literature in three ways. First, it describes five policies that were implemented in one urban school in the Northeastern United States. Second, it describes the effects of these policies on the everyday practices of teachers and administrators. Finally, it explains why these policies did not have the benefits the district expected. Whereas previous work has focused on schools that were already successful, this one strives to examine a school in transition.

The authors wish to express their appreciation to William A. Firestone for his comments on earlier drafts of this paper.

Methods

The study was conducted in a New Jersey urban school district with a large Black and Hispanic enrollment, and began with a review of critical events in the district. Here are the highlights. In 1979, the state board of education required the district to institute a city-wide school improvement plan, primarily because of low student test scores. The local board of education, along with the superintendent, developed such a plan. As a result, new behavioral and performance standards (Kirst, 1987) were implemented for both faculty and students throughout the district. The new standards were implemented over a period of several years.

In 1982, the district implemented a student promotion policy based on academic performance. The district also implemented a new instructional management information system centering on commercially published reading and mathematics materials, packaged instruction throughout the district. By 1983, a new teacher attendance policy and a new student homework policy were also in place. Throughout the 1980s, despite the new policies, the district continued to face adverse publicity from low student test scores and negative external evaluations.

These were some of the events that shaped the district's experience with reform in the 1980s. Because the student assessment and promotion piece was introduced in the lowest grades first, it was not until 1987 that so-called competency-based promotion would have been operative at all grade levels in the school. At the beginning of the decade, only the lower-grade teachers had been directly affected by some of these adjustments. Over the years, however, upper-grade teachers too were directly involved with all of the new policies.

This was a study of state-initiated reforms filtered through the district and their consequences. The school, a K-8 with approximately 1,100 students, was selected on a reputation basis as one of the better schools in the district. The study focused on how teachers reacted to these reforms under relatively favorable circumstances compared with those in more turbulent schools. The school offered a general curriculum. In addition, it offered English as a second language, bilingual education, compensatory education, speech, computer education, and a class for the neurologically impaired.

Extensive interviews began with a series of questions designed to initiate conversation on the effects of five new policies that were implemented since 1981. The interview data were supplemented by an analysis of school handbooks, minutes of staff and committee meetings, attendance records of students and teachers, test scores, classroom registers, plan books, folders of students' work, report cards, and student retention records. Confirmation of evidence was accomplished through repeated conversations with the same individuals and numerous cross checks among persons and documents.

Interviews and analyses of documents required approximately six months of effort. All teachers of second and fourth grades, all sixth grade teachers, compensatory education teachers, ESL (English as a Second Language) teachers, and special education teachers were interviewed. In all, thirty interviews were conducted. Field notes were taken during the interviews and rewritten the same day. To clarify teachers' answers to the questions posed, nearly all interviews were followed by a telephone call or a second interview confirming specific assertions, because all too often empirical research relies on participants whose knowledge may be high but whose objectivity is suspect (Gormley, 1987, p. 158). In this case study, however, the primary investigator was generally familiar with the school in advance of the study, and participants in the study were aware of this fact.

The teachers not only were willing to describe critical events surrounding the new policies, but helped identify background records that supported their comments. It was recognized, however, that a certain amount of reciprocal attitude fitting probably occurred, as interviewer and respondents worked together. Thus, no strong claims are made about the validity of these data, even though every effort was made to improve their internal consistency.

The remainder of this paper is divided into four sections. First, five policy initiatives are described. Second, the effects and outcomes of these initiatives are analyzed, using a modified version of Berman's (1986) compliance theory. Third, a number of explanations are offered for the failure of policy initiatives of produce expected results. Last, implications of the reasearch are drawn. Every research method implies a value position. This paper springs from a sense of the incipient vitality in the school and a sense that state-initiated mandates can be a crucial source of energy needed for school reform. While we listened sympathetically to what teachers said about the effects of these mandates, we also recognized that these policies were filling a power vacuum (Doyle and Finn, 1984) that perhaps needed to be filled.

Policies

The threat of a state education department takeover, along with rumors that top adiministrators were to be fired if the takeover occurred (Doyle and Finn, 1984, p. 94; Kirst, 1987, p. 14), had prompted the school district to implement five district-wide policies. As the study began during spring 1987, it was agreed by nearly all teachers in the study that these policies were likely the result of state pressures upon the school district.

Question: Why, in your opinion, were these policies implemented?
Answers: (Here are some answers that were given.)
"...under pressure from the state..."
"...to get ready for the state's mandated pupil-testing program.'"
"...to show the state we are on track."
"...they were afraid of the state, I guess,"
"...they (the Board) are accountable to the state,...no choice."

Student Attendance Policy

To become eligible for promotion, students in the district were required by the student attendance policy to miss no more than thirty school days per year, except for chronic illness certified by a doctor or school nurse. The student attendance policy closely resembled state guidelines for student attendance applicable to all of its public school districts.

Student Homework Policy

The student homework policy, initiated in 1981-82, required teachers in second grade to assign ten minutes of homework per night. Teachers in higher grades were required to assign an additional ten minutes of homework every year. By 1987-88, according to the policy, eighth grade students would have received seventy minutes per day of homework. The student homework policy had no state-specified counterpart, but was part of the district's overall improvement plan.

Student Achievement Policy

To become eligible for promotion, students were required by the new policies to demonstrate certain levels of achievement on criterion-referenced exams in reading and mathematics. The minimum proficiency levels were 75 percent for reading and 65 percent for mathematics. Those students failing to meet these levels were required to attend summer school. This policy closely resembled state guidelines for districts.

Teacher Attendance Policy

Teachers were permitted under the new policies to accrue no more than five consecutive absences during one year without documentation from a physician. Upon accruing six total absences in a year and failing to submit documentation of illness from a physician, teachers were scheduled for a hearing before the building principal. A nine-day, unexcused teacher absence would have triggered a teacher-board conference, according to this policy.

Classroom Information Management policy

Teachers were required to maintain student records in the classroom that included district-wide academic progress charts in reading and mathematics as a part of a commercial instruction series. The classroom information policy was a district-level initiative, with no direct counterpart in state-level guidelines for districts. The information management system, while potentially useful for diagnostic studies, was intended to improve teacher accountability (Weiss and Gruber, 1984).

Effects of the Policies

Student Attendance and Homework

The student attendance policy was accepted by teachers and students at the school with little complaint or controversy. But, average student attendance at this particular school had not been a serious problem. The average student attendance rate at this school had been approximately 96 percent throughout the 1980s, within district and state guidelines, while the student attendance rate for all elementary school in the district had been approximately 90 percent during this period.

Likewise, the student homework policy seems to have been accepted by teachers as a part of the game (Bardach, 1977, pp. 66-81), although teachers felt that a required minimum amount of homework per day, whether necessary or not for instruction on any given day, reduced their ability to prepare. Little documentation existed, however, to estimate the amount of daily homework actually assigned. No one could demonstrate, for example, that ten minutes of homework per day in the lowest grades and progessively more homework in the upper grades had been, in fact, assigned or graded.

Student Promotions

The data available on student promotions permitted a somewhat deeper analysis of outcomes. The student promotions data indicated, for example, that virtually 100 percent of the school's eighth graders were promoted in two successive years for which information was available. This finding was unexpected, in view of the normal curve equivalent test scores for this period. However, the capacity of teachers to retain students was also a function of local norms. The percentage of nonpromoted students would have been higher if the student achievement policy had been rigorously enforced. By comparison, higher nonpromotion rates were found in the earliest grades. The nonpromotion rate in first grade, for example, was about 12 percent in 1986, somewhat more in line with what one would have expected (Table 3.1).

Table 3.1

Average Student Achievement Test Scores and Promotion Rates*

| | | READING | | | MATH | | % PASSED |
GRADE	1984	1985	1986	1984	1985	1986	1986
1	53	55	59	65	63	69	85.4
2	60	56	59	81	70	63	86.8
3	52	53	54	60	60	70	88.6
4	44	48	46	65	65	66	92.0
5	54	57	50	67	71	72	92.0
6	47	47	50	70	67	72	90.0
7	48	50	52	56	62	64	96.0
8	49	48	54	63	53	64	97.0

*Figures for reading and math are nationally-normed achievement test scores with mean 50, s.d. 10.

The eighth grade scores show that students achieved an average normal curve equivalent percentile score of 54 in reading and 64 in mathematics. This was about twenty points below state and local guidelines for districts in reading. Yet, 97 percent of the students were promoted upward to high school. These figures show the results of poor decision making, particularly in the upper grades. The typical student met the passing standard for districts in neither reading nor mathematics. The basic skills development of the majority of students in the school was not up to the state's (or the district's) minimum academic standards for districts. The only good news was that test scores did not decline.

Teacher Attendance

The teacher attendance policy was less than effective as well. In fact, the teacher attendance policy seemed almost irrelevant to a four-year pattern of teacher attendance documented in the district's files. Teacher attendance remained uneven across the year and below state minimums, despite the teacher attendance policy. At almost no point during the years that were examined did teacher attendance attain the 95 percent level that was required by the district and the state (Figure 3.1).

According to the figure, the average teacher attendance usually peaked in September. The low point of teacher attendance occurred during the winter. This is the season most challenging for teachers whose own school-age children are subject to minor illnesses and those who commute through snowy weather to the suburbs. Although district policies called for building-level

Teacher-Days

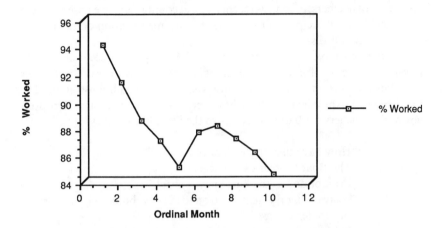

Figure 3.1 Percent scheduled teaching days attended by ordinal month of school year, September through June.

hearings in cases of excess teacher absences, we found that the capacity to hold such hearings was pushed to the limit following the winter periods of high teacher absenteeism. The principal was unable to cope with the many teacher absence hearings that were required. As teacher absences grew during the peak winter periods, the principal could not handle the number of teacher absenteeism hearings.

Deceptive Record Keeping

The new information management system was also widely implemented, yet in a superficial way. Student folders were observed in the classrooms properly organized and labeled. Yet, the whole purpose of using student folders to track the progress of potentially disafffected students, meaning most of the students, appears to have been distorted. One teacher described her own assessment of the information system as follows: "Some teachers do not even give the real achievement tests; they just put plus (+) marks on the students' folders." The most cynical teachers commented that administrators all along had anticipated that conflicts would erupt between teachers and parents if teachers kept accurate records and followed the district's promotion policies rigidly.

The teachers recognized that information contained in student folders could be used to audit promotion recommendations for the following year. Many teachers refused to document student progress in the degree of detail that would have allowed observers to audit the results of ongoing testing in the classroom. Most teachers said that student promotions should be left to the discretion of teachers, as long as teachers are accountable to the parents. Here we see evidence of incipient professional norms in a situation dominated by bureaucratic controls.

On the other hand, teachers reported that they often secured "faked" physicians' excuses for their own absences, and transformed the teacher attendance policy into a cat and mouse game with the administration. The required visits to physicians' offices, however, were not inexpensive. Here are a few of the teachers' verbatim reactions to the attendance policy:

Question:"How have these policies affected you?"
Answers: "The Board forces us to cheat..."
          "Promotion?...the kids know I cheat."
          "[I say to them] you must go on to the next book so I can mark your folder to pass."
          "We keep ourselves covered and go about things in our own way."
          "We are strictly teaching for the tests and not well as you see."
          "I laugh at the [teacher attendance policy]; some of us even present fake doctors' notes, not forgeries, but authentic notes for faked illness."

Additional Paperwork

The new classroom information system resulted in two sets of student records being kept in many classes, a set of records on students that could be shown to officials from the district office and a set of records realistic and practical for daily instructional purposes. In addition, teachers classified more students as handicapped than would otherwise have been the case. The process of classifying more students as handicapped required a substantial increase in paperwork.

Divisiveness

There were three main informal groups of teachers in the school. The first group consisted of the Black teachers who expressed ambivalence and concern that students would be emotionally hurt by nonpromotions. The second group consisted of gregarious, highly spirited teachers. Teachers in this group accepted events at face value, avoiding controversy. Both groups manipulated the system to their own ends. The third group consisted of quiet, thoughtful people anguished by the disasters around them who tried to maintain integrity by working a lot harder. The new policies affected these groups differently, but pushed them apart.

In addition, the young mothers on the faculty had been using their contractual sick days as child care days. The new policies drew attention to problems relating to the maternity conditions faced by these teachers and to their divided responsibilities as teachers and parents. While expressing sympathy for young mothers, the older faculty indicated that if younger ones could have child care days, they (older ones) should be allowed family care days. The teacher attendance policy thus aggravated sensitivities and divisions that were already present.

The teachers recalled a faculty meeting at which the principal compared student test scores by grade and teacher. Such comparisons put special pressure on the lower-grade teachers. These were the ones to whom upper-grade teachers turned in offering explanations for the poor performances of their own classes. Teachers working in the lowest grades, to their credit, did not openly blame students for the low test scores; yet, some deeply resented the unsupportive parents.

Mistrust and Suspiciousness

Many teachers believed that the policies would simply go away over time. They expressed this in statements like the following:

> "The policies will change...every five years...resolve themselves and then dissolve."

> "Today one policy, tomorrow another."

The teachers' mistrust of the administration was reinforced to an extent by the principal who was known to announce over the public address system, concerning circulars from the central office (for example), "The more things change, the more they stay the same." This miscalculated use of an aphorism was more powerful than the principal realized, for it found its way into the speech of teachers and fueled a pervasive expectation that deep realities of the school and district would not (and could not) change.

The teachers were also aware of new programs and educational innovations that had first appeared and then disappeared. "Fads," teachers called them, and teachers were given no good reasons, in this case, to assume the new policies would last any longer than other new policies in the past had lasted. The principal too exhibited little confidence that the new policies would endure. More importantly, perhaps, it was rumored that the principal himself had used sick days, on various occasions, to extend personal vacations. And teachers said they were aware of other administrators who enjoyed this "privilege," which aggravated the distrust between the principal and the teachers.

But the teachers also recognized that their own insights about the policy process would likely not shield them from swift sanctions if the administration decided to impose them. There were rumors and innuendoes about unofficial files being kept on teachers by the principal, and there was a general impression among the teachers that their conduct was under careful scrutiny by an administration that had stopped caring about them. Although the evidence on lack of district support was clear, there was no direct evidence of any threats carried out by the administration.

Discouragement and Frustration

The district, in effect, had required a new basal series in reading and mathematics without providing in-service training opportunities in how to use these materials efficiently. To the extent that these materials may have required different ways of teaching, teachers had not been assisted in making the necessary transitions. The complaints, particularly from the lower-level teachers, were strong in this regard.

The pressure for rapid results experienced by the teachers, combined with a lack of dramatic improvements in test scores, led to open expressions of frustration and bitterness. In effect, teachers were saying, "We are the ones trying to help these kids in school, and look at the grief we are getting in return for it?" Some teachers also expressed the feeling that they had made mistakes in their careers and were now trapped by an unrewarding work situation, unable because of financial reasons to change jobs. These attitudes, however, were inconsistent with any intellectual rationale for teacher tenure.

Explanations

Central policy makers often mistakenly assume that local institutions have the capacity to change without considerable assistance, even when projects require extra effort (Berman and McLaughlin, 1976, p. 358). They then try to overcome the perceived lack of willingness through mandates (Cuban, 1984, p. 214). As local institutions cannot comply with the mandates because they lack organizational capacity, these institutions either resist the mandates or engage in superficial symbolic behavior to keep up appearances. The data support this general view and point to several reasons why one school has failed, thus far, to achieve the results expected.

Capacity Issues

There are at least two meanings of organizational capacity relevant to the data collected in this study. The first meaning concerns availability of material or purchased resources. The second meaning concerns availability of qualified and committed people. Both meanings of capacity refer to conditions that interact with power to produce change (Table 3.2).

Table 3.2

Expected Policy Outcomes by Type of Power and Level of Capacity

		(CAPACITY)	
		High	Low
(Power)/			
	Formal	Compliance	Dissension
	Incentive	Adjustment	Displacement
	Condign	Resistance	Dissimulation
	Routine	Facility	Confidence
	Example	Refinement	Emulation
	Leadership	Commitment	Participation

The first sense of capacity refers to material capacity—the availability of appropriate materials. The availability of appropriate materials varies within schools, between schools within districts, and between districts. Schools without pencils, chalk, or equivalents render moot issues of the willingness of students and teachers to write. Those who argue that purchased resources are not enough to guarantee improvements have a point to make. Material resources or the lack thereof, however,contribute much to shaping the efforts of teachers and students alike. The district's decision to standardize instructional materials at the elementary level resulted in an abundance of the standard materials in well-stocked closets, but a shortage of alternative materials to help teachers tailor or individualize instruction.

The second sense of capacity refers to human capacity—the availability of appropriate skills, knowledge, and values. In urban schools, where the instructional focus is ostensibly on the development of basic literacy and numeration, sopisticated elementary-level competencies are needed. In this regard, effective schools prescriptions seem to have had strange undesirable effects. Many administrators, for example, interpret this research to mean that all teachers should follow a particular set of procedures for instructing no matter what, and they have ritualized and ceremonialized these things to a point where we cannot even conceive of a more-sophisticated technology (Silver, 1986, p. 142). Also contributing to this use of effective schools research has been unquestioning acceptance of bureaucratic norms by administrators and teachers alike.

The evidence gathered on human capacity was limited. It seemed, however, that standard instructional materials purchased by the district, for understandable reasons (e.g., student intra-district mobility), may have neutralized or supplanted, to an extent, the teachers' knowledge. These materials were, in a sense, curriculum substitutes. In addition, there was evidence that teachers had been threatened with lawsuits from parents concerned that their children would not be promoted because of low test scores. The teachers were generally unprepared to deal with packaged instruction and threatened parental lawsuits. The district had not taken aggressive measures to build capacity in areas such as involving parents with helping children through alternative technologies at home, which seems to belie the notion that research and technology are being used to achieve greater capacity in schools (Emery and Trist, 1965; Epstein, 1984).

Issues of human capacity can be further divided into issues of *conceptual capacity, procedural capacity,* and sensitivity, including *normative capacity.* The school under-conceptualized its problems all along, and this has been an obstacle to progress. For example, the emphasis on subordination, command, and compliance makes little sense in a tenure-dominated environment. The school's procedural incapacity, exemplified by the parents' use of summer school to circumvent retentions, the inability of the principal to conduct timely teacher absence hearings, or the mushrooming paperwork associated with tracking student progress, amply demonstrated that school improvement is more than a question of faculty willingness. Finally, more needs to be said than space allows on the pervasiveness of bureaucratic norms in both faculty and administration.

In brief, however, two points seem clear. First, teachers and administrators are confused about values associated with the terms *bureaucrat* and *professional.* As commonly used in one urban school, the term "professional" is most often meant to justify a demand for greater autonomy, not to volunteer for new or even basic challenges. Second, real professional norms may be unachievable in such a top-heavy environment. While downsizing the bureaucracy would be insufficient to generate healthy norms, downsizing could be a step in the right direction. Regardless of the organizational configuration and the ensuing norms that emerge, however, basic questions of human capacity remain.

First, who shall teach? One of the teachers assigned the following essay topic to a class of sixth graders, "The worst thing about my teacher last year, Mr./Miss/Mrs. (name), was..." The teacher then corrected students' mechanical errors and proudly posted the papers on a bulletin board in the main corridor for everyone to read. Although a few colleagues were mortified, most apparently were amused. Furthermore, although events often speak for themselves, opinion was divided in this instance over what, if anything, should be done about a teacher who would criticize colleagues in this manner. Events like these, too frequently raise questions not answered by choice models (Chubb and Moe, 1986), and other proposals, such as site-based management (Guthrie, 1986), proposed to reform urban schools. These questions are on a deeper level, or so it seems.

Second, what shall be the content? Related to the question of who shall teach is the question of instructional objectives. The teachers in this case were confronted by packaged, criterion-test-driven objectives. If content requires continuing refinement of meanings to keep these meanings fresh in the minds of teachers, packaged objectives spoil the very capacity for growth in the faculty since they preempt to an extent the process of deciding *what* to teach. In addition, the push for cognitive gains has led to bland content often lacking in playfulness, and urban educators should not fail to recognize the counterproductiveness of bland, to an extent punitive, content. The emphasis on basic skills development has been unsophisticated, heavy handed, and uninspired.

Finally, who will administer the schools? There are plenty of administrative certificate holders (Bliss, 1988). Quantity is not the problem. Symptomatic of the problem is that teachers in this case were unimpressed, to put it mildly, by levels of administrative participation and commitment below their own. Rigorous administrator preparation programs and requirements for continued professional development are needed. Schools of education must work to overcome problems associated with socioeconomic segregation in the preparation of administrators. New certification provisions such as those now effective in New Jersey, requiring degrees in administration or management, would help a great deal. But urban administrators themselves should certainly take a more active role in upgrading the sophistication and efforts of their group.

Power Issues

Change is a function of power as well as capacity. Legitimate power is said to be that which derives from the formal organization. Legitimate power can be expressed as willingness to comply with mandates or inducements. The state had issued mandates it was reluctant to push. This is another reason why the district failed to achieve anything like the results expected in terms of student and teacher performance. In doing so, however, the district achieved a kind of short-term victory, by seizing the "reform" initiative from the teachers' union and other interest groups. Few would fault the district for expecting its personnel, students and teachers, to at least attend. However, an acceptable way to achieve this was seemingly unknown, which raises the issue of whether state and district policy makers have a clear sense of the difference between controllable from uncontrollable conduct (Landau and Stout, 1979).

Condign power, similar to reward power, is compliance through actual or possible punishment. Condign power relies on increasing the cost or burden associated with the job. Condign power implies, "unless you do this, we will do that..." The exercise of condign power may include dismissal, transfer to undesirable work sites, or assignment of arduous non-teaching duties (e.g., cafeteria duty or advisor to student publications). The teachers were fearful of the system's condign power, which was perhaps the whole point of using it. The use of condign power may also have contributed to a sense of urgency over things like the need to track student progress, if only nominally at first. The data contained little or no evidence that any threats, either real or imagined, had been carried out. But not all power implies external pressure (Elmore, 1983, p. 366).

The power of day-to-day routines concerns how adult men and women get along in the ordinary course of events. Unfortunately, labor-management relations in elementary schools align themselves almost perfectly with male-female relations, which further complicates change. What this means is that elementary teachers are usually women whose perspectives on children and schooling may differ, in a deep sense, from those of men administrators. For example, administrators tended to complain of bafflement, and teachers of disappointment. It should surprise no one that problems between the sexes characterize schools as they do other gender-integrated institutions. Furthermore, to their credit, urban schools employ many nontraditional women with courage to work in sometimes unfavorable conditions. Day-to-day routines indicate how well value conflicts are being handled.

The power of example rests in providing clear examples with which people can identify. In this case, little attention was given to constructive examples of putting the new policies into effective use. For example, teachers missed a number of opportunities to set positive examples for one another in how to use the policies for the benefit of students. They failed to recognize that the policies provided many leverage points to use in working with parents and district subject matter specialists. More importantly, the teachers permitted the district to dominate the policy agenda because of their own inertia on questions of teacher attendance, effective instructional strategies, and student promotion.

The power of leadership is among the more elusive institutional powers. Good leaders seem to exhibit concern for the accomplishment of tasks as well as concern for persons. There was little evidence of instructional leadership of that kind, although the school environment, by creating a subtle balance of autonomy and control, can have a lot to say about whether the principal is able to exert effective leadership (Peterson, 1984, p. 594). The teachers were clustered into three informal groups, each one with its social leaders. But neither the principal nor any of the teachers functioned as instructional leaders, and the lack of instructional leadership was another reason why the district's policies failed to achieve the expected results. Although teacher concerns may have been anchored in the classroom (Cuban, 1986, p. 67), teachers proposed no constructive alternatives.

Conclusions

Summary

In the early 1980s, the district under pressure from the state approved a directive to the superintendent to prepare a program of district improvement. But one event led to another, and teachers came to feel as if they alone were being held responsible for low student achievement in the district. This led to unexpected acts of professional "cheating." The teachers engaged in creating student records that were incomplete to prevent outside criticism of their students' progress. They even went so far as to begin submitting "faked" physicians' excuses for their own absenteeism. The results in this area add weight to Bardach's description of policy implementation games and Berman's thesis that the ideology of compliance tends to stimulate various kinds of distortions by those who are forced to comply when they lack the capacity to do so.

Five new policies were implemented. But the implementation of these policies turned out to be largely superficial. The evidence indicated that school administrators were not eager to expose the system's failure either, although the fact of widespread systemic failure had been no great secret. The building administrator in this case would easily have audited student achievement records and could have called a halt to the practice of promoting students who had failed to reach grade level. The lack of enforcement on the part of the building administrator signaled to the teachers something less than a full commitment to the new policies. What came across as idle threats by the administration did little to build up two-way trust or a healthy faculty consensus (Deal and Kennedy, 1982, pp. 164-169).

The inability of the administrator to bring about constructive change through district mandates demonstrated, among other things, that powers available to school administrators are limited and that administrators too were constrained by environmental forces. External inputs do not usually cause changes in commitment, interest, or concern (Berman and McLaughlin, 1976, p. 365). When material and human constraints seem insurmountable, academics typically recommend inquiry as a way out. But teachers and the principal in this case had not yet even agreed that their school had failed in its mission to promote higher academic achievement.

Implications for Research

When formal and condign power are used in an urban school lacking in capacity to carry out changes, dissension and dissemblance are likely to occur. In this case, goal dissemblance ocurred in the form of teacher cheating on medical accountability records. The cheating was not only an exercise in superficial compliance, but a deliberate self-defensive effort. Similarly, the instructional technology provided by the district in the form of packaged instructional units had not been enough to create an improved environment for test scores, and test scores remained lower perhaps than expected. The teachers felt the new policies had placed them between a rock and a hard place; that is, between parents (or their own families) on the one hand and their employer on the other. Given these conditions, dissension and dissemblance were to be expected. Future studies, based on a systems approach or alternatives (Elmore, 1978), should focus on other kinds of policy experiments designed to improve the environment for test scores. Of special importance would be studies of how urban schools have begun to recover from the effects of mandates.

The effort to improve accountability through additional paperwork reduces the capacity of teachers by restricting preparation time. In this case, there was a substantial increase in the amount of required paperwork. It was estimated, though not precisely established, that the five new policies may have reduced instructional preparation time by as much as 25 percent because many teachers remained adamant about keeping their work within the normal school day. The administrators either did not recognize the trade-off between preparation time and accountability, or else they were striving to achieve a different balance between the two. Time studies, more popular in the 1970s than today, would show how teachers allocate their time to routine paperwork, as opposed to instructional planning, during school improvement projects.

Given the recent emphasis in the literature on instructional leadership, it is useful to recognize that principals are not always free to demonstrate the leadership that society expects. Principals have career concerns too, obviously. The principal, in this case, vacillated between selective enforcement of the policies and failure to capture the spirit of the policies in his own job performance. More importantly, the principal demonstrated he was unwilling to be the first to move toward political abyss by acknowledging the obvious—a failure makes substantial progress in resolving the problem of low student achievement. The situation requires the power to acknowledge the most difficult problems and to create a safety zone in which teachers can work. It would be useful to examine the differences in perspectives on school improvement among principals themselves.

Without effective and humane powers, dissension, displacement, and dissemblance occur when the capacity for change is low. What the teachers failed to recognize, however, was that leadership can spring from almost any part of the school organization. Striking was the extent to which teachers had allowed the new policies to overtake their own school improvement efforts. The main policy agenda had been usurped by the state and district, while the teachers remained relatively passive. Thus, teachers were unprepared to question packaged instruction or resist teaching to the tests. The teachers were operating in a purely reactive mode, and the results were predictable. There is a need for comparative impact studies of differences in reform outcomes between proactive and reactive groups of teachers.

Implications for Practice

The effort to control attendance behavior of tenured teachers through condign power was a failure. Outside responsibilities limited the capacity of teachers to perform well in this area. The teachers were not bad people, but they lacked effective outside support systems. Moreover, the normative culture was unhealthy. Favorite solutions may tend to seek out occasions (March and Olsen, 1983, p. 292). In a nutshell, however, the problem of teacher absences had been referred to the wrong intersection of capacity and power, as if the teachers could solve it *alone* and as if the command to *change or else* would be enough.

The teachers' collective bargaining agreement permitted fifteen days of absence. However, the district improvement policies called for certain punitive documentation after five consecutive days of absence or nine total days of absence; these rules were inconsistent. Furthermore, the district had mistakenly chosen to treat an economic problem as if it were a moral problem, calling for the use of punitive sanctions. The use of condign power rather than leadership was interpreted as paternalistic, and it became a cause for dissemblance and shame. An alternative solution would have been to set the number of sick days at a reasonable level through contract negotiations, to eliminate all punitive documentation, and to institute a system of automatic pay deductions for any absences beyond the negotiated level. This alternative would have shifted the problem from a potential exercise in formal power to leadership, a different intersection of capacity and power.

The emphasis on basic skills was essential. The system as it was, however, required teachers to act in two opposing ways. For example, to win the loyalty of students and parents, teachers were called upon to help and to protect the individual students. Many of the teachers, not only the minority teachers, were responding to this imperative. To become more accountable, however, teachers were called upon to administer promotion tests and to recommend retentions in a universalistic way. Alternative strategies are needed to resolve this classic problem in schools—the dual obligation to help and to evaluate.

While the state attempted to exert formal power over districts, it did not promote teacher participation and commitment at the school level. The time has come for urban teachers and administrators to play a greater role in initiating school improvements if they wish to protect their tenure. As one teacher put it, "We want to have our professional cake and eat it too." Faculties must develop their own capacities through study, experimentation, and collegial effort. This may require teachers to think of their work in new ways (Johnson, 1986, p. 74). The path to urban school improvement seems to lie in the direction of expanded capacity along with more sophisticated and judicious power.

Schools today are asked to do it all (Rosehnoltz, 1985, p. 349; Wildavsky, 1979, pp. 31-52). A single objective, such as raising achievement test scores, educating the whole child into excellence, or even eliminating drugs (according to Wildavsky), *is* possible. But, multiple objectives are problematic. For example, personnel decisions are constrained by licensing procedures, tenure laws, salary scales, collective bargaining agreements, subtle politics of race and class, a segmented labor market for educators, and differences in housing conditions between cities and suburbs. In urban settings, constraints directly opposed to the success of minority students have been almost overwhelming. Many, but not all, of these constraints take the forms of organizational incapacity and inappropriately applied power.

4 Combatting Deculturalization of the African-American Child in the Public School System: A Multicultural Approach

FELIX BOATENG

Introduction

The comparatively poor performance of African-American children in the public school system has been attributed to a variety of factors. One of the most injurious of these factors, and the one that seems to have the most damaging impact, is the continuous deculturalization of the African-American child and the neglect of African-American cultural values in the curriculum (National Alliance of Black School Educators, Inc., 1984; McAdoo and McAdoo, 1985; Oakes, 1985).

Broadly conceived, deculturalization is a process by which the individual is deprived of his or her culture and then conditioned to other cultural values. Anthropologists and sociologists define culture as a way of perceiving, believing, and evaluating (Goodenough, 1976). Culture provides the blueprint that determines the way an individual thinks, feels, and behaves in society. To deculturalize African-American children is, therefore, to deprive them of that which determines the way they think, feel, and behave.

It is important to note that deculturalization does not mean a loss of a group's culture, but rather failure to acknowledge the existence of their culture and the role it plays in their behavior. For example, when a French child speaks English with a French accent and says "ze man" instead of "the man," it is accepted that the child is influenced by the French cultural background. However, if an African-American child says "de man" instead of "the man," the child is accused of speaking a substandard version of English. Some teachers would go to the extent of complaining that that

73

manner of speaking is in itself an obstacle to learning. No acknowledgement is given to the fact that West African languages do not have the "th" sound, and that the children's African background, according to scholars of Ebonics, exerts influence on the way they speak the English language (Stoller, 1975). In other words, unlike the French child, there is a complete denial of the existence of any culture for the African-American.

Culturally Relevant Curriculum and Academic Success

To appreciate the depth of damage deculturalization brings to the academic achievement of the African-American child, it is necessary to call attention to the relationship between academic success and a culturally relevant curriculum. Traditionally, it has been assumed that an understanding of the child is basic to education. More recently, however, educators have realized that this understanding must go beyond basic psychological processes and embrace facets of the child's sociocultural world (Maehr and Stallings, 1975). Children bring different historical backgrounds —religious experiences and day-to-day living experiences to school. These experiences direct the way the child behaves, speaks, thinks, and believes in school. Educators agree that to work effectively with the heterogeneous student populations found in our schools, teachers have the responsibility of acknowledging the cultural backgrounds of their students and the cultural setting in which the school is located in order to develop effective instructional strategies that would help students reach their full potential (Gollnick and Chinn, 1986). Children who come to the teacher are inevitably products of, and are continually influenced by, the cultural world in which they hold membership. According to Maehr and Stallings:

> not only is this cultural influence reflected in patterns of dress, but more importantly, it is evidenced in motivational patterns, intellectual functioning and communicative skills. As a result, social and cultural factors are among the more important influences on the human development (Maehr and Stallings, 1975, p. 1).

This view has been echoed and supported in a number of studies since the 1960s. A striking feature of the Coleman Report (1966), for example, was the revelation that there is a close tie between African-American academic achievement and the social environment of the classroom. Even though the report limited the definition of social environmental to social models, such as sensitive teachers, more recent studies confirm the finding that the total environment of the classroom should have some relevance to the child's experience to ensure effective learning (McAdoo and McAdoo,

1985). Most of these studies reaffirm the long established conclusion that the sociocultural system of which the child is a product must be clearly emphasized if public education is to be effective (Ramirez and Castaneda, 1982).

Effects of Deculturalization

Despite research that rejects deculturalization, many African-American children and other culturally different children are still made to feel that they must reject the culture of their homes in order to succeed in school. Compelling evidence indicates that the underrepresentation of African-American culture in the curriculum and the resulting curricular and instructional inequalities, foster mediocre classroom experiences for African-American children and erect barriers to their academic achievement (Hale-Benson, 1986). More than three decades after the 1954 *Brown vs. Topeka Kansas Board of Education*, there are still well-intentioned, hardworking individuals who are locked into a school structure that operates under the assumption that cultural differences among children cannot be accommodated within a single school curriculum. These individuals are made to believe that the first step in education is to convert all first graders to replicas of white, middle-class suburban children. A Euro-American-centered consciousness has therefore remained the basis of curriculum development and instruction in the public school system. In the published proceedings of six Head Start Research Seminars (1969) held under the auspices of the United States Office of Economic Opportunity, McDavid states:

> Our society is a diverse and heterogeneous one, in which we embrace a variety of subcultures delineated by ethnic, linguistic, racial, geographic, educational, and socioeconomic earmarks. Within each of these subcultures, social standards vary, and corresponding socialization practices vary. Yet we plan public education as a single, massive, uniform Procrustean Institutionalized system of values, beliefs, and habits defined according to some stereotype rising magically out of the middle-class pillars of society. . . . This, then, is the stereotypical target toward which our institutionalized educational system tends to socialize all of its participants, regardless of the adult subculture to which they are bound, and regardless of the relevency or irrelevancy of these values and habits to each one's own real world (McDavid, 1969, pp. 5-6).

McDavid's comments are still applicable and illustrate the persistence of the belief in a single exclusive definition of American character. The influence of this belief in determining curriculum and instructional strategies has been prominent and pervasive. As a consequence, the public school system has become a strategically important vehicle that promotes the deculturalization of African-American children to Euro-American norms and creates confusion in the consciousness of these children. Only if the minds of African-American children are freed from this confusion, can their creativity be released to remove the barriers to academic achievement.

Another barrier to the academic achievement of African-American children is the academic and social alienation they face as a result of deculturalization. Since no recognition is given to the African-American sociocultural experience in the curriculum, the social context of the school is not equipped to elicit maximum effort from the African-American child. The evidence indicates that African-American children do not value themselves less when they perform poorly in school. What is important is the reference group they have established. If African-American children are oriented toward African-American culture, then their lack of achievement in terms of a "Euro-American school culture" may matter less to them (Rosenberg and Simmons, 1972; Coopersmith, 1975).

Combatting Deculturalization

A number of approaches aimed at combatting the deculturalization of the African-American child have been suggested, developed, and implemented. Some of these, such as the establishment of Black Independent Schools and Black Islamic Schools, have made tremendous contributions toward the solution of the problem. However, most African-American children are locked into the public school system for a variety of reasons and, barring a major revolution in this society, this will be the situation for the foreseeable future. There is, therefore, a need for an approach that would address the inequalities in the public school curriculum and remove the barriers to academic achievement for the masses of African-American children and other alienated peoples of color.

Promoting the academic achievement of African-American children is no longer an issue for only African-American people. Considering recent evidence from demographic forecasts which shows that one out of every three school children will be nonwhite by year 2000, the poor academic performance of African-American children should have serious implications not only for the future of African-American people but also for the intellectual, social, and economic health of the entire nation (American Council on Education, 1988).

Secondly, neglecting the experiences of African-American people in the curriculum is not only detrimental to African-American children, it is also a great source of the miseducation of other children who continue to be poorly prepared for a multicultural world. Most educators now agree that society can no longer afford to perpetuate the Euro-American perspective in the school curriculum. Educators are awakening to the need to offer their students an educational experience that will prepare them for the realities of a culturally diverse society.

Multicultural Education

Considering the importance of addressing the inequalities in the curriculum and of preparing all children effectively for a multicultural society, restructuring classroom instruction to reflect the diversity of the society seems to be a viable alternative. From the perspective of educational policy and practice, public education must seek whatever information the social sciences can provide concerning the different sociocultural system from which its children come. Teacher education programs must expose students to the unique communication, human relational, learning, and motivational patterns that are produced in African-American and other culturally different children through the offering of courses on African-American and other minority experiences. Knowing what these unique patterns are, public education must adopt policies and instructional programs that are consistent with the diversity of the society and the unique socialization patterns. This has been referred to as multicultural education.

It is an option that has widespread implications for neutralizing the deculturalization of African-American children and ensuring their academic success. A multicultural instructional approach would integrate African-American and other cultures into the curriculum and provide African-American children with the opportunity to participate fully in the learning process. Unlike the Euro-American-centered curriculum, multicultural curriculum and instruction are inclusive — not exclusive. It gives all children the opportunity to see themselves as being members of the human society.

Goals of Multicultural Education

The major goals of multicultural education are to help all students:

1. reach their potential by drawing on their cultural experiences and by helping them to view events from diverse cultural perspectives.

2. overcome their fear of diversity that leads to cultural misunderstanding and cultural encapsulation.

3. view cultural differences in an egalitarian mode rather than in an inferior-superior mode.

4. expand their conception of what it means to be human in a culturally diverse world and to develop cross-cultural competency — the ability to function within a range of cultures.

To achieve these goals, multicultural instruction needs to be pervasive rather than supplementary. It is a mode of experience and learning that should be infused and integrated throughout the curriculum and through the school program. For example, one does not set aside one hour during the school day to teach about the African-American experience. Since there is a long-standing assumption that only that which is Euro-American is American, an Eurocentric curriculum cannot be changed by simply adding units or lessons here and there about African-American or Chicanos. American history, literature, art, music, and culture should be taught from diverse ethnic and cultural perspectives rather than from only Euro-American perspective. Multicultural education experts recommend using the conceptual approach in reaching this goal (Banks, 1981, 1985).

In the conceptual curriculum, the understanding of such concepts as racism, acculturation, and assimilation is paramount; the cultural group selected to illustrate the concepts becomes a secondary issue. The teacher decides which cultural group can provide the best illustration for the concept being taught. However, since examples have traditionally been drawn from the Euro-American culture, there is a need to strive for a balance by selecting content from other cultures and ethnic groups. In teaching about the westward movement, migration, civil war, etc., the participation of African-Americans and other groups should be presented at the same time. This is an effective way of showing that African-American whites, and other groups have always shared a common humanity and that things have been handled differently because of differing historical and social experiences.

Of course the commitment to provide students with multicultural education is much easier to espouse than to implement. Teachers who want to use multicultural programs in the traditional classroom must first be cognizant of forces that usually militate against the effective introduction of such programs and learn to devise appropriate strategies to minimize their impact. Some of these forces are related to student interest, teacher behavior, textbooks and instructional materials, and school climate.

Student Interest

Since the public school has traditionally used the Euro-American culture as the basis for curriculum development and instruction, a lack of student interest in various cultures is an obstacle in the introduction of a multicultural approach. In Black Independent Schools, it is normal for the African-American students to have a sense of African-American cultural or ethnic identity. There is a special effort on the part of teachers to make students aware of their culture.

In the public school system, the orientation is so Eurocentric that white students take their identity for granted, and African-American students are totally deculturalized. An introduction of different cultural experiences in the curriculum may therefore not be enthusiastically received by students. To circumvent such a problem, teachers are advised to begin multicultural instruction with a strong emphasis on self-awareness of the student's own culture.

As Mitchell *et al.,* (1986) point out, a major strategy is to understand and utilize student cultural background as a first step toward the development of multicultural programs. Teachers need to know something about the family and community of their students and how the students view themselves in the milieu. Without such an understanding, teachers may hurry to introduce multicultural experiences that mean little to the students.

Teachers may begin multicultural instruction by guiding each student in an exploration of his or her cultural background. This is usually accomplished through such activities as the construction of family trees, interviewing parents, and piecing together the study of their own cultural evolution. In this way, the study of history, for example, becomes real for the students, and as a result they are prepared to accept and understand other perspectives on history. White students as well as African-American students are given the opportunity to examine their membership in ethnic groups and to accept ethnicity as a human condition not limited to minority groups. Each ethnic group is given equal attention in the curriculum, and children are guided to view each others' culture as legitimate.

Teacher Behavior

Inappropriate teacher behavior is the second force working against the development of meaningful multicultural programs. The cultivation of student interest in multicultural education is important. However, it is obvious that the interest cannot be fully cultivated without supportive teacher attitude and behavior. A report of the U.S. Commission on Civil Rights states:

The heart of the educational process is in the interaction between teacher and student. It is through this action that the school system

makes its major impact upon a child. The way the teacher interacts
with the student is a major determinant of the quality of education the
child receives (U.S. Commission on Civil Rights, 1973).

An impediment to the development of effective multicultural instructional programs is, in Aragon's (1973) phrase, "culturally deficient
educators attempting to teach culturally different children." Such teachers
are either insensitive to the needs and potential of African-American and
other culturally different children or, in some cases, are positively inimical
to African-Americans and label them as inferior. The teacher who is not
enthusiastic about multicultural education is less likely to encourage
students to develop more egalitarian views and to promote respect for all
cultures. The teacher who views African-American children as culturally
deprived is more likely to promote deculturalization than the one who
acknowledges the implications of America being a culturally diverse
society.

In some cases, the efforts of teachers who are willing may be hampered
by a sense of inadequacy and powerlessness to do anything meaningful in
attempting to combat the legacy of years of Eurocentric education. Such a
feeling of inadequacy may be aggravated by the behavior of those
colleagues who view their efforts with suspicion, lack of understanding, or
as a threat to their own values. For a multicultural instructional approach
to be successful, the element of threat which may come from other teachers
and community members must be acknowledged and dealt with sensitively.
Some teachers who are already using the multicultural approach have
found out that the best approach is to gradually emphasize the positive
outcomes of the project through campus and community-wide activities
involving cross-cultural experiences (Boateng, 1986).

Sadker and Sadker (1982) found in their research that in order for
teachers to maintain a positive multicultural environment in their classrooms, they should make a conscious effort to recognize the subtle and
unintentional biases in their own behavior. For example, teachers who use
race as the basis for assigning students to projects may be reinforcing
outdated cultural stereotypes. In addition, students receive a distorted
image of the American culture when African-Americans and other
minorities are never invited to speak to the class. On the whole, to ensure
the successful introduction of multicultural education, teachers should be
encouraged to examine and analyze their own behavior and classroom
interactions.

Textbooks and Instructional Materials

The third force that often militates against the effective introduction of
multicultural programs relates to the textbooks and instructional materials

which are used and how the teacher uses them. Teachers who are prepared to introduce multicultural education in their classrooms face the problem of inadequate instructional resources. Research shows that many textbooks contain biases that encourage a Eurocentric teaching approach. This is a major deterrent because the textbook is the most standard instructional item in most classrooms.

Although it may seem that the teacher often does not have much control over the textbooks recommended for the class, Gollnick and Chinn (1986) point out that teachers have a lot of latitude in deciding what supplementary materials to use and in how the textbook itself should be used. For instance, no matter how biased the textbooks may be, the teacher can effectively provide multicultural education by taking time to recognize the biases in the text and by developing instructional strategies to counteract them. A biology textbook that uses only the white figure for the study of the human digestive system and other aspects of human anatomy, can still be used effectively if the teacher discusses this bias and provides supplementary materials to counteract it.

These biases can be recognized only when teachers are encouraged to read textbooks critically for multicultural content. Books that contain biases are usually characterized by what Sadker and Sadker (1982) identify as "invisibility" and/or "fragmentation." The terms are used to describe textbooks in which microcultures are underrepresented and in which contributions and information about these groups are separated from the regular text. The separation of information and issues about microcultures from the regular text and instruction suggests that the experiences of these groups are merely an interesting diversion and not an integral part of historical and contemporary developments. This is known in literature as the "add on" approach which still places non-Anglo cultures outside the mainstream of human activity. There are schools that boast of having integrated the African-American experience into the curriculum. However, in some of these schools, the only time the African-American experience is introduced is during Black History Month. This "add on" tactic still isolates the experience of the African-American child as being "something other than" the human experience which is presented in the curriculum throughout the school year. The African-American experience needs to be integrated into all subjects all year round for it to mean anything to both African-American and white children in the class. Society is multicultural, and it is important that textbooks and other instructional materials reflect this diversity.

Language, Culture, and Academic Achievement

An additional bias related to teacher behavior and instructional materials that presents a barrier in the introduction of multicultural instruction is what one might describe as linguistic chauvinism. Linguistic chauvinism, in the United States, is a three-dimensional bias: the use of standard English as the only language of instruction, the attitude that standard English is superior to other dialects, and the failure to acknowledge the existence and legitimacy of other dialects of the English language. For African-American and other minority children who enter the school system with a linguistic experience that is different from that of the mainstream, linguistic chauvinism aggravates the process of deculturalization. Considering the fact that language or dialect is the fundamental medium through which ethnicity is transmitted (Banks, 1981), children are deculturalized if no recognition is given to the existence of the home and community dialect they bring to school.

Since academic success has been shown to have a strong correlation with a culturally relevant curriculum and since language is a key component of culture, proper recognition needs to be given to the child's linguistic experience in the planning of curriculum and instruction. The importance of the child's home language in the learning process was brought out clearly in the United States District Court ruling in *Martin Luther King, Jr. Elementary Children vs. Ann Arbor School District* in 1977 (Banks, 1981). A case was made for students who speak "Black English" or "Black dialect" as a home and community language. The plantiffs argued that language differences impeded the African-American students' equal participation in the school's instructional program because the instructional program was conducted entirely in standard English. Using linguistic and educational research evidence, the lawyers for the students established,

> ...that unless those instructing in reading recognize (1) the existence of a home language used by the children in their own community for much of their non-school communications, and (2) that this home language may be a cause of the superficial difficulties in speaking standard English, great harm will be done. The child may withdraw or may act out frustrations and may not learn to read. A language barrier develops when teachers, in helping the child to switch from the home ("Black English") language to standard English, refuse to admit the existence of a language that is the acceptable way of talking in his local community (U.S. District Court, East District, Michigan Civil Action, No. 7-71861, 1979).

The court ruled in favor of the plaintiffs and required the defendant board to take steps to help its teachers to recognize the home language of the students and to use that dialect as an educational resource rather than a linguistic liability.

Banks (1981) has proposed a policy of linguistic pluralism as an essential component of multicultural education in a milticultural classroom. In a nutshell, the policy provides parameters that help teachers to accommodate linguistic differences as well as teach about linguistic diversity in the United States. The proposal includes the incorporation of linguistic diversity into curriculum materials that does not necessarily require new language learning for the teacher. Aspects of Black English, Southern English, British English, and other forms of English may be introduced to show the different ways English is spoken and the cultural sources of these differences. This approach recognizes Black and other forms of English as resources rather than liabilities in the teaching of standard English. The proposal provides African-American children who speak Black English an equal opportunity to learn school subjects and a sense of belonging to the school system.

School Climate

To ensure the sucess of multicultural education in a classroom, the overall school climate must be supportive of multicultural education (Gollnick and Chinn, 1986). When respect for cultural differences is reflected in major aspects of the students' educational programs, the goals of multicultural education are easier to attain. A school whose choice of speakers, bulletin boards, and displays does not reflect the cultural diversity of our society, provides an environment that militates against the efforts of teachers who are trying to use the multicultural approach in their classrooms. Similarly, a school that has an all-white administration and an all African-American custodial staff, obviously has an improper climate for multicultural education. Teachers can expose and discuss these situations with students in their classrooms and with colleagues at staff meetings in order to help counter the effects of such circumstances.

Efforts can also be made to invite the handicapped, the aged, and members of cultural groups that may be underrepresented in the school to speak at general school functions. In other words, a school climate that reflects a commitment to multicultural education reinforces the contributions of teachers who use multicultural approaches. In the final analysis, it is individuals at the school site — the principal and the teachers — and not the school officials in the state capitol who hold the key to attaining this climate.

Conclusion

These forces—student interest, teacher behavior, textbooks and instructional materials, and school climate—may hinder the efforts of teachers to introduce multicultural instruction in their classrooms. However, one has to attempt a multicultural approach in order for these hindrances to become apparent so that strategies to counteract them can be developed. The first hurdle is overcome when we recognize the nation as a multicultural society and accept the premise that there is a need for a corresponding educational philosophy that would provide all children the knowledge, skills, and the attitudes necessary for living effectively within the society. Multicultural education is an attempt to fill this need.

The ultimate goal of multicultural education is to enable educators to meet the individual needs of their students so that they can progress to their fullest potential. In a multicultural society where African-American children are more likely to receive instruction with other children in the same classroom, the multicultural instructional approach is an answer to the deculturalization of the African-American child. Multicultural education is designed to give serious attention to changing the school and not the child. Many instances have been cited to show how the public school is traditionally structured to deculturalize and discourage the African-American child. The multicultural education approach provides a way that schools can be changed to elicit the most from African-American and all other children of color. The approach would reduce curricular inequalities and provide African-American children with opportunities to see themselves in the learning program and remove barriers to their academic success. Probably the most important message that African-American children can receive from a multicultural education program is that the school is not alien to their world and that somehow it can and does serve their needs. When the experiences of African-American children are treated as significant in the learning process, the school can be an instrument through which the African-American child can combat deculturalization and be led into new possibilities and achievements.

5 Policy Failure in Urban Schools: How Teachers Respond to Increased Accountability for Students

MWALIMU J. SHUJAA

In their report, *An Imperiled Generation: Saving Urban Schools*, the trustees of the Carnegie Foundation for the Advancement of Teaching proclaim that they are "deeply troubled that a reform movement launched to upgrade the education of *all* students is irrelevant to many children —largely Black and Hispanic — in our urban schools" (1988, p. xi). They go on to say, "thus far, the harsh truth is that the reform movement has largely bypassed our most deeply troubled schools" (1988, p. xii). Finally, the urban school crisis is labeled in the report as "a major failure of social policy, a piecemeal approach to a problem that requires a unified response" (1988, p. xv).

These pronouncements by the Carnegie Foundation were made just five years after the publication of *A Nation At Risk*, the report by the National Commission on Excellence in Education (1983) whose recommendations served as guideposts for much of the education reform that occurred throughout the 1980s. Policies that increased student accountability were among the most popular reforms. Student accountability policies are intended to improve educational outcomes by imposing more stringent standards for earning course credit, grade-to-grade promotion, and graduation. High school graduation requirements, for example, were increased in 45 states. Other types of policies that increased standards for students were new or modified high school exit exams, promotion or gate tests, and minimum grade point average (Fuhrman, Clune and Elmore, 1988).

Despite an extraordinary level of reform activity, the Carnegie Foundation concludes that Black and Hispanic students in urban schools were bypassed. What went wrong? If we are to understand why the policies did not work, it is time to take a closer look at what took place in the schools during the course of policy implementation. The intent of this chapter is to examine the perceptions and behaviors of teachers who participated in the implementation of student accountability policies. I focus on teachers because the interaction between students and teachers in the classrooms is where the "rubber meets the road" when it comes to educational change.

Sarason (1987) argues that policy makers' goals generally reflect two assumptions regarding teachers' responses to the implementation of new policies: (1) they will be the agents of change, and (2) their thinking will be consistent with the goals of change.

Sarason's premise is that policy implementation will not be successful without the cooperation of teachers. Yet, policy makers tend to take this cooperation for granted. In this chapter, I evaluate these assumptions by examining how teachers in predominantly Black and/or Hispanic urban high schools perceived and were influenced by new testing and student standards policies. These effects are revealed through analyses of teachers' perceptions and the descriptions they provide of their own and other teachers' behaviors in response to the policies implemented in their districts. Analysis of the teacher data offers insight about what influence increased standards for students may have on teachers' expectations, whether the positives achieved by strengthening the core curriculum are being offset by concomitant phenomena that frustrate both students and teachers, and how pressure to improve student performance on mandated tests is responded to by teachers.

Design of the Study

Data for this study was drawn from the Center for Policy Research in Education's (CPRE) core database.[2] The core database includes information pertaining to six states (Arizona, California, Florida, Georgia, Minnesota, and Pennsylvania) that represent a range on particular characteristics expected to affect the translation of policy into practice. The overall criteria used by CPRE in selecting districts from among the six states were: (a) range of policy impact — the degree of change a district would need to make in response to the policy, and (b) local capacity — the ability of a district to respond more and less easily to the policy.

A total of 29 districts and 59 schools were sampled. The sample of schools represented a range of policy impact and capacity. For example, schools were chosen with varying percentages of high and low achieving students that were representative of the ethnic and SES composition of their districts. Schools were not included from districts in which there was evidence of low change or low problems.

Respondents

This study draws on school-level interview data collected from 30 teachers in the 11 urban high schools in the core database that had predominantly Black and/or Hispanic enrollments. These high schools were located among four districts located in California, Florida, Georgia, and Pennsylvania.

Purposeful sampling was used; individual respondents were selected by their building principals according to the criteria provided by CPRE. These criteria were designed to obtain a sample that would include veteran teachers, teachers with less than two years experience, teachers in subject areas (particularly math and science) that were affected by increased standards for students, teachers participating in career ladder or mentor programs (if they existed). Often, a single respondent satisfied several of the criteria.

Interviews were conducted by CPRE field staff, including myself, between February and June 1987. Notes were taken during the interview sessions, but no electronic recording devices were used. Immediately after each session, interviewers reread their notes and filled in missing details using recall.

Data Analysis

Transcripts of the interviews were content analyzed to determine the respondents' sentiments about policy influence, implementation, and accountability and their descriptions of their own and other teacher's behavior. Each sentiment that a respondent expressed and each behavior that was described was coded. Since some respondents expressed more than one sentiment or described more than one behavior, the total number of sentiments and behaviors is greater than the number of respondents.

Findings

Teachers' Perceptions of Higher Standards for Students

Table 5.1 shows that teachers perceived that rising enrollments in higher level courses were attributable to policies that increased standards for students. This trend was evident in math, science, and English — three of the subjects designated in *A Nation At Risk* as components of the "new basics" that are essential to a strong curriculum. Teachers indicated that as enrollments in the "new basics" were increasing, enrollments in industrial arts, fine arts, and humanities electives were declining. Students found that there were simply not enough hours in the school day to meet graduation requirements and also take elective courses. Something had to give. One high school could not muster sufficient enrollment to continue offering a single course in African-American history even though its enrollment of nearly 2,000 students was 99 percent African-American.

The following interview segments illustrate teachers' opinions about the influence of increased requirements on students' course taking behavior:

Kids need four years of English; it improves their skills. However, if it is not required it gets pushed to the background. [30-c3]

I don't see any disadvantages [to the new requirements]. I suppose that some loss of electives is a problem for some students since they can't take the classes that are plain fun. [38-c11]

It was argued in *A Nation At Risk* that a greater focus on the "new basics" was the remedy for the smorgasbord-like characteristics of many high school curricula. However, the report also stated that courses that allowed students to pursue "personal, educational, and occupational goals" should not be forced out of the curriculum. These courses, it was argued, should be regarded as complementary to the "new basics."

Teachers' concerns about their students' opportunities to enroll in elective courses sometimes varied according to whether or not they taught students in academic tracks. Some teachers felt that fewer electives would discourage students who they considered noncollege bound from finishing high school. The following interview segments are representative of those feelings:

Because of the mandated requirements in academics, there is little time for other things. What happens is they stop attending. There has been an increase in the dropout rate, no question. We are losing 12 kids this year, have you been told that? [122-p7]

Kids are discouraged. Therefore, they drop out because there are no alternatives. There is little room in the schedule for electives. [70-f9]

For the college prep kids, the new requirements are fine. For the average students, they just result in a higher dropout rate. [33-c6]

Table 5.1 also reveals that there were some doubts among teachers about their students' preparation for higher standards. In California, for

Table 5.1

Sentiments Expressed About Increased Student Standards
By Teachers at Predominantly Black and Hispanic High Schools
(n = 30 teachers)

	FREQUENCY OF EXPRESSIONS				
Sentiments related to:	CA (13)	FL (10)	GA (2)	PA (5)	TOT (30)
Teaching					
teaching was more difficult	1	0	0	1	2
anxiety levels were higher	1	1	0	0	2
more pressure to pass athletes	1	0	0	0	1
Student behavior, academic performance and achievement outcomes					
students took important courses they previously avoided	10	4	0	1	15
students took fewer electives	8	3	0	2	13
students' graduation jeopardized	4	4	1	3	12
caused students to take courses for which they were underprepared	4	0	0	1	5
improved quality of graduates	2	2	0	1	5
non-college-bound students affected differently than college bound	3	2	0	0	5
students more aware of standards	0	4	0	0	4
Quality of changes					
did not demand enough of students	0	1	0	1	2
improved curriculum structure	1	0	1	0	2
introduced watered-down and basic skills courses	2	0	0	2	4
Administration					
provided too little information	0	1	0	0	1

responded to a fad	1	0	0	0	1
Number of sentiments expressed	38	22	2	12	74

example, high school graduation requirements are linked to university admissions criteria. Some science, math, and computer teachers indicate they encountered greater numbers of students who lacked the academic background needed to succeed in their courses. Samples of these perceptions are contained in the two teacher interview segments that follow:

> The UC requirements have resulted in a lot of kids enrolling in chemistry who aren't prepared in terms of their math and study skills. The pressure to get into UC is so intense that there are kids in the honors classes who should not be there. I have to lower my level of teaching each year. [38-c11]

> I am expected to teach chemistry and biology to kids who still have trouble with arithmetic skills they should have mastered years ago. To me something is wrong. [31-c4]

Some teachers did not expect lower achieving students to do well in newly added math and science courses and also questioned the necessity of such courses for those students. The following is an example:

> It's unrealistic to believe that all students will need or succeed at a program that requires three years of science. It will increase the dropout rate and reduce the number of students who graduate on time. It will challenge our standards. We are going to water down the curriculum to come up with third-year courses to accommodate the requirements. [124-p9]

In summary, Table 5.1 presented an array of perceptions expressed by teachers in predominantly Black and Hispanic urban high schools about reforms that increased standards for students. Many of these teachers' statements suggest that higher standards were perceived in terms of what they did *to* students rather than *for* them. Teachers reported that the addition of more required math, science, and English courses was getting more students into essential courses but greatly limited their opportunities to take electives.

A number of teachers also expressed concern that the restricted options would lower students' motivations to persist through graduation. Some teachers revealed expectations that students would not measure up to the higher standards unless the course content was watered down. Few teachers perceived higher student standards as improving the quality of high school graduates.

In the next section, I will discuss teachers' descriptions of how higher standards for students influenced their own and other teachers' behavior.

The Impact of Higher Standards for Students on Teachers' Behavior

Table 5.2 shows that teachers did more monitoring of their own planning and instruction because of higher student standards. Two kinds of self-monitoring behavior patterns were described.

In the first pattern, the instructional process was influenced more by new policies than by the teachers' own goals.

I must teach a lot more composition. I can't teach as much literature as I would like or used to teach. [74-f13]

There is now more structure in the classroom because there has been more of an organization imposed on the curriculum...the instructional process is different. It is now a literature-based curriculum that integrates writing and reading. [30-c3]

In the second pattern, teachers placed more emphasis on their own goals for student learning outcomes. The following examples suggest that teachers consciously did more for their students than the standards required because they felt the standards did not go far enough.

I demand a lot from my kids. I go beyond the basic textbooks. I think that a mind should not be limited. [31-c4]

The lesson plans are broader now because fewer elective or supplemental courses are being offered. I have incorporated some Afro-American history into my U.S. history course because I can no longer teach Afro-American history as an elective. [28-c1]

There were some instances in which teachers took advantage of the new student standards to pursue their own goals. The next example is from a district with year-round schools. In this context, the teacher utilized the additional time to address his/her own goals.

I cover topics in more detail. I have time to cover topics we used to skip or just pass over. We get to spend more time looking at all the subjects. [34-c7]

Table 5.2

Behavioral Responses to Increased Student Standards Described
By Teachers at Predominantly Black and Hispanic High Schools
(n = 30 teachers)

	FREQUENCY DESCRIBED				
Increases in curriculum standards and courses required for graduation have resulted in teachers:	CA (13)	FL (10)	GA (2)	PA (5)	TOT (30)
attending more closely to teaching methods, curriculum or course content	6	2	2	1	11
modifying level of teaching and/or materials to compensate for disparate achievement levels	2	4	0	0	6
doing nothing differently	1	2	0	2	5
stressing to students and/or parents that poor academic performance will affect graduation	1	1	0	2	4
encouraging students to enroll in higher level courses	3	0	0	0	3
teaching additional periods during the regular school day or teaching in evening programs or summer sessions	0	2	0	1	3
teaching new required courses, labs or subject matter	1	1	0	0	2
expanding content in required courses to include subject matter covered in elective courses that are no longer offered	1	0	0	0	1
number of behaviors described	15	12	2	6	35

The second most frequently described pattern of teacher behavior in Table 5.2 was the modification of teaching and/or materials to compensate for students' uneven achievement levels. As previously discussed, more students were required to earn additional credits in math, science, and English. Accordingly, teachers reported that they encountered a wider range of academic performance levels among the students enrolling in these courses. While one respondent indicated that he raised his level of instruction for "low-ability" students, teachers in this sample typically decreased their level of instruction to compensate for lower achieving students. These behavior patterns are described in the following statements:

> I have to lower my level of teaching each year. Things you expect to be self-evident are not. There are a lot of kids in the classes who do not have the proper background. [38-c11]

> At one point, I taught average and above-average students. Now, I get those below average, too. They take chemistry because they need another credit. Some don't even know why they're there. In one class, I must do two different things to meet the needs of a variety of students. [72-f11]

Most of the responses that indicated nothing differently was done because of increased student standards were provided by teachers who also indicated that they had experienced little change in the achievement levels of the students who took their courses. Some teachers did nothing differently because they did not teach courses that were affected by policies that increased standards.

To summarize, teachers responded in very different ways to policies that increased student standards. There were teachers who were able to hold on to their own established instructional goals. These teachers responded to the changes in standards for students by monitoring their planning and teaching to make sure that mandated criteria were addressed while they continued to pursue their own objectives. In contrast, there were other teachers whose instructional goals were supplanted by the new policies.

There were still other teachers who addressed the standards because they simply saw it as their job to do so. In performing what they perceived as mandatory tasks, they indicated little expectancy that their students could measure up to higher standards. These teachers reported that they felt forced to lower their standards because they believed their students were incapable of achieving at the levels the new requirements demanded. Thus, it appears likely that students in some predominantly Black and Hispanic urban high schools received instruction of widely variant quality reflective of the expectations of their teachers.

The next two sections discuss how teachers describe the influence of mandated student testing.

Teachers' Perceptions of Mandated Student Testing

Table 5.3 shows the perception expressed most often by teachers was that mandated student testing produced pressure to raise scores. These

Table 5.3

Sentiments Expressed About Mandated Testing
By Teachers at Predominantly Black and Hispanic High Schools
(n = 30 teachers)

	FREQUENCY DESCRIBED				
Sentiments related to:	CA (13)	FL (10)	GA (2)	PA (5)	TOT (30)
Teaching					
felt pressure to raise scores	7	3	0	0	10
no effect	2	3	0	3	8
teaching to the test should be avoided	7	1	0	0	8
teaching to the test is ok in some situations	1	1	0	0	2
quality of instruction has improved	0	1	0	0	1
Student behavior, academic performance and achievement outcomes					
doubted students ability to pass test	1	1	1	0	3
performance hampered by weakness in basic skills	2	0	0	0	2
students not motivated	1	0	0	0	1
increased interest in test results	0	1	0	0	1
improved classroom performance	0	0	0	1	1
Quality of test and process					
test is too basic	1	2	0	0	3
Curriculum supervision and administration					
test shapes curriculum	0	0	1	0	1
Number of sentiments expressed	22	13	2	4	41

perceptions were apparent among some of the California teachers because school funding and test performance were linked by the now discontinued Cash for Cap Program.[3] The relationship is implied in the following examples:

> The school quality reports have given everyone a heightened awareness that students must function well. [30-c3]

> I think that the emphasis on CAP is to get money for the school. [31-c4]

Some of the teachers perceived that teaching test-taking skills took time away from more valued instructional pursuits. Similarly, other teachers felt that too much of their instructional time was devoted to strengthening basic skills that students should have learned previously. Florida teachers may have expressed such feelings because of policies that require pre-test preparation as well as post-test remediation programs for certain at-risk students. When these programs required students to be pulled out of regular classes, they would miss the instruction given the remainder of the class during their absence. If the students received help during class time, teachers complained because the individual attention these students received reduced the time available to cover the planned content.

Teachers expressed opinions about the maligned practice of teaching to the test. Only a couple of teachers were willing to admit they taught to the test, such as the Florida teacher who stated:

> We must teach to the test at lower levels. It's only fair to the lower ability students. It's so important to them. [73-f12]

Most of the sentiments reflected opinions that were opposed to this practice. However, there was great variation in opinions about what is actually teaching to the test. This can be seen more clearly in the section that follows when the discussion turns to these teachers' descriptions of what they did instead of teaching to the test. Some statements implied that teachers perceived tests to be of little value because they expected that most of the students they taught would not pass them. An example of such feelings is found in the following statement:

> The [test] did affect students in the beginning because students had more interest. The low-achieving kids had interest in it. . . Sometimes I don't see how some of them pass the test. [63-f2]

Other teachers gave indications that they perceived testing to be of low utility by stating that the tests did not motivate students, were emphasized to obtain money, were too easy, or simply were "no good."

To summarize, teachers perceive that mandated testing places pressure on them to improve scores. They feel compelled to devote instructional time to preparing for the tests, but they see little instructional value in them. Teachers regard mandated tests as interferences that often undermine their professional judgment and obstruct the pursuit of educational goals more worthy of their time.

The Impact of Mandated Student Testing on Teachers' Behavior

Table 5.4 shows that teaching test-taking techniques and basic skills were the most frequently mentioned teacher behaviors related to mandated student testing. Teachers' descriptions of their own and other teachers' behavior revealed that they often divided their instructional time between the preparation of their students to take mandated tests and teaching the content they believed the subject area demanded.

At the beginning of the year, we give practice tests, then we review and keep records, remediate and work on items they've missed . . A lot of time is taken away from subjects to work on basic skills [63-f2].

Some teachers attempted to reduce the amount of classroom time lost to test preparation by trying to teach subject area content using methods they believed would also help students improve their test-taking skills. These actions are described below:

Teachers have to make a pointed effort to teach test strategies... When I'm teaching a vocabulary lesson, I interject how to answer a vocabulary test [30-c3].

I try to teach problem solving skills rather than teach students how to answer CAP test questions [32-c5].

Teachers' behavior sometimes gave indications that testing concerns held precedence over subject area instruction.

I would say about 40 percent of my time is either preparing students for a test, taking tests, tracking down students who have missed tests, and so on. There's not much time left for English [91-g6].

...this state and county are test crazy. I structure the tests that I

Table 5.4

Behavioral Responses To Mandated Testing Described By Teachers at Predominantly Black and Hispanic High Schools
(n = 30 teachers)

Mandated testing has resulted in teachers...:	FREQUENCY DESCRIBED				
	CA (13)	FL (10)	GA (2)	PA (5)	TOT (30)
teaching test-taking skills and strategies and emphasizing test consciousness	5	3	1	0	9
working with students before they take the test to improve basic skills in reading comprehension, vocabulary, math, etc.	3	3	1	1	8
not "teaching to the test"	6	1	0	0	7
doing nothing differently	1	1	1	4	7
using materials that cover subject areas on the test or incorporating areas covered by the test into subject area instruction	4	1	0	0	5
placing emphasis on weak areas identified by the test (remediation)	2	3	0	0	5
reviewing test results to identify strengths and weaknesses and to group students	2	2	0	1	5
"teaching to the test"	1	2	0	0	3
devoting some time to test administration (packaging materials, proctoring, make-ups, etc.)	1	1	0	1	3
scheduling time to review subject area content before test is given	1	1	0	0	2
encouraging students to attend school on the day the test is given	1	0	0	0	1
motivating students to do their best on the test ("gearing them up")	1	0	0	0	1
Number of behaviors described	28	18	3	7	56

administer in class so that they're similar to the state assessment. I
want students to be familiar with that test form so that they will do
well. I build in time in every class to teach the content of those tests
[65-f4]

A look at some examples of "not teaching to the test" clearly suggests
that teachers do not object when the alignment between test content and
curriculum content permits them to satisfy accountability demands
without altering subject area content.

We are not teaching to the test, but trying to keep the skills and
subject areas tested in our curriculum [35-c8].

I work with math skills and reading comprehension, but I don't teach
to the test [31-c4]

Avoiding the appearance of "teaching to the test" was a way for teachers
to protect their sense of professional autonomy from accountability's
intrusion. When teachers said they did not teach to the test, they usually
described behaviors that they believed would show that they did not allow
their teaching to be dictated by pressure to improve test performance.

To summarize, there is evidence that mandated student testing had
considerable impact on teachers. Their behavior was primarily influenced
by the tension between their own instructional goals and the learning
outcomes measured by mandated tests. The impact of this tension was
greatest when teachers were constrained in pursuing their own instructional
goals because they were doing things in their classrooms that seemed to
serve no purpose other than to improve test performance. The tension was
least in those situations where there was alignment between test content
and curriculum content. When there was such alignment, teachers could
follow routinized behavior patterns without the fear that their students
would come up short on the tests.

Teachers found walking the line difficult. Efforts by some teachers to
modify their instruction so that their own goals and the accountability
goals would both be satisfied did little to allay feelings that students were
being shortchanged.

Discussion

Three phenomena linked to policies that increased standards for students
are suggested as contributors to the ineffectiveness of these policies in
urban schools:

1. The policies had varying effects on teachers' expectations; therefore, students were likely to have received instruction of discrepant quality.

2. Tightening of the curriculum left students with too many chances to fail and too few choices.

3. Testing and subject area instruction were poorly integrated.

Inconsistent Instructional Quality

The sentiments teachers expressed about increased standards for students covered the gamut of feelings from frustration to motivation. We can expect that the range of instructional quality that these teachers' students experienced was just as broad. For students, the risk of being assigned to teachers who have been frustrated rather than motivated by higher standards meant their likelihood of exposure to top-quality instruction was strictly a matter of chance.

Some students were lucky enough to be assigned to the teachers who perceived higher standards for students as a challenge to be met. These were the teachers whose sentiments conveyed a belief that their students needed everything they could give them. These teachers did more than they were required to do. They expanded subject area content to make it more exciting and challenging for their students.

Unfortunately, there were also students who were assigned to the teachers who felt the new, higher standards were unattainable because their students could not meet the old ones. Some of these teachers suggested not failing their students was the best way they could help them to graduate. These teachers watered down the subject area content of their courses and placed disproportionate emphasis on material students were likely to encounter on achievement tests.

To paraphrase Welch (1979), policies alone are insufficient to change the basic interaction between a teacher and a student. Teacher expectations, for example, are shaped by many factors including the teachers' experiences, prior knowledge of students, and the teachers' own values and beliefs. Teachers who began with low expectations of their students tended to lower them even more when confronted with increased standards. In contrast, teachers who believed in their students were likely to struggle to find ways to motivate their students to meet the demands of higher standards.

Too Many Chances to Fail and Too Few Choices

A number of teachers described situations in which higher standards were implemented without providing additional time for students to take electives or repeat courses that were failed. Students generally were required to pass five major courses during each of their four years in high school. Graduation requirements in each of the four states sampled were increased to include four years of English; thus a failed course meant evening school or even a fifth year in high school.

Concern among teachers that increased standards would jeopardize graduation for some students was evident in all four states. For the most part, teachers complained that they had too little time to cover required materials and students had too little time to take anything but the required courses. As mentioned in the previous section, some teachers lowered their level of instruction so that their students could earn passing marks. These teachers expressed concern that students would become frustrated and drop out of school because their chances of graduating within four years were diminished.

Policy makers at the state level increased course requirements for high school graduation. However, it was local school districts that had to pay teachers and absorb other costs connected with providing students additional time to make up failed courses or take electives. A few teachers in California and Florida reported that their districts had lengthened the school day or implemented year-round schools. However, the costs associated with providing these options in the absence of state support were prohibitive for most districts and especially so for urban districts.

Imbalanced Integration of Testing and Instruction

Glaser (1987) argues that achievement testing and instruction should be integrated to improve learning. For this to occur, tests should assess students' competence "through indicators of the development of knowledge, skills, and cognitive processes." He adds that achievement measures should also provide diagnostic insight into the forms of error and misconception that interfere with the attainment of learning objectives. With this type of information, teachers would be prepared to deal directly with the areas that impede their students' progress. Teachers' descriptions of the influence that mandated achievement tests had on their teaching suggest that the integration of mandated tests with their instructional practices has been awkward.

Conclusions

The failure of educational reform policies to improve the overall quality of urban education should not be attributed to a lack of implementation. Teachers provide clear indications that many of the student accountability policies embraced by the reform movement were implemented in predominantly Black and/or Hispanic urban schools. Teachers complied with the implementation of these policies, but they clearly did not view them as answers to the problems they contend with from day to day in urban schools.

A Nation At Risk argued that curriculum standards needed to be raised in order to keep pace with other industrialized countries. Teachers in many urban schools, however, are more likely to perceive higher standards in the core curriculum as contributing factors to a higher dropout rate. There are other differences in teachers' perceptions and policy makers' intent as well.

Increased course requirements and exit exams often produced lowered teacher expectations for students who were considered to be "non-academic." Teachers who felt they did not have the necessary resources and support to meet the existing standards tended to view policies that increased student accountability with cynicism and frustration.

Policies that mandated student testing were often perceived negatively by teachers who were forced to devote instructional time to preparing their students to take tests. These practices often conflicted with teachers' ideas about what should be emphasized in the classroom.

If the premise underlying Sarason's (1971) assertions about the assumptions of policy makers' regarding teachers is correct, we should not expect that reforms will be successful where teachers' thinking is inconsistent with the intended goals of policy makers. In the case of student accountability reforms, teachers' experiences with policy implementation in predominantly Black and Hispanic urban schools have helped them to acquire an outlook that is often quite different from the goals outlined in *A Nation At Risk*. The success of future reform efforts will depend upon our ability to reduce the gap between teachers perceptions of what is wrong with urban schools and policy makers' goals. This will require the development of more effective ways to predict the impact that proposed policies will have over a wide range of school environments. Further, in those school environments where teachers' energies are subsumed by the pressures of meeting the most minimal requirements, there must also be a greater commitment on the part of policy makers to build the capacity to attain excellence.

Notes

1. I wish to thank Profs. Craig E. Richards, William A. Firestone and Nobuo K. Shimahara for their comments on an earlier draft. I am also indebted to Prof. Richards for his suggestions regarding analysis of the data.

2. The Center for Policy Research in Education (CPRE), a consortium of Rutgers University, Michigan State University, Stanford University, and the

University of Wisconsin-Madison, is funded by the Office of Educational Research and Improvement (OERI-G008690011-88) to study state and local policies to improve schooling. This chapter draws on data from a multiyear study conducted by Rutgers University, the RAND Corporation, and the University of Wisconsin-Madison. The opinions expressed are those of the author and are not necessarily shared by CPRE or the U.S. Department of Education.

3. This program used student gains on the California Assessment Program (CAP) test as an indicator in determining the size of cash incentives awarded to schools.

6 Helping Black Children Succeed: The Significance of Some Social Factors

NORRIS M. HAYNES

and

JAMES P. COMER

Introduction

Academic underachievement among Black students in inner-city public schools continues to be a serious problem despite recent assessments that American public education in general, has improved (College Entrance Examination Board, 1985). Educators continue to express great concern regarding the many problems that still plague many schools. Achievement and other school-related problems appear to be particularly severe among minority children in urban schools. For example, among Black and Hispanic students in New York City, Philadelphia, and Chicago, the average dropout rate exceeds 45 percent (McLure, 1986). Among Black males, the problem appears to be much more acute. It is estimated that the high school dropout rate among them is approximately 72 percent (Jones, 1986). Generally, the academic achievement of Black students has improved, but it is still below acceptable levels. They still lag behind their white counterparts on standardized achievement tests (College Entrance Examination Board, 1985).

To address the problem of underachievement among Black students, we first need to understand what the probable causes are. The causes, we believe, are deeply rooted in the socioeconomically disadvantaged condition of Black children and the failure of educational institutions to respond appropriately and humanistically to the needs created by these conditions.

Mary Wright Edelman (1987) quoted Dr. W. E. B. Dubois who

103

eloquently expressed the need for careful analysis of the social conditions of Blacks when he wrote: "There is only one sure basis of social reform and that is truth, a careful detailed knowledge of the essential facts of each social problem. Without this there is no logical starting place for reform and uplift." (p.1) We need then to carefully examine the conditions that create and perpetuate failure. In doing so, we offer the premise that when large numbers of children from socioeconomically disadvantaged families experience academic failure, this is most likely attributable to factors inherent in that disadvantaged condition. In this chapter, we discuss several of these factors, including poverty, racial discrimination, social inequalities, support groups, the mass media, schools, and business.

Poverty

A major cause of underachievement among Black children is poverty (Committee for Economic Development, 1987). Recent data indicate that a Black child is about three times as likely as a white child to be poor (Hodgkinson, 1985; Edelman, 1987). Census data reported by the College Entrance Examination Board indicate that 52 percent of Black children ages 3-5 are poor compared to 18 percent of white children in that age group. Among Black children in age groups 6-13 and 14-15, 47 percent and 48 percent respectively are poor compared to 19 percent and 17 percent respectively for white children (College Entrance Examination Board, 1985). To live in poverty is to live under stress. Maslow (1970) noted that lower level needs, when unfulfilled, assume prepotency over higher level ones and become the main motivating drives that energize and direct behavior. Children who are hungry, who feel unsafe, or who lack a sense of belonging are most concerned about getting their hunger, safety, and belonging needs satisfied. They are least concerned about deriving self-esteem or self-actualization through high academic achievement.

The alleviation of poverty, then, is seen, as an important condition for the elevation of academic performance among Black children. Here we have an intersecting of social policy with educational concerns. The failure of society to meet the basic needs of poor children can and will have catastrophic social implications. A nation that turns its back on its children is, "a nation at risk." Edelman (1987) noted that poverty among children in America could have been completely obliterated in 1986 for less than the 1987 fiscal year defense budget. The point is that politicians and policy makers seem to attach greater importance to superfluous ammunition than to the welfare of children.

Children's ability to achieve academically is influenced by their socioeconomic condition. Federal, state, and city government agencies must develop policies that move families off welfare rolls and out of unemployment lines to meaningful jobs. The restoration of economic strength to socioeconomically deprived families will contribute to academic success among many Black children.

Poverty, though a significant cause of academic failure among Black children, is by no means the only cause. It is one of several factors that serve to depress and stunt the psychoeducational development of Black children.

Racial Discrimination

Economic dislocation among Blacks is the result of many years of racial discrimination and concerted attempts on the part of the white majority to exclude Blacks from participating in the American dream. The militancy of the Black liberation movement and the strident vociferous demands for justice and equality that echoed around the country in the 1960s won for Blacks limited access to educational and employment opportunity. Twenty years after Dr. Martin Luther King's dream of an America where Blacks and whites share equally in the richness of the American economy, many Blacks are still locked out—and in larger numbers than before. The small gains made through affirmative action are being rapidly eroded. The ascendency of neoconservative groups to positions of political power and influence has brought about a deplorable reversal in the nation's commitment to equal opportunity for all its citizens. Comer (1983) noted:

> it is therefore not surprising that social programs that social programs and affirmative action are under attack, especially in light of a contracting economy in which there are more qualified people than there are available positions. Social policy development, needed to improve opportunities for blacks and decrease the potential for racial conflict is hampered by efforts to justify political economic theories. (p. 147)

Black children are heirs to the effects of the bigotry and racial prejudice that have guided national policy prior to the 1960s and that have resurfaced during the 1980s. To protect Black children and ensure that their rights as American citizens are protected, an effective national policy that addresses racial prejudice in all its forms must be developed. In particular, policies that divide local school systems racially, so that there are schools for Blacks that are substandard and schools for whites that are superior, must be changed.

In every urban school system in the United States where there is a large Black population there tends to be a two-tiered system of education with Black children receiving the inferior quality (Fordham and Ogby, 1986). Yet the policy makers in Washington issue statements regarding educational practice and academic achievement without addressing such glaring inequalities. Black children, therefore, face double jeopardy. Not only are they socioeconomically deprived but they are also educationally disadvantaged. Effective action requires the political mobilization of Blacks to assert the rights of their children to a superior education. Blacks must use their voting power to elect local, state, and federal officials who care enough about Black children to seek the eradication of inferior schools.

Social Inequalities

Access to effective social services and adequate health care is another major concern that confronts poor Black families and impacts on the ability of Black children to perform in school. One middle school in the city of New Haven recognized this as a major problem and held a community services information day. Service providers ranging from social welfare agencies to substance abuse counseling programs visited the school and shared information about their services with hundreds of parents. The reaction of parents was that of surprise. There was so much available to them that they knew so little about. They expressed deep gratitude to the school's principal and suggested that the event be held annually (Haynes and Hamilton-Lee, 1988).

Apart from information dissemination, the range of social and support services available to Black families appears to be too limited and uncoordinated. There is great need for more comprehensive and integrated services for Black youth in particular. Edelman (1987) identified several kinds of activities that can help prevent undesirable outcomes such as teen pregnancy. We believe that they can also enhance the overall quality of life for Black youth. These are: (1) many and varied opportunities for success; (2) academic skills enhancement; (3) work-related, skill-building, and work exposure; (4) family-life education and life planning; and (5) comprehensive adolescent health services.

At the end of the average school day, most children spend their time in unproductive, sometimes mischievous, activity. A minority of them work to earn needed money. Some turn to drugs and are co-opted by seasoned drug pushers to become drug runners or couriers for attractive remuneration. There have been instances where others have engaged in illicit sexual activities to earn money to buy attractive clothes. Still others become so bored and disenchanted with life that they commit suicide or run away in search of something meaningful or at least better.

A young Black male student who currently attends the Massachusetts Institute of Technology as an electrical engineering student was recently interviewed by *People Magazine* about his friends, school, and neighborhood in South Jamaica, Queens. His response summarized the feeling of despair which is pervasive in many poor Black neighborhoods. He stated: "most of the people I knew from Junior High are either dead or in jail. And most of the girls have babies now. There's a lot of drugs. Education is not important there, money is" (*People Magazine,* April 4, 1988).

The availability of meaningful, enjoyable and productive activities outside of school can serve to reduce the susceptibility of Black youth to the lure of drugs, unsafe sexual activity, and propensity toward violence. The existence of basketball courts in some derelict sections of the city is not enough. Community resources must be invested with proper planning, and the involvement of parents, churches, businesses, schools, and city governments. The commitment to effect positive change must be made by those who control the financial resources.

To provide such a program of activities in such an integrated and comprehensive fashion may seem like a radical idea, and indeed it is. But consider the potential benefits: lowered rates of teen pregnancy, reduced use of illicit drugs, increased school attendance, higher achievement, and safer and better communities.

Support Groups

Despite poverty, racial discrimination, and social inequities encountered by Blacks, there are many impressive examples of Black children from impoverished backgrounds who have succeeded academically and have gone on to excel in different professional and career fields. A major contributing factor to the success of the individual has been the existence of a support system consisting of either one individual or a group of individuals that motivated, inspired, cared for, and sustained them (Comer, 1980; Gordon, in press). In some instances, the support was found within the primary social network where a thoughtful aunt or uncle or a caring minister assumed responsibility and offered guidance. In other instances, support came from outside. Some benefactor or teacher took an interest and provided moral and material support.

Invariably, individuals who survived the horrors of poverty and the mental oppression of marginal existence made it because someone cared enough to share time, wisdom, and a vision of the future with them. This spirit of altruism and selflessness is fast disappearing even among families and friends in the Black community. The extended family as a source of nurturance and guidance is all but vanished. At one time the Black church was a bastion of hope. Comer (1983) noted:

> Destruction of the Black community in the post-slavery period might have been even more far-reaching had it not been for the role of the black church. The church almost single handedly provided the structure of attitudes, values and behavior so crucial for adequate

group performance. Indeed the black church was virtually a substitute society. (pp. 145-146)

The ability and will of the church to successfully intervene on behalf of floundering Black youth appears to have been overwhelmed by the enormity of the problems confronting the Black community. Its effectiveness, we suspect, may have been diluted by religious indifference and disillusionment on the part of the young people. In the same *People Magazine* article cited earlier, a young Black man imprisoned at the Oak Glen Youth Conservation Group in California's San Bernadino mountains remarked "I am not a bad person, but my life took a bad turn." (*People Magazine,* April 4, 1988, p. 37). Maybe if there had been a strong enough support system, the good in this young man would have prevailed.

The point being made is that the Black nuclear and extended family, as well as the Black community, are no longer as galvanized around a common set of values, goals, and guiding principles as they once were. The Black family has been under socioeconomic attack and is, in the judgment of many, seriously imperiled. Many social scientists have written morbidly about the disintegration of the Black family (Rainwater and Yancey, 1967; Coleman, 1985; Edelman, 1987). It is estimated that 40 percent of Black children are being raised in fatherless homes (Jones, 1986). Pregnancy rates among adolescent Black females are decreasing but are still very high and are much higher than for white females. In 1985, there were 89 births per 1000 unmarried Black teenagers between ages 15 and 19. This compared to 21 per 1000 unmarried white females in the same age group (Children's Defense Fund, 1988). The chances are great that the children of teen parents will live out their childhood days in homes headed by single mothers where poverty rates are highest. Seventy five percent of all households headed by a female under age 25 are poor (Children's Defense Fund, 1988).

Certainly then, the crisis of instability in the Black family is contributory to underachievement and general psychoeducational depression among Black children. The Black community, therefore, has to accept responsibility for rebuilding its infrastructure, the main building block of which is the family unit. We must begin by addressing the adolescent pregnancy problem aggressively. We must inculcate wholesome moral values, while at the same time providing useful educational information that will direct and channel children's energies and emotions in constructive and edifying enterprises.

The entire Black community must be involved in this effort. It ought not to be left entirely to government agencies or schools. Black communities must once again become so cohesive and their fabric, the people, so tightly interwoven in mutual respect and concern that, even in the face of the potentially deleterious effect of poverty, their integrity and strength are maintained. The Black child ought to be able to look at the Black adult next door or in church or on the street corner and feel good about being Black. We must rid our communities of the negative role models, such as the drug pushers, and work to eliminate homelessness, substance abuse, and alcoholism in our communities. Black children must have decent wholesome environments in which to live and grow. They are entitled to conditions that are conducive to healthy social, psychological, emotional, and educational growth.

The Mass Media

The role of the mass media, particularly television, in influencing children's behavior and attitudes has been well documented (Comstock, 1980; Singer and Singer, 1986; Pierce, 1978). However, little attention has been paid to how the power of television can be used to address the problems of low achievement and high dropout rates. Children spend many hours daily looking at television. Yet, there is a disappointing lack of educational programming on the major networks. There is apparently no commitment to use the media influence to at least motivate children to want to learn and achieve.

Academic attainments and educational pursuits could be elevated to the prestigious and important position that sports, for example, now occupies in the American psyche. Television producers, supported by the business community, must decide that it is possible and necessary to do so. We must get to the point in this country where scholastic achievement and performance in other school-related activities are talked about, sung about, and acted out in television.

To engender keener interest in and greater fervor for academic pursuits and to instill a sense of pride in children for academic achievement, there must be a national campaign to address this issue. The media has to be at the forefront of this campaign. There have been scores of editorials on television, in newspapers, and on radio deploring the condition of public education and the failure of schools to educate poor and disadvantaged children. However, the media has not been active in doing anything about the problem. An agreement has to be reached between business and television stations that business sponsors will support prime-time academically oriented programs. The future of this country to a large extent is being shaped by television and a major portion of that future is the lives and minds of children.

There are those who would no doubt argue that television programming reflects the mood and taste of the nation; the viewers decide what television should produce. The argument has been advanced time and time again that Nielsen ratings determine television programming. That is not an entirely false position, but it is a misleading one. Viewers can only rate programs that they see. There has been little or no prime-time or even off-time educational programming on the major networks. The only prime-time programs with educational implications or focus have been special reports which have aired very infrequently, emphasized educational problems, and offered no solutions. An important question to be asked is "What influence do the poor and disadvantaged, who live in our inner cities and whose children are failing, dropping out, being victimized by school violence, and being entrapped by drugs, have on television programming?"

It is incumbent on all of us as citizens and viewers of television to insist and demand that excellence in education, school reform, quality education, self-esteem, effective social skills, and high academic expectations for all children become pervasive themes in television programming.

The Role of Schools

Most of our work is done in schools. Schools, therefore, constitute an important constituency for us. Schools, after all, are the main conduits of educational information to our children. Schools are where children's abilities to think, to speak, to create, and to analyze are nurtured, refined, and assessed. When large numbers of children, regardless of their socioeconomic backgrounds, fail to achieve at an acceptable level, schools must accept culpability and be held accountable. Despite the views of Maslow and others about the strangling consequences of poverty, we state categorically that the poorest child can learn if the school makes that child want to learn. Hills and David (1986) articulated this point well when they stated: "Although schools cannot right all the wrongs in our society and cannot compenstate for inadequacies of some homes they can make a significant difference in fostering good behavior and higher achievement (p. 4). They further recognized that "self-esteem and a sense of achievement can partially protect children and youth from the disadvantaged effects present in some of their environments" (p.4).

For schools to be successful in elevating the academic achievement of disadvantaged children, they must be responsive to their psychoeducational needs. The emphasis in schools cannot be on academic achievement alone. The psychoemotional and intellectual development of children are inextricably tied to each other. Teachers, whether they know it or not, contribute either positively or negatively to the emotional adjustment of children in school. Often when children do well in a class or subject area, it is because they like the teacher and feel good about being in that class.

Children seldom do well in classes they dislike. High absenteeism and soaring dropout rates are no doubt related to children's sense of affiliation with the adults in the school (Comer, 1980). The more children bond with adults in their schools, the greater their chance of academic success.

Recognizing and meeting the psychoeducational needs of Black, minority, and disadvantaged children does not necessarily mean lowering academic standards. It is a myth that cultural sensitivity and responsiveness in educational results in the compromise of high academic standards. Expectations for poor Black children ought to be the same as for middle-class, white children.

Teachers must expect, encourage, and promote excellence among all children regardless of race, gender, or socioeconomic status. We well know that low expectations result in low performance. Recognition of cultural differences affects the educational process, not standards. Differences in learning styles among children, when addressed appropriately, can enhance the learning process. Instruction can be organized so that the disadvantaged child learns the mainstream ways of working, learning, and acting, and the mainstream child becomes aware of and learns from non-mainstream ways of adapting, learning, and coping. Teachers are sensitized and they too learn from their interactions with children whose cultural norms are different from theirs.

The Role of Business

In collaboration with schools, local businesses and other institutions have an important role to play in making the educational experience of disadvantaged children meaningful and relevant. Cooperative learning opportunitites in which business and industry work with schools to provide practical experiences for students to complement classroom instruction must be expanded and improved. Abstract concepts come alive when they are applied to real world situations. Classroom learning is meaningful only as it is transferable to life experiences outside of the classroom. For disadvantaged children, a vision for the future is tied to concrete experiences in the present. Thus, plans which include graduating from high school, going to college, and pursuing a professional career are formed, shaped, and nurtured by experiences that these children are exposed to during the school years. Children from poor families generally do not have the social networks to provide them with easy access to good job experiences during summer holidays or meaningful internships as other more privileged children have. It is necessary, therefore, for businesses, schools, and government agencies to provide opportunities for the students to combine abstract learning with concrete experience, the ideal with the real, the future with the present. Schools must take the lead in this.

Summary

Several important social factors which influence the intellectual development and educational performance of Black children have been identified. These include: poverty, racial discrimination, social inequalities, support groups, the mass media, the instructional and affective nature of schools, work opportunities, and community-based programs that provide an outlet for constructive expression of basic human drives and aggressive energies. All of these factors can and should be addressed through the collaborative and coordinated efforts of schools, families, community-based organizations, local businesses, local, state, and federal government agencies and the mass media.

The problem of underachievement is related to and caused by the failure of society to adequately address in a comprehensive, integrated way the psychoeducational, socioeconomic, and emotional needs of economically disadvantaged children and their families. What results is high absenteeism, high dropout rates, substance abuse, adolescent pregnancy, and violence.

Strategies for improving academic performance among black children are too often undertaken in isolation without adequate attention to the social contexts in which they occur. We have argued here not only for a more realistic approach but also for a much more culturally sensitive approach. Until policy makers and educators recognize the important relationship of sociology and economics to education and learning, significant progress in realizing major academic advances among Black children in the inner cities of this country will continue to be elusive.

7 Literacy and Schooling in Subordinate Cultures: The Case of Black Americans

JOHN U. OGBU

Introduction

Literacy is currently receiving a good deal of attention from researchers, policy makers, and professional educators. Common concerns are the development of literacy among children and the problem of literacy competence of functional literacy among adults. In industrialized nations like the United States these problems are regarded as particularly acute among the lower class and subordinate minorities.

The literacy problem of subordinate minorities, the focus of this paper, is threefold and relative, the latter because it derives partly from comparing minorities with the dominant group. One aspect of the problem is that a larger proportion of minorities has not successfully learned to read, write, and compute. Another is that a greater proportion of minorities is not functionally literate. That is, they are unable to demonstrate the ability to read, write, or compute in social and economic situations that require these skills; for example, they cannot fill out job applications and income-tax forms or read and comprehend instructional manuals and utilize the information. Third, school children among subordinate minorities lag behind their dominant-group peers in reading and computation as judged by classroom grades and scores on standardized tests.

Our research since the late 1960s has been on this lag in minority student's performance, and we have compared the situation in the United

Previously published in *Literacy in Historical Perspective,* edited by Daniel P. Resnick for the Center for the Book in the Library of Congress. Published by the Library of Congress. Reprinted by permission.

States with those in other countries like Britain, India, Israel, Japan, and New Zealand. For this paper, we will limit our discussion to Black Americans, beginning with the current hypothesis that Black children fail disporportionately in school because they come from a predominantly oral culture which engenders a discontinuity in their participation in the literate culture of the school. We will then suggest an alternative interpretation of the disproportionate school failure of Black children in its historical and structural context.

Oral Culture, Literate Culture, and School Performance

Shifting Theories of Language Research

Over the past two decades, there has been a continuing shift in theories generated by language studies to explain the disproportionate failure among Blacks to learn to read. A brief review of these theories, as provided by Simons (1976), will take us to the current hypothesis that school failure among Blacks, especially in reading, is due to the fact that they come from an essentially oral culture.

Initially, the field of language studies was dominated by a deficit perspective, whose hypothesis (which still survives in some quarters) is that Black dialect is inferior to standard English and constitutes a handicap in the thinking and learning of Blacks. Ethnographic studies by Labov (1972) and others showed that this model was false, and it was replaced by the difference perspective, whose initial hypothesis asserted that Black dialect is different from standard English but still constitutes a viable system of thinking and learning. Black children failed, especially in reading, because a "mismatch between children's language and the language used in school and in the reading texts interfered with Black children's acquisition of reading skills" (Simons, 1976, p. 3). That is, schools did not use Black dialect as a medium of teaching and learning.

Efforts to use Black dialect in texts and in the classroom, while teaching standard English, did not, however, improve reading achievement among Black children. Critics charged that the difference hypothesis focused too much on materials and teachers and failed to specify the mechanisms by which the interference or mismatch occurred. Critics proposed two types of interference, the first of which was phono-logical. It was thought that differences in pronunciation "might interfere with the acquisition of word recognition skills," but this was subsequently shown not to be a significant factor (Simons 1976, p. 8; see also Rentel and Kennedy, 1972). The second hypothesized interference was grammatical; that is, a "mismatch between Black child's syntax and the standard English syntax of the texts used by the teacher" (Baratz, 1969; Stewart, 1969). But reading achievement among Black children who read materials written in Black dialect grammar did not significantly improve. It was concluded from these studies that Black dialect was not the source of the failure of children to learn to read (Simons, 1976, p. 11).

In the early 1970s a new hypothesis moved beyond language per se to the broader area of communication strategies, speculating that school failure is caused by a mismatch between communicative etiquettes of teachers and students, especially during reading. The hypothesis holds that teachers and minority students who come from different cultures have different communicative strategies and interpretations of situated meanings that lead to miscommunication during reading activities. This interferes with children's acquisition of reading skills.

What is at issue is what is *communicated* by the classroom environment, not the differences in the cultural backgrounds or languages of the teacher and students. The goal of research is to isolate the processes that are meaningful to the participants in classroom communication. Philip's notion of participant structure (1972) provides the conceptual framework for this research. Basically, a participant structure is "a constellation of norms, mutual rights and obligations that shape social relationships, determine participants' perceptions about what is going on and influence learning" (Simons, 1976). Subordinate minority-group children have different participant structures at home than at school, and their generally poor school performance is attributed to this discontinuity.

I have criticized this mismatch hypothesis (Ogbu, 1980a), on three grounds. First, it does not warrant generalization about minority school failure because it is based primarily on research into only one type of minority group, namely, castelike minorities. It does not explain why other minorities, who also have different participant structures at home than at school, learn to read in the same classrooms where Blacks and similar groups fail. Second, the mismatch model ignores historical and societal forces which may actually generate the pattern of classroom processes. And third, although data and insights from studies based on the mismatch model can be used for remedial efforts (Simons, 1976; Erickson, 1978), they cannot lead to social change that would eventually eliminate the need for remedial efforts.

Oral Culture and Literacy

The most recent development in language studies focuses on literacy and attributes the disproportionate school failure of Blacks and similar minorities to a discontinuity between their essentially oral cultures and the literate culture of the white middle-class represented by the public schools.

This hypothesis is based on studies of literacy and its consequences in traditional or small-scale societies (Goody, 1977; Luria, 1976); on studies of language and communicative styles in minority communities (Labov, 1969; Abrahams, 1970; Kochman, 1973); and on microethnographic studies of teacher-pupil interactions in classrooms (Erickson and Mohatt, 1977, cited in Koehler, 1978; Gumperz, 1979; Philips, 1972).

Reviewing studies of both nonliterate, small-scale societies and literate Western societies, Lewis (1979) argues that participants in oral cultures differ significantly from participants in literate cultures, whose sensory orientations are aural rather than oral. She cites a large body of evidence that these two sensory orientations generate contrasting notions of time, causality, space, and the self "which affect the way children are raised and interact with adults" (p. 2). Although the contrast is primarily between non-Western nonliterate populations and Western middle-class populations, she coins the term "residual oral cultures" or "residual oral peoples" to designate segments of Western societies (e.g., subordinate minorities and the lower class) in which many people have minimal knowledge of reading and writing, arguing that these populations resemble in many respects those of nonliterate small-scale societies. Lewis claims that the disproportionate school failure of minority and lower-class children in the United States is due to their participation in those essentially oral cultures. As she puts it,

[In] our society, the schools as key institutions of literate culture tend to reject the oral tradition. As a result, the relatively illiterate find their assumptions about reality in conflict with school expectations. This conflict insures failure and exacerbates other experiences of race and class exclusion (p. 2).

One difficulty with Lewis's formulation is the questionable extent to which one can generalize from small-scale Asian and African societies to groups historically subordinated by their class, ethnic, and racial backgrounds in complex industrial societies. Furthermore, the introduction of literacy of schooling in the small-scale societies does not usually result in the same types of problems it often creates among subordinate minorities and the lower class in the United States (Heyneman, 1979; van den Berghe, 1979). To the contrary, the introduction of schooling in small-scale societies tends to increase cognitive and linguistic or communicate similarities to the pattern of middle-class populations of industrialized societies (Cole and Scribner, 1973; Greenfield, 1966; Luria, 1976). Why, then, after generations of school attendance by Blacks and centuries of interaction with whites, haven't their cognitive and communicative strategies changed to those of the white middle class?

Finally, we know that descendants of illiterate Asian and European immigrants (who might be regarded as "residual oral peoples") have achieved greater success in American public schools than subordinate minorities. For example, studies of Chinese peasant villages in the 1930s (Pepper, 1971, p. 199; Snow, 1961, p. 69) showed that illiteracy rates were often as high as 90 percent. But children of illiterate Chinese peasant immigrants have done quite well in American schools. Gumperz and Cook-Gumperz have proposed a sociolinguistic formulation of the problem (1979). Drawing from the work of Goody (1977) and Luria (1976), they contrast oral and literate cultures in terms of: (1) storage and transmission of knowledge, (2) decontextualization of knowledge, and (3) cognitive strategies in communication and learning. They argue: (1) that in oral cultures stored knowledge is static and its transmission inaccurate, whereas in literate cultures change is built into knowledge and its transmission is accurate; (2) that knowledge acquisition and transmission in literate cultures, unlike oral cultures, are decontextualized; and (3) that in literate cultures a distinctive mode of reasoning emerges that is separate from everyday activities. Using these three domains of change as criteria, the authors contend that the *home*, in contrast to *school*, is a place of oral culture, and they suggest the changes children must make in their cognitive and communicative strategies in order to learn and use written language effectively. They summarize the process involved in the transition from oral to written culture for all children as follows:

Developmentally the transition from speaking to writing as a medium for learning about the world of others requires a change from the interpretative strategies of oral cultures in which children grow up, to the interpretative principles of discursive written language. The move into literacy requires children to make some basic adjustments to the way they socially attribute meaning to events and the processes of every day world in order to be able to loosen their dependence upon contextually specific information and to adopt a decontextualized perspective. Among other things, they must learn to rely on an incrementally acquired knowledge rather than on what is said within any one context. In another dimension the move into literacy requires children linguistically to change their process of interpretation (p. 16).

Gumperz and Cook-Gumperz imply that literacy problems began in the present century with industrialization, bureaucratization, and other socio-economic changes which have tended to: (a) erase the boundaries between elite and popular education, (b) increase the dichotomy between speaking and writing, (c) make literacy prerequisite to economic survival, and (d) institute evaluation of literacy competence through methods which take no account of the socioeconomic changes (Gumperz and Cook-Gumperz, 1979, pp. 11-12).

If this twentieth-century situation creates problems for all children, why do some children make the transition to literacy more easily than others? According to the authors, some oral cultures prepare children better than others: "The argument we have been developing," they state, "is that for all children the literacy experience requires essential changes in the processing of verbal information. For some children, however, the shift of under-standing of written language is sometimes facilitated by early language experience; the child is able early in life to gain processing experience of the written word" (p. 27). Elsewhere, after reviewing several microethnographic studies of communicative interaction between teachers and children of subordinate groups (*e.g.,* Native Americans, Blacks, Native Hawaiians, rural Appalachians, and working-class British), Gumperz sums up the underlying cause of their disproportionate school failure as follows:

> This work highlights the point that children's responses to school tasks are directly influenced by values and presuppositions learned in the home. It demonstrates moreover that classroom equipments, spatial arrangements or social groupings of teachers and students are not the primary determinants of learning. What is important is what is *communicated* in the classroom as a result of complex processes of interaction between educational goals, background knowledge and what various participants perceive over time as taking place (1980, p. 5).

The authors have certainly made an important contribution to our understanding of the cognitive and linguistic changes all children make in learning to use written language. But their implicit and explicit explana-tions of the special problem of minorities is essentially one of the mismatch of communicative etiquettes which we previously criticized. Furthermore, in looking at the problem historically, we find that the educational experiences of Blacks and other subordinate minorities in the United States (*e.g.,* Chicanos, Indians) do not conform to the nineteenth-century situation described by the authors (Ogbu, 1978). Though many Americans idealize education for its own sake, for most Americans, and for Blacks in particular, it has been aimed at developing marketable skills. We shall return to this point later.

The oral culture-literate culture discontinuity hypothesis seems inade-quate to explain the disproportionate school failure of subordinate minority children. We shall suggest an adequate hypothesis which considers both historical and macro-structural forces that shape classroom processes under which children acquire their literacy. But first we wish to distinguish subordinate minorities from other minorities who do not necessarily share similar problems in school and from lower-class people for the same reason.

Stratification as a Context: Castelike and Class

We define a given population as a minority group if it is in a subordinate power relation to another population in the same society. A minority status is not determined by mere number because the subordinate group might outnumber the dominant group, as the Bantu in South Africa outnumber whites by more than 2 to 1. For some purposes, such as education, it is useful to distinguish different types of minorities, and in our work we have classified minorities into autonomous, castelike, and immigrant types.

Autonomous minorities, which are represented in the United States by Jews and Mormons, are also found in most developing Asian and African nations. They are primarily numerical minorities who may be victims of prejudice but are not totally subordinated in systems of stratification, and their separateness is not based on specialized denigrated economic, political, or ritual roles. Moreover, they often have a cultural frame of reference which demonstrates and encourages success in education and other areas as defined by the larger society.

Castelike Minorities — those we have referred to as subordinate minorities — are either incorporated into a society more or less involuntarily and permanently or are forced to seek incorporation and then relegated to inferior status. In America, for example, Blacks were incorporated through slavery; Chicanos and Indians through conquest.

Castelike minorities are generally regarded as inherently inferior by the dominant group, who thus rationalize their relegation to inferior social, political, economic, and other roles. Until recently it was (and in many instances still is) more difficult for castelike minority-group members than for dominant-group members to advance on the basis of individual training and ability. The concept of a job ceiling (Ogbu, 1978) at best describes the circumscribed occupational and economic opportunities historically faced by castelike minorities. A job ceiling is set by the pressures and obstacles that consign minorities to jobs at the lowest levels of status, power, dignity, and income and meanwhile allow the dominant group to acquire the jobs and rewards above those levels. As we shall argue, the access of castelike minorities to schooling and their perceptions of and responses to schooling have historically been shaped by the job ceiling and related barriers.

Immigrant minorities are those who have come more or less voluntarily (unless they are refugees) to their new society for economic, political, and social self-betterment. Immigrants may be subject to pillory and discrimination but have usually not internalized their effects. That is, at least in the first generation, they have not experienced such treatment as an ingrained part of their culture and thus have not been disillusioned to the same extent as castelike minorities. This is true even when the two minority types are faced with the same job ceiling and other barriers. Immigrants also tend to measure their success or failure against that of their peers in their homeland and not against the higher classes of their host society. (See Ogbu, 1978, for further elaboration of these and other factors that differentiate immigrants from castelike minorities.)

Minority groups do not usually accept subordination passively, though their responses vary. Some groups reduce or eliminate aspects of their subordination; others may actually reinforce some aspects of that subordination. Moreover, different types of minorities respond differently. Except for political emigres, the immigrants have the symbolic option of returning to their homeland or re-emigrating elsewhere. This option may, in fact, motivate the acquisition of education and literacy because immigrants can transfer these skills elsewhere for greater rewards. Because this option is usually not open to castelike minorities, they tend to develop various gross and subtle devices to raise, eliminate, or circumvent the job ceiling and other barriers. We shall explore the important implications that these devices have for schooling and literacy.

Lower-Class and Castelike Minorities

Current discussion tends strongly to equate the education and literacy problems of castelike minorities with those of the lower class. But the differences between them appear in the attempt to distinguish castelike stratification from class stratification. "Caste" or "castelike" in this chapter is a purely methodological reference to the structural form underlying the history of minority subordination in America and similar societies.

In a class stratification, people are ranked by their education, their jobs, their behavior, and how much money they make; that is, by achieved criteria. Lower-class individuals have difficulty advancing into higher classes by achieving more wealth and education or better jobs and social positions because they lack requisite training (education), ability, or proper connections. But class stratification, at least in the United States, has an ideology which encourages lower-class people to strive for social and economic self-betterment that would put them and/or their children into higher classes. This social mobility occurs enough among white Americans that they view America as a land of great opportunity and success as a matter of ability, perserverance, and education (Berreman, 1972; Warner et al., 1945).

In a castelike stratification people are, by contrast, assigned to their respective groups at birth or by ascribed criteria such as skin color, and they have few options to escape that designation. Each caste group (*e.g.,* blacks in America) has its own class system but less opportunity for class differentiation and mobility than the dominant class system. For example, the job ceiling in the United States affects Black-white racial stratification but not the stratification of social classes within the white group or within the Black group. Caste thus gives class in the minority population added disadvantages: a white, lower-class American is only lower class; a Black, lower-class American is also faced with a job ceiling and other caste barriers.

There is current debate over whether and to what extent class stratification has replaced racial or castelike stratification in America (Willie, 1979; Wilson, 1978). Since the 1960s, civil rights legislation and other efforts have raised the job ceiling and somewhat reduced other racial barriers, but they have not eliminated these barriers altogether. No one knows the extent to which Blacks are now employed in more desirable jobs as a matter of compliance with the law. What is certain is that the number of Blacks in top jobs more than doubled after affirmative action legislation went into effect in 1966 and 1972, that there is a strong white resistance to these laws, and that Blacks are still underrepresented in desirable jobs and overqualified for the jobs that they do (Brimmer, 1974; U.S. Commission on Civil Rights, 1978).

Furthermore, the positive changes have not reached far enough to affect significantly the social and economic conditions of the Black lower class; nor have they been consistent through the years because of economic recessions, white backlash, and changes in political climate. Statistics easily conceal the single most important indication that castelike stratification persists in America: the extraordinary supports (affirmative action, Equal Employment Opportunities Commission Appeals, Special Programs) that Blacks need, but that whites do not, in order to move into the middle class. The pattern of change is significant for the problem of education and literacy in that Black perceptions of American racial stratification and their opportunities within it have not grown to resemble the perceptions of the white population.

A Cultural Ecological Explanation of Black School Failure

The Framework

Cultural ecology provides a more adequate framework for understanding the literacy problems of Black and similar minorities, whether we focus on school completion, functional literacy, or performance on classroom and standardized tests. This framework enables us to study the connections between the school or learning processes *and* societal forces (such as economic patterns and opportunities, intergroup relations, and status mobility in a given society) which affect school curricula, classroom attitudes and efforts, and various activities of school personnel and other members of the educational system.

Cultural ecology is the study of institutionalized and socially transmitted patterns of behavior interdependent with features of the environment (Netting, 1968, p. 11; see also Geertz, 1962; Goldschmidt, 1971; Bennett, 1969). It does not deal with the overall physical environment but with the effective environment, that is, those aspects that directly affect subsistence quest (technoeconomic activities) and physical survival. In modern societies the effective environment is primarily the bureaucratized industrial economy. A given population's effective environment generally consists, however, of its resources, its ability to exploit these resources, and its level of technology. The principal economic activities or subsistence strategies depend upon the effective environment. And each mode of exploitation calls for specific skills, knowledge, and other attributes which facilitate subsistence and survival under the specific condition. Ecological adaptation for a given population consists of the congruence or fit between the population's strategies for subsistence, survival, and status and the instrumental competencies and related behaviors of its members. Adaptation for an individual consists of learning about resources and exploitative strategies and acquiring appropriate instrumental competencies and rules of behaviors for achievement as it is defined by for his or her social group.

Childrearing and formal education are culturally organized to ensure that children in a given population meet these criteria for adaptation (Ogbu, 1980). In modern societies, the school is the principal institution adapting children to bureaucratized industrial economy in four ways: teaching them the basic practical skills of reading, writing, and computation essential for almost every subsistence activity in the economy; preparing them for more specialized job training when they later enter the labor force (Wilson, 1973); socializing them by means of organizational features (teacher-pupil authority relations, the grading system, etc.) to develop social-emotional attributes essential for participation in the work force (Scrupski, 1975; Wilcox, 1978); and providing the credentials young adults need to enter the work force (Jencks, 1972). In the latter role, schooling is more or less a culturally institutionalized device for allocating and rewarding individuals in society's status system, particularly in the economy (Ogbu, 1979; 1980 a, b).

While ideologically most Americans do not see their schools this way, it is a reasonable analysis based on our own study of school and economic behaviors in Stockton, California. In our research, we asked people why they go to school; why they send their children to school; and why they pay taxes to support schools; we listened to public and private discussions and gossip about schooling, jobs, and related matters; we examined documents from local school systems and from city and county planning departments, as well as from employment and welfare agencies. These sources suggest that Stocktonians do not seek education for its own sake, to satisfy their curiosity, or for self-fulfillment, but in order to get jobs as adults and thereby achieve full adult status as defined by their community. Not only do Stocktonians believe that more and better schooling leads to more desirable jobs, higher income, and other social and economic benefits, but local statistics also tend to support their belief — for the majority whites. In Stockton, as elsewhere in the nation, whites with high school diplomas generally have a better chance at more desirable jobs and greater lifetime earning power than their peers with only elementary school diplomas; however, they have less chance at desirable jobs and less earning power than their peers with college degrees.

The belief that economic opportunities are commensurate with educational achievement is a part of local white epistemology and is borne out historically by the actual experiences of most whites in the job market. The belief is communicated to local white children and reinforced in a variety of ways. These observations lead us to conclude that the school efforts of local whites are greatly influenced by their experiences in and perceptions of the connection between schooling and adult economic participation.

A major ecological consequence of castelike stratification and job ceiling is that Blacks in Stockton and elsewhere in the United States have traditionally occupied economic positions characterized by scarce, dead-end, peripheral, or unstable jobs and by low wages, few chances for advancement on the job, and little social credit as measured by values of the larger society. Some ghetto Blacks occupy economic positions that are almost devoid of any wage labor but that contain social resources such as other ghetto residents and caretaker institutions (Harrison, 1972; Ross and Hill, 1967). Equally important is the fact that the Blacks' effective environment contains, in addition to these conventional resources, a subeconomy or "street economy" defined as "a market for the distribution of goods and services which are in demand but have been outlawed officially for social and moral reasons" (Bullock, 1973, p. 100; see also Foster, 1974; Heard, 1968; Milner, 1970; Wolfe, 1970).

Educational Consequences

What are the educational consequences of the Black effective environment? Because the traditional social and economic positions of Blacks have not required much formal education or rewarded education accomplishments highly, the pattern of schooling which has evolved for Blacks generally prepares them for inferior roles. It does not qualify Blacks for the more desirable social and economic positions open to whites, nor does it encourage Blacks to achieve their maximum. These combined factors have traditionally affected Black literacy as measured by school completion, functional literacy, and performance on classroom and standardized tests. We now want to suggest four specific ways in which these factors sustain the lag in Black school performance by: (a) promoting certain treatment or experiences of Blacks in school and classroom and (b) fostering certain classroom attitudes, orientations, and behavior.

White Perceptions of Blacks and Black Access to Education

Blacks have had some access to formal schooling ever since they were brought to America in the early seventeenth century. Although formal education was available to only a few in the South (where most Blacks lived before emancipation), and although there was strong opposition to Black education in both the South and the North, actual legal prohibitions against Black education were instituted in the South only from 1832 to about 1861 after Nat Turner's Revolt (Bond, 1966, p. 21; Bullock, 1970). Black access to the public schools increased after emancipation, and, as table 7.1 shows, their illiteracy rates steadily declined.

However, factors important to understanding the present situation are concealed by the table. First, Blacks have had to fight for almost every increase in their access to public schools; in neither the South nor the North have they been free as a matter of right to attend their community public schools (Bond, 1966; Bullock, 1970; Kluger, 1977; Ogbu, 1978). Second, Black education in both the South and North has usually been inferior, often separate, and generally based on white perceptions and stereotypes of Black status in society and especially in the economy. Third, because Blacks do not share white perceptions of their status, they tend not to accept white standards of education for them. Consequently, since the second half of the nineteenth century, Blacks have been fighting whites against both inferior and separate education (Kluger, 1977).

Let us briefly summarize how white perceptions of Black status have shaped Black education historically and affected the quality of Black literacy.

Before emancipation, Blacks received occasional biblical education because their masters believed it would make them more obedient and faithful. After the Civil War, when Blacks were relegated to peon-like status as sharecroppers or were limited to "Negro jobs" in domestic service and unskilled labor, education followed suit. The ruling white elites believed the tenant farming system would break down if Black children received the same education as white children. They would, for example, learn to question the high rates of interest and the exploitative accounting methods the planters imposed on illiterate tenants. Thus, Black education was starved of funds.

As the South urbanized, Blacks at first received some "industrial" education, chiefly in cooking and low-grade building skills. But when many desirable factory jobs began to require special training, Black school curricula began, ironically, to emphasize classical and academic rather than industrial education, which was now offered in white schools (Bond, 1966, p. 404; Myrdal, 1944, pp. 897-98; Ogbu, 1978, p. 117).

We can conclude that, historically, if Blacks did not qualify for desirable jobs, it was because their education was designed to disqualify them, not because they were incompetent. Until perhaps the 1960s, American society never seriously intended Blacks to achieve social and occupational equality with whites through education.

Even now, "subtle mechanisms" continue to adapt Black and white graduates to different futures. One such mechanism for lowering the job ceiling is the disproportionate labeling of Black children as educationally "handicapped." For example, in a recent court case brought by Blacks against the San Francisco School District, evidence showed that Blacks made up only 31.1 percent of the school enrollment in 1976-77, but constituted 53.8 percent of those categorized as educable mentally retarded and relegated to special classes. In the same year, in the twenty California school districts which enrolled 80 percent of Black children, Black students comprised about 27.5 percent of the school population but 62 percent of those labeled educable mentally retarded. In his decision favoring Blacks the judge concluded that:

> The statistical analyses of the statewide and district-by-district figures indicate the obvious. Their (i.e., Black) apparent over-enrollment could not be the result of chance. For example, there is less than one in a million chance that the overenrollment of Black children and the underenrollment of non-Black children in the E.M.R. classes in 1976-77 would have resulted under a color-blind system of placement (U.S. District Court for Northern California, 1979, pp. 21-22).

The figures are similar to those of other large American cities, including Chicago and New York (see, for example, U.S. Commission on Civil Rights, 1974).

Black Responses

We pointed out earlier that castelike minorities do not usually accept their subordination passively and that Blacks have been fighting since emancipa-

Table 7.1

Black and White Illiteracy, 14 Years Old and Over, by Region for Selected
Years: 1890-1969

(Numbers in thousands)

Area and Year	BLACK ILLITERATE			WHITE ILLITERATE		
	Total	Number	Percent	Total	Number	Percent
United States:						
1890..........	4259	2607	61	35818	2880	8
1910..........	823	91	11	43091	1944	5
1930..........	8027	1445	18	77357	2350	3
1947..........	10471	1152	11	95952	1919	2
1959..........	12210	910	7	109163	1709	2
1969..........	14280	509	4	127449	891	1
South:						
1890..........	3769	2462	65	7755	1170	15
1910..........	5308	1906	36	12790	1087	8
1930..........	6116	1351	22	18390	780	4
North and West:						
1890..........	631	208	33	28063	1710	6
1910..........	823	91	11	43091	1944	5
1930..........	1911	94	5	58967	1570	3

Source: U.S. Department of Commerce, Bureau of the Census. *Current Population Reports,
Special Studies, Series P-23, No. 80, The Social and Economic Status of the Black Population
in the United States: An Historical View, 1790-1978.* Table 68, p. 91.

tion for more and better schooling and against the job ceiling. Those
responses, as they relate to schooling and jobs, may in fact contribute to the
lag in the school performance, as we shall demonstrate

Black school conflict and mistrust.   History has left Blacks with a
feeling that whites and their institutions cannot be trusted to benefit Blacks
equitably. Public schools, particularly in the ghetto, are generally not
trusted by Blacks to provide Black children with the "right education." This
mistrust of schools arises partly from Black perceptions of past and current
discriminatory treatment by public schools. This treatment is fully
documented in several studies (see Bond, 1966, 1969; Kluger, 1977;
Weinberg, 1977).

For over a century, having first "fought" against total exclusion from
the public schools, Blacks have been "fighting" against inferior education
in both segregated and integrated schools. In the totally segregated

Southern school systems, Blacks of course identified strongly and therefore cooperated with "black schools." But their effectiveness was undermined by their simultaneous rejection of these same schools as inferior to white schools and thus their need to "fight" for school desegregation. Their attention, commitment, and efforts were diverted from maximizing achievement in Black schools to the pursuit of equal resources and an ideal learning setting, namely, desegregated schools.

But in desegregated schools throughout the nation disaffection and mistrust also abound because Blacks see inferior education perpetuated through many subtle devices they suspected the schools of using (e.g., biased testing, misclassification, tracking, biased textbooks, biased counseling, etc.), and because they doubt that these schools understand Black children and their needs.

This doubt is particularly widespread at the moment: it was openly expressed by many Blacks at public meetings and in ethnographic interviews during our fieldwork in Stockton. In a study of a desegregated high school, Slawski and Scherer (1977) also found that local Blacks tended to attribute low school performance of Black males to the school's inability to "relate to Black males in ways that will help them learn." The point we would like to stress is that Black mistrust and conflict with schools reduce the degree to which Black parents and their children can accept as legitimate the schools' goals, standards, and instructional approaches. As a result they tend not to experience a need to cooperate with the schools or to follow their rules and requirements for achievement.

The same conflicts and mistrust also force the schools into defensive approaches to Black education — control, paternalism, or actual "contests" — which divert the attention of both Blacks and schools from the real task of educating Black children. This contrasts sharply with the experience of white, middle-class parents and their children, who tend to see the completion of school tasks and conformity with school standards as necessary, desirable, and compatible with their own goals. Ghetto Blacks tend sometimes to interpret the same demands as deceptions or as unnecessary impositions incompatible with their "real educational goals." Perseverance at academic tasks thus becomes difficult for Black children.

Disillusionment over job ceiling and academic efforts.
Throughout history a greater proportion of Blacks than whites have been educationally better qualified or overqualified for their jobs yet underpaid for their educational achievements (Henderson, 1967; Norgren and Hill, 1964; Newman et al., 1978; Sharp, 1970; U.S. Commission on Civil Rights, 1978). Even in recent years their gradual penetration into more desirable jobs has been accomplished mainly through collective struggle for civil rights (Newman et al., 1978; Scott, 1976; Ogbu, 1978). Job opportunities remain the primary concern of Black Americans today.

The job ceiling and related discriminatory practices shape Black operations, which in turn influence their perceptions of and responses to schooling. Blacks are generally bitter, frustrated, and resentful at the job ceiling and other barriers to the full benefits of their education. The extent of this bitterness is evident in the time and resources they expend in efforts to break or circumvent the job ceiling (see Davis, Gardner, and Gardner, 1965; Dollard, 1957; Drake and Cayton, 1970; Ogbu, 1974; Powdermaker, 1968; Newman et al., 1978; Scott, 1976) as are their strategies for achieving their objectives, such as "uncle tomming," boycotting white businesses, protesting, rioting, and appealing to the courts, to Fair Employment Practices Commissions, to the Equal Employment Opportunity Commission, and the like (see Drake and Cayton, 1970, p. 745; National Advisory Commission on Civil Disorders, 1968, p. 61; Newman et al., 1978, pp. 10-26; Ogbu, 1978; Powdermaker, 1968, pp. 107,100,112; Schemer, 1965, p. 85).

When Civil Rights effectively expand Black employment opportunities and other rewards for education, as they appeared to be doing in the 1960s, this encourages Black students to work hard in school (Ginsberg et al., 1967). But a discouraging message is also communicated, namely, that without such a collective civil rights struggle, Blacks automatically have fewer opportunities than whites to benefit from education.

Black children learn about the job ceiling and other barriers quite early in life, though not necessarily from explicit statements by their parents and other adults in their community. In our ethnographic research in Stockton, California, we have found, however, that Black parents communicate contradictory attitudes toward schooling. They emphasize the need for their children to get more education than they did, and they insist that their children work hard in order to get good grades and to graduate from high school or college. However, the same parents, by being unemployed, underemployed, and discriminated against, and by gossiping about the similar experiences of relatives and other adults in the community, imply that even if the children succeed in school, their chances at good jobs and other societal rewards are not as good as those of their white peers. It is also a part of local Black epistemology that a Black person must be "twice as good" or "twice as qualified" as the white in order to compete successfully in any situation where whites are judges. Thus the actual example of the lives of Black parents can undercut their stated encouragements.

Black children also learn about the job ceiling from public demonstrations calling for more jobs and better wages and from mass media reports of these and related events. These sources convey to Black children that the connection between school success and one's ability to get ahead is not as good for Blacks as for whites. As Black children get older and experience personal failures and frustrations in looking for part-time jobs and summer jobs, these negative messages are reinforced. Some perceptions of young Blacks, such as their impression of unlimited employment opportunities for their white peers, may not be accurate (Ogbu, 1974); they nonetheless lead to increasing disillusionment among Blacks about their future and to doubts about the value of schooling (Ogbu, 1974, p. 100; see also Frazier, 1940, pp. 134-47; Schulz, 1969, p. 159; Powdermaker, 1968, p. 321).

Not only do these perceptions discourage Black children from developing serious attitudes toward school and from persevering in their schoolwork, they also teach them to "blame the system" rather than themselves for their failures. In our research in Stockton we have found that Black children learn very early to blame the school system for their failures, just as their parents and Black adults in general blame their failures on the larger "system." A resulting paradox is that Black students may express high educational aspirations coupled with low academic effort and perseverance and thus low school performance.

Survival strategies and competencies incongruent with demands of schooling.

Another Black response to the job ceiling is the evolution of "survival strategies." This effects even children much too young to understand the labor market and other barriers and has serious implications for school performance and classroom processes. There are two kinds of survival strategies. The purpose of the first kind is to increase conventional economic and social resources of the Black community and to make available conventional jobs and other societal rewards. These strategies include collective struggles or civil rights activities (Newman et al., 1978; Scott, 1976), clientship or uncle tomming (Dollard, 1957; Myrdal, 1944; Farmer, 1968; Ogbu, 1978). Civil rights strategy is well known to most people; but clientship also arises from the job ceiling and other barriers. Blacks learned long ago that one key to self-betterment within the caste system is through white patronage (i.e., favoritism, not merit alone), which can be solicited through some verson of the old "Uncle Tom" role; that is, through compliance, dependence, and manipulation. More recently, the reverse strategy of "shuckin' and jivin'" has been adopted, which is another defensive way to manipulate white patronage. The second kind of survival strategy, which includes hustling, pimping, and the like, exploits nonconventional economic and social resources or "the street economy" (Bullock, 1973; Foster, 1974; Heard, 1968; Milner, 1970; Wolfe, 1970).

Thus, within the Black community success in terms of conventional jobs and resources often requires collective struggles and/or clientship *in addition to educational credentials*. Nonconventional forms of success and ways of making a living are also open to Blacks. Thus "successful people" are not only those who succeed in conventional terms either with school credentials alone or with clientship and collective struggle as well but also those who make it in the street through hustling and related strategies. They are admired, and they influence the efforts of others, including children, to succeed.

We have suggested that survival strategies may require knowledge, attitudes, and skills that are not wholly compatible with white, middle-class teaching and learning behavior. We have also suggested that children learn the survival strategies during preschool years as a normal part of their cultural learning; consequently, the potential for learning difficulties may already exist when children enter school. Whether and to what extent those difficulties arise depends on the individual child's experience in school and the classroom. We suspect that insofar as children have become competent in these survival strategies they may lack serious attitudes toward school and toward academic tasks in general, including test taking.

Conclusion

In this chapter we have argued that the disproportionate school failure of Black children is not because they come from an oral culture, though we have not challenged that assertion that Black culture is an oral culture. We have only noted that members of the so-called oral cultures of small-scale societies and immigrants into the United States from residual cultures of more complex societies do not manifest the same learning problems in school that are found among Black and similar castelike minorities.

We have suggested an alternative view of the problem within an ecological framework in which schooling is a culturally organized means of preparing children for adult roles in the social and economic life of their society or social group. Within this framework the traditional social and economic positions of Blacks have not required much education nor rewarded Blacks highly for educational accomplishments. Black menial position enforced by castelike or racial stratification has influenced how the dominant whites who control their schooling perceive them and define their educational needs. It has also influenced how Blacks themselves perceive their opportunities and the importance of schooling.

The perceptions of whites have led them to provide Blacks with inadequate schooling and to communicate attitudes in school settings that do not encourage Blacks to maximum efforts. Black perceptions generate disillusionment about schooling and a lack of perseverance toward schoolwork; they lead to survival strategies that require knowledge, attitudes, and skills which may be incompatible with school requirements. Furthermore, it is likely that perennial conflict and mistrust between Blacks and the schools interfere with the willingness of Blacks to comply with school rules and standards and place the schools in a defensive posture toward Blacks. Closer study is needed to determine how these factors contribute, singly and in combination, to the learning difficulties observed in classrooms.

Since the 1960s, some efforts have been made to change Black status and schooling, for example, through legislative and administrative channels noted earlier in the chapter. The magnitude and quality of these changes, however, have not broken the job ceiling or significantly altered Black expectations, especially among the lower segments of the Black community.

During the same period, efforts have also been made to improve Black schooling and raise academic achievement levels through school desegregation, compensatory education, preschool (Headstart) education, parent education and training, Follow-Through, special admissions, special scholarships, and many others (Ogbu, 1978). These programs have helped many Blacks to complete higher levels of schooling, to achieve greater functional literacy, and to improve their performance in classroom and on standardized tests. But the number benefiting from such programs remains small and many who do benefit probably do not come from the lower segments of the community. These programs remain ineffective for or unavailable to the majority. Moreover, they are essentially remedial and often based on misconceptions of the underlying causes of Black school problems (Ogbu, 1978). Preventing learning problems before they develop will require a strategy that will simultaneously have to: (a) consider the economic expectations of Blacks as a root cause rather than a consequence of the school failure and literacy problem; (b) eliminate the gross and subtle mechanisms which differentiate Black schooling from white schooling; and (c) examine Black perceptions and "adaptive" responses, including the problem of mistrust and conflict in Black relations with the schools.

Part Three

Limitations of Academic Achievement Measures

8 Limitations of Current Academic Achievement Measures

ASA G. HILLIARD, III

Introduction

The measurement of "academic achievement" in America is big business, indeed. In order for the producers of academic achievement tests to make a profit easily, certain *economic* requirements must be met. First, the test should be very short, taking a minimum of time to administer. It should be easy to record answers. It should be easily scored. And above all, a single test must be used for every test taker.

Test makers assume that there is a common body of academic content to which every child has been or ought to have been exposed. Since this is not the case, the generic word "achievement" should be qualified in some way if it is to have scientific meaning. Yet, those who develop tests for profit would find it nearly impossible to admit to the diversity that exists in the human experience.

Sometimes educators and psychologists try to rationalize the use of standardized achievement tests on professional grounds. They state the tests are valid and imply that they are useful. The public raises few questions about tests. In fact, few are knowledgeable enough about tests to know precisely which questions should be raised. As a result, standardized testing in America enjoys an unprecedented acceptance by the general public and by the teaching profession.

The pattern of use of tests in the United States is quite different from that in other industrial nations of the world. Some nations do have a standard curriculum. Until recently, the United States has permitted, even encouraged, a wide diversity in curricular offerings. The tracking system that is almost universal in the United States guarantees that students will be exposed to different curricular content. Indeed, the United States may be farther from a common curriculum than any other industrial nation (Lomotey and Swanson, 1990).

It is the purpose of this chapter to explore issues surrounding the use of standardized achievement tests with African-Americans. I will discuss issues associated with the possible *benefits* of this testing to African-American students, criteria for evaluating standardized achievement tests, and efforts to improve standardized achievement testing practices. In the history of standardized testing, little has been said regarding their beneficial use. Rules for test construction have emphasized the need for tests to produce consistent results (reliability) from one time to the next or from one test to another (American Psychological Association, 1974). Sometimes, the rule is that the tests predict future performance (predictive validity) for students. However, the literature has been virtually silent in providing evidence that the use of different types of academic achievement tests has produced benefits or limited opportunities for children, especially for African-American children.

I will restrict my discussion of academic achievement tests to tests that are usually classified into two categories. First, I will consider the well-known general test of academic skills or achievement. Second, I will discuss intelligence quotient or simply "intelligence" tests. Although, IQ or intelligence tests are considered by some scholars to provide measures of general capacities in students, they too can best be described as academic achievement tests, as material on these tests can be mastered with good coaching and practice (Messick, 1980).

It is important to consider IQ tests and traditional achievement tests separately since they are developed for different purposes. Each one may be evaluated on a slightly different basis because of the use to which each is put in school settings.

Achievement Tests: Beyond Black and White

At least four primary criteria should be utilized in the evaluation of any academic achievement test. The statement of these criteria should suggest the need for culturally salient development and use of such tests.

Academic achievement tests are designed to assess the competency of test takers in some domain of knowledge. Most often educators seek to determine what a student has learned after exposure to instruction in a given area. There are reasons for testing students who may not have been exposed to the content on the test; however, the educator must know about the degree of exposure in order to make a meaningful interpretation of the test results.

In order for such tests to be scientifically valid and fair, several rules should apply. First, the tests should be content valid. this means that the material on the academic achievement test should match material in the curriculum that is offered to students. Additionally, validity determintaion relies heavily upon the opinion of experts who generally base those opinions upon an armchair analysis of sample copies on the test. A more scientific approach is to do an empirical content analysis, comparing carefully the actual course offerings to which students are exposed with the content of the standardized test. When such empirical checks have been performed in the past, gross mismatches have been demonstrated between popular nationally standardized tests and locally offered school curricula (Hilliard, 1982). In fact, the best matches result in a situation where the average student who takes a nationally standardized test will be looking at a test where nearly half the material is being seen for the first time. There is no nationally standardized curriculum. The curriculum determination is and has always been a local matter. Even then, the prescribed or authorized curriculum may vary considerably from the offered curriculum.

It seem irrational then to use nationally standarized tests as if the meaning of scores in relationship to the curriculum in one school district is the same as it is for other school districts. In short, few nationally standardized academic achievement tests meet rigorous scientific criteria for empirical content validity determination.

In some school systems, criterion-referenced standardized tests have been developed. This means that careful attention is given to matching the content of the test with the content of the school curriculum as best it can be ascertained. In addition, criterion-referenced scores usually are reported without concern for the rank of students, being concerned, rather, with whether or not a student has mastered the required content on the test. A student's performance is not really compared with that of another student, but with content criteria. When the content validity of such a criterion referenced test is determined empirically, most of the objections to achievement tests disappear.

Second, tests used for different groups should be universally appropriate. It is possible to be arbitrary when determining the content for a standardized academic achievement test. Those who produce tests have great latitude in making decisions about the content that should be included. Tests can have good content validity and yet the content might not be appropriate. For example, if an academic achievement test in social studies matches the actual content of the social studies curriculum by approximately 90 percent, it would be said to have good content validity. However, if that content is racially biased, it may be said to be inappropriate; philosophical positions determine the selection of particular content. In such a case, the appropriateness of the content may be related to the philosophical orientation of users. It is matters such as these that make it difficult to produce a test that will be universally appropriate for all students on all occasions.

Third, tests should include representative samples of the course content and should be given to a representative sample of the population under study. The content on a test would rarely, if ever, be exactly like the content offered in coursework. As a result, it is necessary to select a sample of course content to include in an academic achievement test. In addition, where a large group of people is concerned, it is not possible to try to test everyone. Therefore, attempts are made to select a representative sample from the general population.

Good academic achievement tests are said to have representative samples of content and the test takers are said to be representative of the population that is supposed to have been exposed to the content. In the past, African-American children were not included in standardization samples. As a result, the experience of European-American children was given greater weight on the test than those of African-American children. Most recently, attempts have been made to correct this deficiency by adding more African-American students to standardization samples for nationally standardized academic achievement tests.

Fourth, there should be a consideration, in the development and utilization of tests, of student's relative access to knowledge. Many standardized academic achievement test users assume that all students in the testing population have had an equal opportunity to master the knowledge presented on the tests. As a result, a low score on an academic achievement test by a student is interpreted to mean that the student did not know certain information and *could* know such information. In reality, the student may score low merely because that student has not had the necessary exposure to do well on such a test.

Observers of schools can see that few African-American students are exposed to high quality instruction (Lomotey, 1989). The interpretation that is placed on their low performance tends to penalize the student rather than to direct attention toward the systems that have withheld their benefits from the African-American student.

IQ Testing

Everything that applies to achievement tests may also be applied in general, to IQ tests and their use. However, IQ tests have been developed for a highly specialized purpose. The primary purpose has been to forecast student achievement at some specified time in the future. While in a general sense, the concept of content validity is appropriate here, IQ testing emphasizes a different type of validity. It is called *predictive validity.*

According to the rules for determining the validity of IQ testing, a student's score on the IQ test is to be compared to that student's score on some valid measure of academic achievement (American Psychological Association, 1974). Of course, if a valid achievement measure is not available, then the predictive validity of IQ cannot be determined. If, on the other hand, a content valid achievement test exists, then it is possible to determine the predictive value of an IQ test.

The *utilitarian* question from an educator's perspective is, "Of what value is an IQ test, *even if it has the highest level of predictive validity?"* The fact that an IQ test had high predictive validity merely shows that two scores (IQ and achievement) are associated with each other. However, in psychometrics, correlation does not equal causation. We may also say that correlation does not equal explanation. In other words, the reason for the high correlation is unknown. Therefore, the IQ test score cannot be said to be a measure of the mind, since that would imply that we knew the reason for the score.

If the student's IQ test performance does not cause the achievement test performance, and if it does not explain it, then the IQ test has no value that is known to the educational community. So what does prediction tell us? It tells us virtually nothing that any good test of achievement could not tell us. The use of IQ test information does not result in any changes in instructional outcomes for children.

The use of IQ in the assignment of students to special education would be an example of decision making related to instruction. Yet the data are overwhelming. Children do not do better in achievement because of their participation in special education. In fact some do worse (Glass, 1983; Heller, Holtzman, and Messick, 1982).

The practice of using IQ tests in school is inappropriate for the simple reason that it makes no meaningful contribution to the education of children. The use of IQ tests does not inform educational decision making in any pedagogically valid way. Yet the IQ test makers assume that there is a science of pedagogy. This means that both valid pedagogy and valid tests must exist. At present, neither teachers nor psychologists learn anything from IQ test use that helps in the design of instruction to make it better than would have been offered without information from the IQ test.

IQ testing in education is nothing more than a bad habit. Therefore, to speak of the validity of IQ tends to be somewhat misleading. Technically, IQ tests may be valid; however, the predictive validity may not be valuable. We need to determine some concrete benefit of the IQ test. That is, can it have prescriptive or instructive utility? Given the low performance of African-American students with respect to normative performance on IQ tests, we must ask what benefit to the children is provided through the use of such tests. At present, there is no evidence of any prescriptive validity at all (Kaufman and Kaufman, 1983).

The Failure of Standardized Testing

The contribution of standardized achievement measurement is flawed in five fundamental ways. First, it is not "measurement" in any scientific sense of the word. In science, one measures when one has an interval scale. At present, there is no way of utilizing cultural content of linguistic data so as to produce an interval scale. An interval scale is one where the measurement instrument is divided into equal amounts of the thing being measured. Linguistic data simply do not behave that way, especially in cross-cultural situations (Hoover, Politzer, and Taylor, 1987).

Second, there is a failure to link assessment to instruction in any meaningful way, especially in the case of IQ testing. In the case of achievement testing, the situation is better in that some educators do design remedial instruction based upon what is learned from the test.

Third, instruction cannot meaningfully be sorted into categorical types. In other words, there is not one way to teach a "normal" child and another way to teach a "retarded" child or a "learning disabled" child. At least, there has been no professional articulation of such differentiated pedagogy. Therefore, it is impossible to use psychological tests in making decisions about the nature of differentiated pedagogy yet to be manifest.

Fourth, coaching of African-American children raises scores significantly, especially where IQ testing is concerned. If this is true, then the predictive validity of the IQ test does not exist since scores are not fixed.

Fifth, there is abundant literature to show that achievement testing, in particular IQ testing, has a long and shady history that has been mixed with racism (Gould, 1981; Kamin, 1974). In spite of whatever improvements there may have been made in the measurement of cognition and learning in recent years, the past leaves much to be desired. Unfortunately, it is the past that we rely upon, for the most part, today.

Improving the Testing Practice

Test developers and advocates have responded gradually and reluctantly over the years to criticisms that have been made of academic achievement tests and IQ tests. The kinds of responses that they have made have been superficial. For example, test developers have been willing to change the makeup of the sample upon which their nationally standardized tests are standardized (Kaufman and Kaufman, 1983). However, changing the makeup of the sample does not deal with the issue of cultural bias.

Sample modification merely allows the minority culture(s) to be marginally influential in the shaping of test items. Yet, each child, minority and majority, is immersed 100 percent in their respective cultures. One child, the African-American child, for example, may only use a fraction of his or her culture in responding to test questions. In discussing this dilemma, Hoover, Politzer, and Taylor (1987) have said:

> African-American children and European-American children tend to learn very different vocabularies and even very different languages. An African-American child learns all of his or her language. Yet much of the vocabulary that he or she may learn is of no use at all in most standardized testing situations.

Another response to criticisms of standardized tests is to change the item writers or to add reviewers by race or by cultural origin. These changes may result in some positive outcomes, provided new item writers and reviewers have developed systematic information on their cultural group. Merely being a member of a cultural group does not place a person in the position to be helpful. These new reviewers should have systematic knowledge about the culture of their own cultural group.

Some standardized test developers respond to criticisms of bias in the content of their items by changing the content of the test to include percentages of items that reflect the culture of the minority cultural group(s).

Finally, test developers have been willing to modify item analysis techniques; however, these are statistical changes that may not be sensitive to cultural nuances (Hoover, Politzer, and Taylor, 1987). This is also an inadequate response because by looking at African-American statistical differences in response patterns, reality may be identified (a difference in pattern) while the meaning of the pattern may not be identified. Two people may use the same word; however, as linguists know, they may not use them with the same meaning. Identical words do not necessarily mean identical semantics for two people. A computer-scored answer sheet may rate them the same. It is the semantics that we are after in the mental measurements — the deep structure rather than the surface structure. The fact is that there are few cultural universals, and it is, after all, culture that psychometrists must use to fashion their instruments. They "measure" using words, but which words?

Summary

While the comments made here may seem to be unduly harsh, this is not an antitest position. It is rather a call for theoretical grounding in the use of standardized achievement tests. In the past we have used many poorly developed standardized tests of academic achievement. Clearly, the way in which they have been used has resulted in limiting the frames of mind of educators. Instead of helping us develop an appreciation for the unlimited potential of children, it makes us think of their limits. Instead of allowing us to appreciate the wonderful flexibility of the human mind, tests cause us to think of the mind as constrained in narrow channels of operation. Further, instead of causing us to look at the failure of systems that serve children, it causes us to focus on the children themselves as the cause of their own failure.

We need adequate academic achievement information about African-American children. Once we have clear agreement on educational goals, then such instruments can be constructed or selected. Then, of course, we will need to require equity in the delivery of educational services to students. At that point, content valid measures of academic achievement may become useful. However, no matter how good such instruments are, if they follow the present pattern they are likely to be multiple choice, paper and pencil tests. We need to hold out for more. There is a need to broaden the assessment process, for we need detailed information on the progress of our children in many academic areas. In particular, we need detailed information on their writing, speaking, discussion, and dialogue. In the past, the economic imperative has caused these important areas to be neglected. If standardized academic achievement tests are to be beneficial to the education of African-American children, then radical changes must be made in the *purposes* for which they are developed, the *validity of the validation process,* and *clarity about the manner of their use* with our children.

9 Standardized Test Scores and the Black College Environment

JACQUELINE FLEMING

Introduction

The Black college environment facilitates intellectual growth for Black students (Fleming, 1984). In the past, critics of Black colleges have assailed their physical and financial resources, and even the lower standardized test scores of many of their students. These critics have simply assumed that lesser facilities automatically meant lesser educational development. New studies on standardized test scores show, however, that the value of the Black college experience has been underestimated by those outside these colleges.

The Southern Education Foundation has funded an investigation into the usefulness of standardized test scores in predicting college success on Black college campuses (Fleming, 1985). The impetus for this study comes from a desire to ask more quantitative questions as to the development of students in Black colleges. This chapter reports on this study.

The prevailing assumption among Black educators is that standardized test scores such as the SAT and the ACT are inadequate predictors of college success measured by grade point average. Yet all of the studies on which this opinion was based were conducted with Black students attending predominantly white colleges. In contrast, this study found that test scores of students in Black colleges were quite good predictors of college success. It now appears that the environment in which the test score potential comes to fruition plays a critical role in facilitating the development of intellectual aptitude. While the test may not tap under-developed student potential, it does seem to indicate the extent to which students can benefit from a supportive educational environment.

General Findings

Five predominantly Black colleges participated in the study. Each submitted test scores (either SAT or ACT), high school grade point averages, and college grade point averages for freshmen and seniors for whom all three indices were available. A total of 1,551 students were included in the analysis.

The five colleges chosen were different in key respects. The first was a single-sex institution. The second was a nonselective institution with an open admissions policy. The third was a Catholic college. The fourth was a large urban university. The fifth was a small private school in the rural South. These institutional differences account for the variety of college experiences found among predominantly Black institutions.

Table 9.1

Prediction of Grades at Five Black Colleges from Standardized Test Scores

COLLEGE	CORRELATION
1) Spelman (N = 641)	.341 moderate
2) Morris Brown (N = 159)	.395 moderate
3) Xavier (N = 535)	.565 strong
4) Tougaloo (N = 70)	.555 strong
5) Texas Southern (N = 146)	.424 moderate

The results, shown in table 9.1, indicate that in all five colleges' standardized test scores predict college grade point average exceptionally well. The statistic used to determine degree of prediction is the correlation coefficient. The higher this number is, the stronger the relationship between test scores and college grades. The usual range among white students is from .30 to .45. The table indicates that in these five Black colleges the degree of prediction is even higher. The correlations range from .34 to .57.

A correlation below .30 means the degree of prediction is weak. A correlation between .30 and .50 is moderate, while a correlation over .50 is strong. Thus, the relationship between test scores and college success in this group of colleges is moderate to strong. Such figures cast doubt on the notion that test scores are inadequate predictors of college grades for Black students.

In addition to the study of these five schools, similar information was gathered from three unpublished studies. The results of all three are consistent with the findings of this study (see table 9.2). An unpublished study from Morehouse College finds that test scores correlate well with college grades (from .41 to .48) (Morehouse College, 1984). Another unpublished study from Xavier University reports that test scores provide very strong prediction of college grades (Xavier University of Louisiana, 1984). The correlation is .61. Finally, in an unpublished study, L. Ramist (1984) of the Educational Testing Service found that SAT scores predict college grades moderately well at eleven predominantly Black colleges. The average correlation is .38.

Table 9.2

Prediction of Grades from Standardized Test Scores in Three Unpublished Studies of Black Colleges

STUDY	CORRELATION
1) Morehouse College (1984): SATM	.48 moderate
SATV	.41 moderate
2) Xavier University (1984)	.61 strong
3) L. Ramist, Educational Testing Service	.38 moderate

The fact that such impressive results occurred in eight different samples, one of which included eleven colleges, demonstrates a consistency of effect that is unusual among the studies of Black students. This degree of consistency has occurred only among white students in white colleges as is discussed later.

Findings for Black Students in White Colleges

While I did not collect new data on Black students in predominantly white colleges for the current study, a sampling of previous studies was gathered, reporting relationships between test scores and college grades. Table 9.3 lists these studies and indicates whether the degree of prediction is weak, moderate, or strong.

The most likely conclusion to be drawn from these studies is that in white college environments test scores are inconsistent predictors of college grades for Black students. Half of the studies indicate weak prediction. Half show moderate prediction. None provides strong prediction.

The notion that test scores are not important in predicting college success for Black students is overly simplistic. Some studies find that test

Table 9.3

Prediction of Grades from Standardized Test Scores among Blacks in White Colleges

STUDY	CORRELATION
1) Miller & O'Connor (1969):	
Females, 1961	.48 moderate
Females, 1965	.01 weak
2) Wilson (1980): SATM	.410 moderate
SATV	.371 moderate
3) Wilson (1981): SATM	.191 weak
SATV	.236 weak
4) Fleming & DuBois (1981)	.01 weak
5) L. Ramist, Educational Testing Service	.30 moderate

scores bear no relationship to college grades, so that knowing a student's test score will not tell us how that student might fare in college (Miller and O'Conner, 1969). Other studies find that test scores "under predict": the student will perform better than the test score suggests. Still other studies find that test scores "over predict." That is, the student will not perform as well as the test score indicates (Temp, 1971). It is no wonder, then, that many social scientists and educators feel that test scores should not be relied upon in selecting Black students for admission into predominantly white colleges.

Some educators and scientists feel that the test itself is at fault. They insist that the tests are biased against minority students and fail to measure important abilities that minority students bring to the college setting. While there is always this possibility, the continuing validity studies conducted by the Educational Testing Service indicates no systematic bias against minorities (The College Entrance Examination Board, 1983).

In view of the findings of this study that test scores can be helpful in predicting college success, the problem with test scores of Black students may not lie as much in the test itself as in the environment in which test potential comes to fruition.

Findings for White Students in White Colleges

Table 9.4 lists the major studies that have been conducted using white students. Many of these are long-term validity studies conducted by the Educational Testing Service or by researchers working under its auspices. Most of these studies were conducted each year for periods of up to thirteen years. Others include up to 11 different colleges, creating highly reliable statistics. This listing, however, also includes studies by nonpartisan researchers and single-sample studies.

Table 9.4

Prediction of Grades from Standardized Test Scores for White Students

STUDY	CORRELATION
1) Fincher (1974)	.49 moderate
2) Ford & Campus (1977): SATM	.32 moderate
SATV	.37 moderate
3) Wilson (1980): SATM	.388 moderate
SATV	.392 moderate
4) Wilson (1981): SATM	.301 moderate
SATV	.338 moderate
5) Fleming & DuBois (1981)	.41 moderate
6) Willingham & Breland (1982)	.53 strong
7) L. Ramist, Educational Testing Service	.42 moderate

The most obvious aspect of this table is the consistency with which studies of white student test scores show either moderate or strong prediction of college grades. Most of these studies include a fair representation of minority students in the samples.

Such consistent results have convinced psychometricians that test scores are reliable predictors of college grades and could be used as one factor in selecting students. There are not many measures that rival test scores in consistency of prediction. The high school grade point average is another and virtually the only other measure that is considered to indicate how a student will fare in college.

High School Grades and College Success

High school grade point average is generally considered the best predictor of college grades. On the average, high school grades are usually slightly better predictors than test scores. Yet in any given study, it is a toss-up as to which factor will yield the most information on how a student will fare in college.

In this study, high school grades were slightly better predictors of college grades in three of the five colleges. High school grades predict moderately well in four colleges and strong in one, table 9.5.

Table 9.5

Prediction of Grades from High School Average at Five Black Colleges

	CORRELATION OF H.S. AVERAGE WITH COLLEGE GRADES	COMBINED CORRELATION OF H.S. AVERAGE AND TEST SCORES WITH COLLEGE GRADES
1) Spelman	.420 moderate	.476 moderate
2) Morris Brown	.461 moderate	.540 strong
3) Texas Southern	.516 strong	.565 strong
4) Xavier	.460 moderate	.603 strong
5) Tougaloo	.494 moderate	.603 strong

In the final analysis, there was very little difference in how well each of these factors contributed to college success. The average level of prediction for high school grades was .476, compared with .453 test scores. Both averages are in the high moderate range. The difference is negligible.

When these two factors are used together to predict college success, the average level of prediction is now in the strong range. Thus, both factors used jointly contribute more information about a student's future performance than either used alone. For this reason, the College Board insists that test scores be considered along with the high school record (The College Entrance Examination Board, 1983).

According to past research, the picture is essentially the same among white students. High school average and test scores are both good predictors, but high school grades predict somewhat better. They are both in the same basic range of accuracy—moderate to high moderate, When these two are used in combination, the degree of prediction is usually elevated into the strong range.

When Personal Qualities are Important to College Success

This study, like many others, fails to show that personal qualities have anything like the predictive power of test scores. It seems clear that test scores (when used with the high school record) are the best indicators of the extent to which academic potential has been developed in the college-bound student. Many researchers still hope to show that the individual characteristics of the student are important. Yet our understanding of when and how to use personal qualities has not progressed very far.

At three of the five colleges in this study, measures of the following personal qualities were administered to select classes of freshmen:

Fear of failure
Fear of success
Need for achievement
Time spent in extracurricular activities
Time spent in developing special talents
The aspiration level of career plans

While these qualities are considered important to the achievement process, none possess great power to predict college grades. Most of the correlation coefficients fall in the weak range. The level of career plans produces the strongest relationship to grades in one college (r=.42), indicating that the more ambitious a student's career goals are, the better his or her grades will be. However, not even this personal attribute was important in more than one college.

The findings for Black students in Black colleges are very much like the findings in other studies for white students in white colleges. Willingham and Breland (Willingham and Breland, 1982), devoted considerable attention to finding out just how important personal qualities are in predicting success for students in 18 different colleges. They found that considering 22 personal qualities did not add predictive power beyond that obtained by using test scores and the high school record. On the other hand, studies of Black students in white colleges indicate that personal qualities such as motivation often predict college grades when test scores do not (Miller and O'Conner, 1969).

Apparently, developed aptitude measured by standardized tests or high school grades is the best spot measure of future performance, *unless* there is a poor adjustment in the college environment as appears to be the case for Black students in many white colleges.

The College Environment as Mediator of Test Potential

White students in white colleges and Black students in Black colleges experience similar normal conditions of support. Students in each of these situations have a reasonable opportunity to avail themselves of the essential supports. In *Blacks in College*, I isolate the three most important supports as:

1. The opportunity to talk to friends, which discharges harmful emotional tension.

2. The opportunity to receive encouragement from teachers or mentor figures, essential in sustaining and enhancing motivation.

3. The opportunity to work with others on campus in constructive extracurricular activities (Fleming, 1984).

Without an opportunity to establish an adequate number of inter-personal supports, students become alienated from the college and motivation deteriorates. With the student's lifeline severed, "normal" functioning is difficult.

Whether a Black student manages to survive the alienation is an individual matter. It depends on whether that student possesses inner strengths that he can fall back on under stress. Some students possess sufficient inner strengths and others do not. In any case, it is difficult to determine before college which strengths will make the critical difference.

Test scores, then, would tell more about how a student will perform under conditions of reasonable supportiveness from critical persons and influences. Adequate support assures the translation of academic potential into performance in college.

An appropriate conclusion is that test scores in and of themselves are inadequate measures of Black student potential for academic achievement. It is far more likely that predominantly white college environments fail to provide normal supports for Black students, supports necessary to intellectual development.

The Black College Attitude Toward Standardized Tests

The study reported in this chapter was undertaken to determine how United Negro College Fund (UNFC) colleges view and use test scores. With 35 of the 43 member colleges responding to the survey, the results indicate that Black colleges pay little attention to test scores as admission tools but do use them for placement purposes.

The vast majority, or 80 percent of the schools surveyed, do require test scores for entering freshmen. However, these scores are rarely used to reject students. Only three (11 percent) of the colleges reject prospective students because their test scores are too low.

Most of the colleges do not feel that test scores are an important criterion in selecting students. Only 26 percent feel that test scores are important in this respect, while 66 percent feel that the high school average is the most important criterion.

Regardless of the assessment of the usefulness of test scores in admissions, most, or 92 percent, use SAT and ACT test scores for placement purposes along with other placement tests. Thus, scores are used largely for retention purposes after admission.

UNCF institutions pay little attention to the testing issue. Only three of the 35 colleges had conducted studies of test scores in their college environments. Virtually none had conducted systematic studies of what contributed to good performance on graduate admissions tests. It may be that Black colleges share a general feeling that test scores are unimportant for Black students. This feeling might lead them to value tests less than other colleges do.

However, this study suggests that Black colleges possess environments that are facilitative of test score potential and presumably for enhancing test-taking abilities. The Black college environment could be critical to learning more about Black standardized tests and to finding solutions to test-taking problems among Black students.

Recommendations

There is now a great deal of evidence that the Black college environment is a useful one for Black students. The normal availability of support, encouragement and acceptance provides an atmosphere in which test score potential is translated into college achievement in a stable and predictable way. With this advantage, Black colleges could use their naturally supportive environments to enhance test-taking abilities. The problem in relation to Black test taking is largely due to inattention, rather than to a lack of solutions. The following recommendations might guide colleges toward assuming the role they would like to take in relation to this important issue:

1. Black colleges should systematically collect and examine more concrete information on how test scores function for their particular student populations. It is the lack of data that has lead to invalid assumptions about Blacks and standardized tests.

2. Black colleges should consider several ways in which they would like to approach the problem of Black test taking, such as instituting new programs, reorganizing existing resources, improving test scores, and instilling the confidence that students will need in test-taking situations later in life. The possible approaches are virtually endless, limited only by the individual school, its unique student body, and its students' needs. Many remedies are possible without large amounts of new money.

3. The colleges should make a serious commitment to remedying some aspect of the testing problem by choosing one approach and making the commitment clear to all in the institution.

4. The schools should evaluate their efforts in areas such as improving graduate tests versus SATs, increasing the number of students who pass competency tests, increasing the number who take tests at the graduate level, lifting student confidence in testing abilities, or discovering other ways that are important to the college and its students.

Part Four

Programs that Work

10 The Madison Elementary School: A Turnaround Case

BARBARA A. SIZEMORE

Background

The high-achieving African-American school was an abashing anomaly in the Pittsburgh, Pennsylvania, Public School System in 1979 and was not the result of approved organizational routines. It forced the system to explain the existence of low-achieving African-American schools and raised questions about standard operating procedures and policies that allowed such schools to operate. The National Institute of Education (NIE) funded a study in school year (SY) 1979-80 permitting the author to investigate the organizational factors important to producing high achievement in three predominantly African-American and poor elementary schools—Madison, Vann, and Beltzhoover, kindergarten through fifth grade—in the Pittsburgh Public Schools (PPS) (Sizemore et al., 1983).

Of the 21 elementary schools that were 70 percent or more African-American in 1979, only five were high achieving as reflected on the Metropolitan Achievement Test (MAT), which means reading and mathematics scores exceeding or reaching the national and/or city norms were received by more than a majority of students in the school (at least 51 percent). In this study, reported in a previous article in *The Journal of Negro Education* (Sizemore, 1985) and a chapter in *Schooling and Social Context: Qualitative Studies* (Sizemore, 1987), the findings revealed an outcome of high achievement and high growth in reading and mathematics

Previously published in *The Journal of Negro Education* 57(3), pp. 243-266. Reprinted by permission.

at Beltzhoover and Vann Elementary Schools; high achievement and high growth in mathematics and low achievement and high growth in reading at Madison.

We found that these anomalies were set in motion by the following organizational factors:

1. The recruitment and selection of a moderately authoritarian principal who believed that African-American students could and would learn.

2. The willingness of this principal to risk differing with the system's norm of low achievement of African-American, poor schools. He or she dared to be different in order to create this anomaly.

3. The mobilization of consensus among school and community actors around high achievement as the highest priority goal.

4. The generation of a climate of high expectations for student achievement conducive to teaching and learning.

5. The choice of functional routines,[1] scenarios, and processes for the achievement of this highest priority.

6. The willingness to disagree with superior officers around the choices of these routines and their implementation.

The organizational output of high achievement seemed to be the consequence of several essential functional routines:

1. The principal's assumption of responsibility for all student discipline, attendance, and parental conflict through the publication of processes to be followed when violations, infractions, or confrontations occurred and prompt enforcement of the same with selective sanctions understood by all school actors.

2. Rigorous supervision of teacher and staff performance and daily visitations of classrooms and programs.

3. Consistent monitoring of students' reading and mathematics skill mastery process.

4. The use of staff and teacher expertise, skills, information, and knowledge to conduct problem-directed searches for the resolution of school concerns and dilemmas.

5. The involvement of parents in some participatory and meaningful way in the school's program.

6. The prompt evaluation of teacher and staff performances and the provision of assistance, help, and in-service where necessary; however, the rating of performances as unsatisfactory where warranted, including persuading such teachers to transfer in spite of central office resistance.

7. The establishment of the school's office as the central business command post by communicating routines which control information and coordinate school activities.

8. The implementation of a horizontal organization based on some kind of reading skill mastery grouping determined by criterion-referenced tests with no more than three reading groups per class, within which arrangement grouping and regrouping for mathematics is permitted; teacher assignments dictated by teacher expertise with a particular kind of learner rather than on teacher desire; self-contained classrooms modified by some kind of nongrading, team teaching, and departmentalization; the provision of support of the diagnosis of student problems related to pacing and progress; and highly structured classrooms moderated by affection and consideration.

9. The expansion of the school day by using teacher aides, teacher preparation periods, staff development time, special subject, social studies, science, and recess periods for tutoring and small group instruction for students who need reinforcement, reteaching, and remediation; and an increase in student attendance patterns.

10. The demand for the use of materials which prove functional for elevating achievement when such are not approved by the board of education, especially in the areas of phonics, African-American history and culture, and mathematics problem solving.

11. The denial of student placement in educable mentally retarded divisions unless all strategies for regular learning had occurred and had been exhausted.

12. The refusal to accept system programs that consumed administration and supervision time normally given to the regular program—unless such programs increased the school day.

How Madison Looked In 1980

We found differences between the schools. Madison appeared to be a declining school with many routines which differed from those at

Beltzhoover and Vann. Beltzhoover was the highest achieving school of the three in April 1980, using MAT scores. Beltzhoover parents were treated as equals in a partnership. They could monitor teacher performance, bring their observations to the principal, and demand redress. At Vann, parental roles were prescribed by the principal; at Madison their roles were defined by the teachers. Vann and Beltzhoover were more alike in other characteristics. In both schools there was a mid-range consensus among the school actors around high achievement as the highest priority goal. At Madison, on the other hand, there was a low consensus around this goal.

At Beltzhoover and Vann, the principals were more authoritarian, although the degree differed. At Madison, the principal was guided by collegiality and specialization and was firmly based in teacher professionalism and the adherence to standards. Vann and Beltzhoover were both loosely coupled[2] with central office (Weick, 1976). Both principals, twelve-year veterans, were viewed as "renegades," "non-team players," "uncooperative," and "loners" by central office personnel. On the other hand, the principal of Madison, a new principal of only three years, was tightly coupled with central office, running her school as best she knew how by the rules. At Beltzhoover and Vann, each principal assumed the responsibility for student discipline and parental conflict, generating loyalty among their teachers through the sense of obligation engendered by the action. At Madison, an undercover war, generally led by veteran teachers, was created by the principal's failure to assume this responsibility.

At Vann and Beltzhoover, the principals monitored student progress and pacing, supervised teacher performance consistently, and evaluated teachers promptly. At Madison, the principal relied on her supervisory specialist for assistance in evaluation and in-service and on external sources for help in supervision. At Vann and Beltzhoover, the principals persuaded unsatisfactory personnel to transfer under the threat of receipt of an unsatisfactory rating. At Madison, the principal underwent the long, red-tape process prescribed by the board of education and the Pittsburgh Federation of Teachers. Additionally, the principal of Madison was proscribed by the presence of a union official on her faculty and forced to submit to the process. By the same condition, the principal was constrained from using the preparation, special subject, social studies, science, and staff development period for tutoring, remediation, reinforcement, and reteaching.

In 1980, Madison had a higher faculty and student mobility rate, higher student absenteeism, a lower student population, a larger number of extra programs, more loosely structured classrooms,[3] fewer poor students, and a newer principal than either Beltzhoover or Vann. Because of Madison's higher socioeconomic status, investigators thought the achievement would be higher as an effect. This proved not to be the case. In fact, the data show a school in transition.

The offices at Beltzhoover and Vann were highly centralized and characterized by a business-like atmosphere. On the other hand, Madison's office was somewhat of a central social meeting place. It housed a soda pop machine inside the principal's office into which teachers and staff trekked for purchases. Unattended student disciplinary referrals often played with messengers or students passing by until the clerk noticed their behavior, and visitors often failed to notify the principal that they were in the school.

The principals of Beltzhoover and Vann spent a great deal of their work time interacting with students; the principal of Madison spent most of her time with her own faculty and staff from central office and the university regarding the extra programs housed in her school.[4] At Madison, teachers spent more time handling discipline problems in their classrooms than did the teachers at Beltzhoover and Vann. Madison teachers were less cooperative with each other and more informal in their own behavior. Only at Madison did some teachers fail to teach reading and mathematics every day and only here did teachers interrupt each other's classes with consistent regularity for trivial and frivolous reasons.

Recommendations

The following policy and administrative recommendations were given to the board of education and the superintendent in order to create and maintain high-achieving schools for African-American and poor students:

1. Designate student achievement as one of the most important criteria on which teacher and principal performance will be judged.

2. Lengthen the school day in schools where the population demands reinforcement, repetition, and reteaching; pay staff accordingly; and increase student attendance.

3. Require evidence that teachers can teach reading and mathematics before hiring or require principals to provide proof of this ability during the probationary period. Use student achievement as the basic criterion in cases where probationary teachers receive satisfactory marks or better.

4. Provide probationary periods for principals and decentralize more authority at the building level for veterans, but monitor these principals' performances in elevating achievement.

5. Place research teams in schools that are high achieving in hopes of

increasing the knowledge base about how this is accomplished, especially for African-American students.

6. Recruit and hire more teachers and principals who believe that African-American and poor students can learn; make this a requirement for working in these schools.

7. Monitor more stringently the selection and purchase of textbooks and educational materials for cultural bias and selected emphases for different populations, such as phonics, linguistics, word problems, and ethnic history and culture.

8. Monitor the proliferation of programs in schools that serve African-American and poor students. Where these programs are desirable, principals should be given assistance in dealing with their administration and supervision.

Changes in the School System

In February 1981, in reponse to district-wide needs assessment surveys conducted by the Learning Research and Development Center of the University of Pittsburgh, the Pittsburgh Board of Education (PBOE) adopted an action plan for increasing the effectiveness of individual schools. The School Improvement Program (SIP) was designed to develop and test school improvement strategies in seven low-achieving schools. The long-range goal was to disseminate effective school improvement strategies developed in this project to schools in the district. The time line for the project was three to five years. The former principal of Beltzhoover was selected as the director of this program with the full support of the African-American board members who wanted someone who had already demonstrated the ability to produce a high-achieving all-African-American school. One of these schools has made dramatic improvements.[5]

In September 1981, the new principal, a twenty-five year veteran in the PPS, was appointed at Madison. Her teaching career began in an African-American and poor elementary school where she was soon promoted by the first African-American principal in the PPS to Primary Team Lead Teacher. The next principal made her his building designee to serve as head in his absence. Her next appointment was as an assistant principal of an African-American elementary school in one of the city's low-income public-housing projects, and, finally, she was appointed principal of Madison.

By the 1984-85 school year, the PBOE had undergone many changes. All middle schools (6-8) and some elementary schools were desegregated.

Beltzhoover was one of the desegregated schools because it was closest to the white community. But, if any schools had to remain segregated, the African-American members wanted the other high-achieving African-American schools to remain so. This compromise saved Madison and Vann. With the desegregation problem resolved, African-American members developed a consensus around excellence as their goal and a new superintendent was hired. A new majority formed on the PBOE, and, in December 1983, the African-American school board director for District 3, in which Madison is located, was selected to be president of the PBOE by his fellow board members. He is still president at the writing of this chapter. The new majority had twin interests: (1) to eliminate the achievement gap between African-American and white students in the PPS, and (2) to attract white students back to the PPS.

By 1985, with a new superintendent, a new board president, and new priorities stressing high achievement, the high-achieving African-American school was no longer an abashing anomaly in the PPS. In response to the new PBOE majority and its priorities, the new superintendent institutionalized the Monitoring Achievement Pittsburgh Plan (MAP),[6] the Pittsburgh Research-Based Instructional Supervisory Program (PRISM),[7] the School Improvement Program (SIP), the Schenley High School Teachers' Center (SHSTC),[8] and the Brookline Elementary School Teachers' Center (BESTC).[9]

The Present Study

In 1984, the author sought permission to observe once again in Madison, which appeared to be a turnaround school in the face of new testing data reported for school years 1982-83 and 1983-84 (see table 10.1). The author wanted to determine what, if any, changes had occurred and whether or not any of these changes confirmed the findings that we had reported and/or had resulted from the recommendations we had made.

The New Madison

The Madison School of 1985 looked more like the Vann School of 1980. While it now had students of a lower socioeconomic status, Madison did not have the reservoir of veteran expertise available to Vann, and the new teachers acquired as replacements for the transfers out[10] were often inimical to new routines at Madison.

Moreover, new teachers required more supervision, monitoring, in-service education, and materials. The new principal was moderately

Table 10.1

Madison Elementary School's California Achievement Test (CAT)
Data: 1980-1987

YEAR TESTED	% BLACK	NUMBER TESTED	% AT OR ABOVE NNR	% IN TQR	% AT OR ABOVE NNM	% IN TQM
1980***	99.4	175	45	*	60	*
1981	97.8	(275)**	52	*	58	*
1982	99.2	(298)**	50	*	66	*
1983	99.4	(234)**	60	*	76	*
1984	99.2	238	80	42	84	53
1985	98.5	246	77	46	77	46
1986	99.0	242	81	44	79	43
1987	98.5	230	84	48	78	47

Source: The data for this table were secured from the Division of Testing and Evaluation, Pittsburgh Public Schools.
* Data unavailable.
** Estimated figure. Special education and kindergarten not included in any number tested figure.
***In 1980, the Metropolitan Achievement Test was given.
Key: NNR—National norm in reading on the CAT.
   TQR—Top Quarter in reading on the CAT.
   NNM—National norm in mathematics on the CAT.
   TQM—Top Quarter in mathematics on the CAT.

authoritarian, but she did not need to differ with the system's norm, for the PBOE had set high achievement as a priority for African-American and poor students. Nor did she need to differ with her superiors around choices of routines necessary for reaching this goal. In fact, she had the support of her board member representative, the school board president, the superintendent, the associate superintendent, and her neighbor—the principal of Vann. She did need, however, to mobilize consensus among school and community actors around high achievement as the highest priority at Madison, to generate a climate of high expectations for student achievement, and to choose functional routines for the achievement of these priorities.

Mobilizing school actors and the community around high achievement as the highest priority heightened the conflict that had developed around discipline under the former principal. But the new principal proceeded, undaunted by that problem. Using PRISM, her rigorous evaluations and monitoring influenced weak teachers to leave, and those who stubbornly stuck it out without exhibiting merit finally were moved through unsatisfactory evaluations. Frequently, incompetent, insubordinate, or uncooperative teachers were received from central office as replacements. One teacher transfer organized teacher and parent opposition to the principal's thrust for improvement and resisted her approach to Madison's problems.

Parents who worked in the lunchroom as aides and the lunchroom manager were recruited by dissident teachers to file grievances over changes in the lunchroom and the school schedule during the 1982-83 school year. Several of these parents called a meeting with the assistant superintendent in charge of elementary schools. At this meeting, it became clear that these school actors wanted to oust the principal. After documenting several acts of insubordination, the principal fired all of the parent aides and transferred the lunchroom manager. Several of those fired appealed to local politicians and ministers for help. The local school board member, whose three children attended Madison, supported the principal in her struggle to improve the school. The parent aides placed petitions in local business enterprises that sought the removal of the principal. Their campaign ended by supporting a candidate in opposition to the local school board member in the 1984 election. All of these attempts failed to win enough community support to succeed.

One teacher who had been rated unsatisfactory in another school was transferred into Madison and became the subject of stringent monitoring, using PRISM. She attempted to usurp the union leadership in the school, but failed in her attempt. Later she retired rather than receive another unsatisfactory mark, which would have resulted in her being fired.

To increase the amount of time required for instructional leadership, the principal sought to remove the extra programs in Madison School. Teacher Corps ran out of funding and was terminated. The principal, then, sought the removal of the Elementary Scholars' Program (ESP). This, too, brought community conflict. The two ESP teachers organized the parents and the community proponents to oppose the principal's request for the removal of this program so that she could provide additional classrooms for an expanding enrollment and implement the magnet kindergarten, an Early Learning Skills (ELS) program, and Project Pass.[11] Since most of the ESP students came from other neighborhoods, the principal won out with the community and the local school board member. The removal of this program did much to unify the school community. One parent said, "Now Madison is one school again."

The principal perceives an authoritarian principal as one who "has to make hard decisions, many times when the necessary decision is not popular." She is willing to make these hard decisions and to take the consequences for doing so. Even so, her style, in comparison with her predecessor's, gave the school's teachers a sense of lost power. The building committee, which consisted of the union representative and four other teachers, began to solicit more complaints from faculty and to stir up concern among the new faculty, which came and went, about the need to replace unsatisfactory teachers. This proved to be a losing battle in the face of increasing community support, and, by 1985, three teachers who were part of the 1979-80 Madison faculty had left. Only one remained.

The principal believes that there is now consensus among school actors in Madison around school goals. She is an ardent follower of PRISM, a rigorous but flexible user of MAP and California Achievement Test (CAT)[12] data, and an untiring monitor and disciplinarian. She told the author:

> There are no major obstacles to goal achievement here now. There just must be opportunities for teachers and the principal to talk and for teachers to talk together across grade-level meetings. Students must learn to be more responsible for their own behavior; to accept responsibility for completing assignments in class and out of class; to make an honest effort to abide by school rules; to conduct themselves respectfully, and to be prepared to work when they arrive. It is equally important for students to feel at all times they can discuss their problems with the teacher and principal rather than to act on their own and implement their own rules.
>
> I hold staff meetings and communicate with faculty a lot. I write notes, reproduce directives, submit responses or requests promptly, and solicit suggestions and comments on policy. Anytime anyone wants to see me, I try to be available when I am in the building. I have an open-door policy. There is a wire basket on the counter in which anyone can leave me a note to see him or her. I either stop by the classroom or write a note designating a period to talk.

Because discipline was a problem at Madison, the principal has implemented several disciplinary routines. She insists on proactive discipline that seeks to prevent the recurrence of problems. This includes in-house suspension; student, parent, and teacher conferences; improved instruction; and counseling. Student referrals for discipline are made to the principal by teachers. Whenever a student is sent to the office for discipline, the teacher must also send a note explaining the violation and what action the teacher has already taken. The teachers work with the student who has committed an infraction and try to get him or her to comply. When necessary, they talk to the parent. Finally, if there is no improvement, a parent-principal conference is held. If this does not work, a teacher-parent-student conference is held with the principal and some dispensation is made.

The disciplinary routines were discussed by one teacher in whose room the principal often deposited students with problems when the in-house suspension room was not in operation. This teacher said the following in response to the query about the role of the principal in bringing about high achievement:

> I know that she has high expectations for teachers. We have grade-level meetings where we have to show and discuss test results. She focuses on certain skills and reminds us to reinforce them. There was a change in discipline problem solution for this school year. This year I really noticed consequences coming down on the students. Students were being punished for misbehavior. Most suspensions were at home in the beginning of the school year. In-house was not used as much as in the past. I'm not sure when it began, but it was most noticeable this year.
>
> Before this year, students were talked to about their behavior and they would sit in the office for a period or two, and often the principal would send students who misbehaved to my room and the rooms of other teachers who were perceived as strong disciplinarians. Even now that happens. Students were not forced to bear the consequences of their own conduct. At the beginning of this year, there was a lot of support. You could see the difference. Students were being punished and suspended. That's something they needed. I believe that students should be sent home when they misbehave. . . . But this relaxed as the year went on. . . .

The principal's response to the teacher's comment was:

> Behavior problems were not just sent to certain teachers who were perceived as strong disciplinarians. These teachers were selected based on their ability to maintain good discipline in the classroom, but they were asked whether they would be willing to use any available time they could provide to counsel and work with the chronic discipline problems. On occasion, but not often, rather than have these students sit in the office for disciplinary purposes, they would be placed in one of these classrooms for no more than three periods to complete assignments and benefit from this teacher's expertise. Students are held accountable for their misbehavior. They are reprimanded commensurate with the infraction and in many forms. Not every child who is sent to the office will be suspended, nor will they necessarily be punished at all. Punishment depends on the

circumstances and where the majority of the blame lies.

Generally, the student is at fault, but, on occasion actions or lack of them by the teacher can precipitate student misbehavior. Discipline never relaxes. It remains consistently the same for the entire year.

By 1987, a teacher committee on discipline had been formed to make recommendations to the principal on individual cases. Probably the best way to show the changes in Madison now is to look in on a teacher who has been there since 1979.

A Teacher's Teacher in a Flexible Classroom

On the first day of observations, this teacher told the observer assigned to her, "Don't do me in now." The observer asked why she said this to him and she replied, "The other teachers said that you cleaned us out when you were here before and now it's my turn to go."[13] The observer protested, saying that the study had nothing to do with the unsatisfactory ratings that had occurred subsequently and the transfer of so many teachers. The teacher's response was a raised eyebrow and shrugged shoulders. She had taught school for ten years, and all of those years had been spent in first grade. She felt that the staff at Madison was more at ease in 1987 when she was interviewed than it had ever been before.

> There is not so much tension now. At first there was a lot of confusion. Much of it was racial...just because she (the new principal) was Black. Some white teachers resented her. Our principal has a great deal to do with the elevation of achievement in this school. She is consistent and strong, but not very flexible. In fact, she is authoritarian...constantly supervising...just the opposite of our former principal. But I do what I think is best still and she generally supports me. She is not unreasonable.

According to this teacher, there was cooperation among the teachers at Madison, but, she continued, "it would be better if people could go more to the principal with their concerns. I'm not afraid and nobody should be. But many teachers here are new, and they just don't know how to respond yet. The principal will help any teacher who needs it. You must work here, and your students must achieve. That's the bottom line. The principal just won't stand for less. If you don't do it, you can forget about staying here."

One of the changes made in the PPS to elevate achievement in reading was the choice of the *Open Court* reading series for the primary grades because of its strong phonics content.[14] This teacher didn't think the students were getting enough skills practice in *Open Court* in the kindergarten program, but she liked *Open Court*. Let me report her views.

Open Court is not an easy program. You cannot push kids on if they don't know. When you come into first grade now, you must be ready. Since *Open Court* does not provide for grouping but for whole group instruction, we have cross-grouping during the year to reinforce those who fall behind. We all teach the same lessons. If you look at the CAT scores, some are ready, but, some test well yet can't read. We don't have enough meetings with the kindergarten teachers on these problems. I have discussed this with the principal.

But all in all, *Open Court* is the next most important factor in high achievement here at Madison, after the principal's impact. I love it. Since we've had it, it's amazing to see the students' progress in reading. It's fantastic. If it's taught correctly, they will learn it well.

One thing though...I'm going out on maternity leave in two months, and the substitute teachers don't know the first thing about *Open Court*. This means that my children may not achieve so well this year on the CAT. I hate that.

There are times when I pull out those who are really slow for reinforcement. I have a preparation period and we do a lot of drill and repetition with these children. I guess I do *Open Court* three or four periods a day. In *Open Court* you have to be on the same pacing...this is hard to do sometimes...and takes more time....

See, *Open Court* has to be taught thoroughly and correctly. There is a problem when transfers from out of the PPS come in here. They simply can't catch up, even in October. Slower paced kids are worked with differently and at different times.

This teacher constantly repeats her desire for more time to correct pacing differences among her students, but she thinks that all of her teaching-learning problems can be solved. She thinks she can get anything she wants out of her students and doesn't expect help from her parents to do it. Yet, she wishes her parents were more involved. She says:

I am the best parent some of my children have, unfortunately. But I know this to be true, and I try to be a good parent to them. Parents are different, just like everything else. Some don't have the time. Others don't want to be bothered. Some help and others don't. I have two parents who are truly parents in the full custodial sense. Teachers have to call all of the time and take more of a parental role ourselves. Sometimes, the work is too difficult for parents to help with. For example, *Open Court* is so difficult that parents have to be taught

what to do to help. Some parents are just too young and don't have
the experience to parent. There is no doubt in my mind that as the
family condition changes so does the role of the teacher....

This teacher felt that she had a good relationship with her parents and
observations of her seemed to confirm her belief.

She thought that the MAP was a waste of time for her students. She
said, "It's too easy and my students work beyond the objectives set for them
here. MAP represents minimum standards; yet, some teachers feel this is
the maximum that African-American youngsters can do." But she said that
she took her students as far as she could. She grouped for mathematics, but
complained about insufficient time to pull out the slow children who
needed more reinforcement. She encouraged peer tutoring and help. She
liked the new Silver-Burdett text for math because it got more into daily
situations and provided more word problems. She wanted a change in the
science book. "It's too elementary and 'babyish' for the first grade," she
said. When asked about supervisory help in meeting some of these
problems, this teacher flatly and unhesitatingly declared that the instructional supervisor was useless. "I really don't know why we have one
anymore. I don't see whoever is assigned here. Our principal gives us most
of our help. I think that the BESTC should hire her." Several other teachers
commented on their appraisal of the new BESTC (described earlier.) They
felt that the teachers at BESTC needed to come to Madison to learn how to
elevate the achievement of the African-American students (see table 10.2).

Students were assigned to classes by their CAT reading scores, and these
classes were rotated among the teachers. However, in first grade, the lowest
performing readers were always placed with the teacher who specifically
requested this assignment, one other than the one we observed. During
1986, the observed teacher had the average readers in the first grade. Her
room was large and well decorated, but plaster had been damaged by a
leaking roof, which since has been repaired. Although the peeled paint had
been removed, the ceiling and walls were still unpainted. On the chalk-
boards in the front of the room, the teacher had written her vocabulary
words from the lesson being studied. There was an *Open Court* alphabet
streamer above the front chalkboard, which had one African-American
person on it. There was a calendar on the small front bulletin board for
January (the month of observation). The side bulletin boards were
"Getting Down With Math" where math papers were hung; "Science/
Health" where science and health articles were displayed; "Black is
Beautiful Because" where several articles and excellent work papers were
exhibited. Work tables were placed around the room with work group
designations above them.

Table 10.2

Performance in Reading and Mathematics on the California Achievement Test (CAT) of Pittsburgh Public Elementary Schools, 75 Percent or More African-American, April 1987; Also Included, Brookline Elementary School Teachers' Center and Westwood Elementary

SCHOOL	% BLACK	% AT OR ABOVE NNR/TQR	% AT OR ABOVE NNM/TQM
Madison	98.5	84/48*	78/47
Miller	99.3	75/51	78/52
Crescent	99.6	70/36	61/31**
McKelvy	99.3	66/24	74/40
Belmar	98.8	65/24**	67/26
Vann	98.8	61/27**	76/35
Weil	100.0	62/29**	63/32**
Lemington	99.6	60/26**	60/26**
Clayton	76.9	60/24**	50/20**
Lincoln	98.3	48/13**	55/22**
Brookline	48.0	53/16**	62/23**
Westwood	56.4	84/43*	84/56*

Source: These data were provided by the Division of Testing and Evaluation, Pittsburgh Public Schools. Data presented here are for African-American students only.
* Reached or exceeded the Pittsburgh Public Schools white norm.
**Failed to reach the Pittsburgh Public Schools Black norm.
Key: NNR—National norm in reading on the CAT.
     TQR—Top Quarter in reading on the CAT.

There was an experience chart with stories hung on it in the front of the room. The following classroom rules were listed on the bulletin board.

- Don't slam down the desk tops.
- No gum or candy.
- No pushing in line.
- No destruction of property.
- Respect the rights of others.
- No fighting.
- No profanity.
- No talking out loud. Raise your hand.
- Keep your hands off items that do not belong to you.

Generally, the children in this class were well behaved, but there were two children with problems severe enough to require the principal's intervention. We will call them Amelia and Emil.

Amelia had emotional tantrums. She sulked a lot and frequently balked when the teacher insisted that she do her seat work. Whenever the teacher would tell her to go to the office, she would not always obey. The teacher would sometimes have to drag her across the hall to the office. At other times, the principal would come and get her. From time to time, Amelia would run away, would not board the bus to go home, and would cry, though unprovoked. She had a younger sister in the all-day kindergarten. Sometimes the teacher would send her to the half-day kindergarten room when she "acted like a baby."

The principal had several conferences with Amelia's mother, who was a very young, pleasant woman. She admittedly did not know what was wrong with Amelia. Both children seemed to be well-kept. The mother said that Amelia always did do strange things. "She told me once that she felt very sad, and she cries for no reason," the mother told the principal who advised her to have Amelia evaluated by the school psychologist. The principal then asked the mother to sign the appropriate school forms granting permission for such testing and told her that the school psychologist would schedule an appointment and after testing would discuss the results with her. In spite of all of these efforts, Amelia and her sister were placed in a foster home with relatives in 1987 when their mother was diagnosed as too chemically dependent to take care of them. Yet, when Amelia left Madison, she tested at grade level in reading and mathematics.

Emil wanted to live with his biological mother instead of with his father and stepmother. He acted out in school in spite of his father's great interest in his doing well academically. Emil was very mobile in class, as was Amelia, and talked a lot. The teacher was constantly reprimanding him and warning him about his conduct. Emil did not disrupt the class as often as Amelia did; yet, he did consume too much of the teacher's time. One day Emil took out a ring and showed it to his classmates. The teacher saw it and asked him why he hadn't told his father where the ring was when he came to school looking for it. Emil hung his head in response and the teacher took him to the office to call his father. Emil had been enrolled in the full-day magnet kindergarten and lived far enough away from Madison to come in a van. Because he wanted to live with his biological mother, who lived near enough to Madison for him to walk to school, he misbehaved on the van. One time he vandalized the seats with a screwdriver. On another occasion, he convinced an older student to forge his father's signature to a note giving him permission to visit his mother, avoiding the van and making the school cooperate in his scheme, thus giving it legitimacy. During the 1986-87 school year, Emil's father sent him to live with his mother.

This teacher has several routines for teaching her curriculum. Mostly, she would teach a lesson, demonstrate the concept or skill, permit the students to demonstrate the skill or concept on the chalkboard, and then let them practice what they had learned in a workbook or with seat work (prepared dittos). After this, she would provide immediate feedback by walking around the room from student to student. When she noted incorrect responses, she would reteach the skill or concept there on the spot. If too many students gave incorrect responses, she would stop the class and return to a demonstration lesson. The teacher expected all of her students to learn the skills at a 90 percent level of mastery.

In reading for comprehension, the teacher called on students to read the story aloud, then she corrected mistakes or gave help where necessary to the reader. Afterward, she asked questions about the part read aloud and called on a student for the answer. When the entire story had been read aloud, she called on students to read the questions she has prepared or which appeared in the workbook and to answer same. She continued this routine until all questions had been answered. Then the students were assigned pages in the workbook which asked similar questions or which stressed comprehension skills.

In this teacher's room, the day opened with the calendar routine and questions about the day of the week, time of year, the class schedule, daily school events, and the weather. Next, the students participated in *Open Court* phonics routines using the sound cards, the phonograph, and the cheers (raising the hands up and down several times). The *Open Court* routine started with two sets of cards, one for consonants and one for vowels. It proceeded as follows:

- Students reviewed all the learned sounds from the cards and the streamer above the chalkboard.
- Everyone pulled out a set of cards.
- Teacher called out a vocabulary word.
- Teacher asked students to identify the ending sound.
- Group responded.
- Teacher approved or disapproved the answers.
- Students showed the sound card.
- Teacher called for a new card sound.
- Teacher played a record demonstrating the new sound.
- Students practiced the new sound.
- Teacher wrote vocabulary words on the chalkboard with the new sound.

The students seemed to enjoy these activities. Everyone participated enthusiastically.

This teacher gave homework every day except on Fridays. Every Monday, she sent home a notebook with her students containing the homework assignments for the entire week and explanatory notes for parents to use. This was done for reading and mathematics. Dictation was given in class on the vocabulary and spelling words. These lists also were sent home each week. Students had assignments with these words each day. The teacher reviewed the vocabulary, read the story, and answered the questions. Then the students read the story as a group. When they had done well, they gave themselves an *Open Court* cheer.

This teacher read her students stories with morals, values, and lessons after lunch to quiet them down and get them into a serious mood for the afternoon's work. If they misbehaved in the lunchroom, she would use a few minutes to review the rules of conduct for the lunchroom and reprimand those who were disorderly or disobedient. Lines were used to move the students from place to place. The boys and girls formed separate lines and each had its own leaders and monitors. The teacher had classroom jobs for the students. Students' seats were moved when they disturbed their neighbors, talked continuously, or disrupted the classroom routines. Sometimes an offender was sent to sit at one of the tables under the windows away from the class. At other times, violators were seated at the table nearest the teacher's desk. When the teacher's tolerance barrier was broken, students were sent to the principal's office.

From time to time, the principal would peer into the classroom from the door's window. Once in a while, she would enter and sit down for a few minutes. The teacher appreciated the principal's help with Amelia and Emil. She tried to deal with the other discipline problems herself. She had one hyperactive student, but he was untroubled by severe social and emotional problems. She had had trouble getting his mother to come in for conferences. On one occasion when his mother came after school to get him, the teacher stopped her and had an impromptu conference. This happened on a day when the principal was holding a PRISM meeting. Since the teacher had not informed the principal of her absence, the teacher was questioned and advised to inform the principal in the future. Since the encounter with this parent had been serendipitous, the teacher felt that it was impossible for her to have informed the principal beforehand. She used this as an illustration of the principal's "by the book" approach.

There were twenty-two students in the class (twelve boys and ten girls), all African-American. Each child had two workbooks to complete, one in reading and the other in mathematics; spelling and vocabulary words to learn to use in sentences; social studies; science; music; art; physical education; and library. *Open Court* provides for proofreading activities with red marking pens which the teacher distributes at the start of the lesson and collects at its end. The students seemed to enjoy the proofreading lessons. The teacher assigned an exercise in writing, using the vocabulary words. Students were to write complete sentences. The work was corrected in class at its completion. Students proofread each others' papers. Mathematics was taught in the afternoon; however, mathematics seat work was distributed throughout the day when students completed their other work assignments in language arts, social studies, and science. Students often asked the teacher for permission to do "baby math." These were problems on skills which the students had already mastered.

During the observations in 1986, the teacher was teaching place value, adding, and subtracting simple facts without regrouping. She followed the teaching, demonstration practice, test, corrective-feedback, demonstration practice, retest routine. Students demonstrated their understanding on the chalkboard. Each day, most of the morning time was spent on reading, phonics, and dictation (spelling). Science and social studies were taught periodically. In the afternoons, English and mathematics were taught daily and health and special subjects were taught twice a week. The students went to other teachers for special subjects: music, art, physical education, and library.

This teacher is a sensitive teacher who sees changes in her students immediately. The following is an example:

Amelía didn't line up. The teacher went up to her to inquire about her refusal. Amelia was crying.

"Why are you crying?" the teacher asked, putting her arms around Amelia.

"I got 18 wrong on the test."

"No, you didn't. Is that what you thought? No! You had 18 right. And that's excellent. That's nothing to cry about. If you had gotten 18 wrong, I'd have been upset. You had 18 right. That's good. You get an *Open Court* cheer!"

All of the children gave Amelia an *Open Court* cheer. She stopped crying when the teacher gave her a big hug. Then she quietly got in line.

The teacher is described as "laid back" by the older students who have passed through her. This means she is easy-going, pleasant, and understanding. She believes that African-American history should be integrated into the curriculum and she usually assumes the responsibility for the African-American history program.

The New Principal Who Made the Changes

The principal was interested in improving instructional skills for teachers, and she set about to do just that. She stated:

I look at and study anything which has to do with the academic progress of children. I talk with the teachers about these data. Printouts for MAP come into the building, the class summary sheet lists the name of every child in a given room. It indicates how well each child has done. I look at several things: how well the class mastered objectives, the total number of objectives mastered, and students' individual scores. I write lengthy comments on these summary sheets, especially on students who are missing consistently large numbers of objectives. We confer over these data. In the individual conferences, I am interested in knowing if the youngster has a critical problem. I seek to identify these problems if and where they exist. I try to get the teachers to do a lot of talking and planning. If the teacher is having trouble planning, I make suggestions and provide resources. I also pull instructional supervisors in.

The principal sets individual goals with teachers at their first meeting in August. They plan these goals at the end of school in June. Principals receive PRISM training in July for adopting and planning for the Superintendent's goals. During the 1983-84 school year the school system adopted science goals for emphasis. The principal described that process in this way:

These science goals surfaced and I introduced them in the spring of 1984. Teachers were instructed about MAP science at staff meetings. I told teachers that principals would be providing in-service training for teachers who were interested in science, and they should indicate their interest. We would be headed toward more hands-on. More materials would be purchased and principals would be looking for ways to buy equipment.

The principal has an open door for parents as well as faculty and staff. She acts as a buffer between the two groups. Parents and visitors are required to sign in at the office before proceeding to classrooms. There are signs throughout the building advising of this school rule, a routine which varies from the previous principal's practice. The principal wants very much to improve community and parent relations:

I want my parents to become involved in the school, to become knowledgeable about what the school is doing, to support the teachers and administrators, and to make suggestions about what they would like to see happen. Many parents work, and the desire is there although the time isn't. You know that the concern is there. You can call them on the telephone. I try to stimulate this involvement by individual encounters, conferences, PTA meetings, school meetings, special events, and programs. We send home letters, newsletters, bulletins, and we make telephone calls.

The principal has a more supportive community since the school has become high achieving.

The principal uses her support services to the maximum. She has special praise for her school social worker and the instructional supervisor, although her assessment of the latter varies with that of the teacher described above. In addition to her support service workers, the principal commends her special subject teachers. Many attribute the full-day magnet kindergarten and the Early Learning Skills (ELS) class to her since they did not exist at Madison before her arrival. The principal believes that ELS is a good experience for her students, and she makes a point of seeing that they get out of ELS and into the higher first grade reading levels at Madison successfully. Parents were apprehensive at first, but now they want their children in ELS if they need to be there.

The principal sees herself as an instructional leader, but she tries to be a good manager as well. While she attempts to fill this bill, she does not have the kind of power she would like to have to do it. She does have the right to interview teacher aides and staff but is not always given the right to interview teachers. Because teachers are unionized, teachers have rights which must be respected regarding their placement, transfer, and assignments. The principal has never received a list of candidates for her consideration. She would like to have more input there.

A meticulous follower of the rules, like her predecessor, the principal complies with the union contract and relentlessly pursues due process for all employees. So thorough is her work and so complete are her reports that she has rarely lost a case for unsatisfactory marks. Other principals visit her to observe her techniques. She takes copious notes in her observations of teachers and makes detailed accounts of teacher conferences, which she produces for her superiors when necessary.

She doesn't believe it makes sense to have a curriculum which doesn't meet student needs. The student is not supposed to adjust to the curriculum. The principal sees the formal curriculum as the courses which are required and the informal curriculum as those facets which principals and teachers add on because the students need them. She says:

The formal curriculum has changed. It now includes MAP testing, *Open Court* reading series, and Harcourt Brace Jovanovich for the intermediate grades in reading. Yet, the informal curriculum hasn't changed much. African-American history is not written into our curriculum. It should be integrated into the formal curriculum.

Children need a more positive self-image and self-pride. I consider music, art, and physical education the formal curriculum.

She wants the informal curriculum to make the children feel good about themselves and have a positive feel toward school.

Students are placed in classrooms by scholastic ability, focusing on reading based on total performance using the CAT, MAP, grades in reading, reading level, and teacher judgment. Board policy is followed for student promotion and placement in special education. Failure is watched closely to see what works. The principal believes that first grade failures did better in 1985. When teachers make requests to refer students for special education, the principal wants to see the students' records. Conferences are held even before referrals take place to determine number of failures, test scores, attendance, teacher programs, teacher responses, parental conferences, and family characteristics. Ancillary service workers and psychologists are consulted before referrals to the mentally handicapped, socially and emotionally disturbed, and learning disability programs are made. It is indeed a routine of last resort.

The principal has very good relations with her superiors, including her school board member whose children were students in Madison School during the time of the observations. In addition, she has good relations with her janitorial staff, including the head engineer. She says she has too much to do to perform others' jobs for them. In order to handle her busy schedule, she looks at those things which are most critical and works down from there. She arrives at school each day at 8:00 a.m., handles paperwork, makes phone calls, and, if any teachers are out, checks on the substitute service. She considers special subject teacher assignment or student distribution as the appropriate standard operating procedure to remedy any substitute unavailability.

"Most teachers at Madison are interested in doing a good job," she said unequivocally. "The high scores at Madison are due to an increased awareness on the part of teachers who care more about what they do than they did in my first year, although teachers were more cohesive then. Teachers pay more attention to instructional skills, and students are learning to be responsible for their own behavior now." She lists the following as primary contributing factors to Madison's high achievement in 1984: improved student and teacher attendance, increased time on task, improved instructional skills, good parental cooperation, close monitoring of student achievement, and a strong demand for good discipline.

Conclusion

The high-achieving African-American elementary school is no longer an abashing anomaly in Pittsburgh. Supported by school board policy and system routines, the principal is now held responsible for the attainment of the system goal of high achievement for all students. Schools are placed in SIP when they do not perform, and principals are removed when they have failed to succeed after a reasonable length of time judged by the Assistant Superintendent.

In Pittsburgh, schools can be classified in four categories according to their achievement of the school system priority of eliminating the achievement gap: (1) those which have eliminated the gap between white and African-American system norms; (2) those which have narrowed the gap between the African-American and white norms in the system; (3) those which still fall below the African-American norms; and (4) those which fall below the 50th percentile. Schools classified in category four are placed in SIP and provided with Chapter 1 services. Several types of routines are developed for these schools: assessment, placement, pacing, monitoring, measurement, discipline, instructional, evaluation, staff development, and decision making.[15]

The new Madison confirmed our findings in the previous (1979-80) study. We found the twelve routines which had been seen before. While there is much in the literature citing teacher leadership and parent involvement as important criteria for high achievement, our findings do not confirm these notions. It may be that the African-American school needs a different mix of ingredients for a successful recipe. Since there has never been a consensus among the American polity around full citizenshp for the African-American (Morris, 1975), and since the institutional value of white superiority still dominates the social reality (Sizemore, 1972), strong leadership may continue to emerge as the most important factor in the elevation of achievement in African-American schools until the education of teachers comes to include content which reflects the true history and condition of African-Americans so that they are enlightened and better prepared to teach African-American children.

The National Conference on Educating Black Children has produced a monograph titled *A Blueprint for Action* which is being considered in Pittsburgh along with the present programs of the Pittsburgh Public Schools. The first Western Pennsylvania Conference on Educating Black Children sponsored by the Greater Pittsburgh Alliance of Black School Educators was held at the Allegheny Middle School in Pittsburgh on April

23, 1988. Over 500 teachers, administrators, parents, community organization representatives, students, and policy makers attended.

Ronald Edmonds said that we do know enough to educate all of the children of all of the people. It is no longer an educational question, it is a political question: "How do we feel about the fact that we haven't done it already, and when do we intend to do it?" (Edmonds, 1979). The Pittsburgh Board of Education has made that decision. Hopefully its enlightened leadership will continue. Its highest priority is to eliminate this inequity. More school systems should follow the board's action. Additionally, more school communities should adopt the blueprint and begin to help their policy makers in this effort.

Notes

1. A *routine* is a series of activities designed to achieve a goal; a *scenario* is a series of routines; a *process* is a series of scenarios. This definition came from the use of the Organizational Process Model created by Graham T. Allison in his study of the Cuban missile crisis discussed in his book, *Essence of Decision: Explaining the Cuban Missile Crisis* (Boston: Little, Brown and Company, 1971). In this model the outcome of an organization is the result of what the people do or the implementation of routines (standard operating procedures).

2. The loosely coupled view of organizations stresses the autonomy of the individual actor in the system and the absence of centralized control of behavior, especially with regard to instruction.

3. *Structure* is defined here as the presence of rules, regulations, and directives and the dominance of routines for their execution enforced by a hierarchical authority. Classrooms were classified as high, flexible, and loose according to the amount of structure observed in the organization and operation of their routines.

4. In 1980, Madison had the following programs: The Elementary Scholars' Center, the PPS program for the gifted and the talented, Headstart, and a Day Care program. Two programs generally not a formal part of the system were in the school also: Teacher Corps and Project '81. Teacher Corps mainly provided systematic demonstrations at in-service meetings and conducted classroom studies on low- and high-achieving students' actual time-on-task during mathematics and science. Project '81 was a statewide demonstration project on Competency Based Education (CBE) for the State Department of Education, generating local options before long-term policy emerged. Madison was a testing site for simple competencies in financing.

5. Miller Elementary School. Also the African-American students at Westwood under the former principal of Madison reached or exceeded the system's white norm in both reading and mathematics in 1987. See table 10.2. The author plans to observe there next to determine what changes, if any, this principal has made in her routines.

6. MAP is a pre-post instructional testing system designed to increase student achievement in basic skills. The core of the MAP project is the diagnostic testing program. In the MAP plan, all teachers of the subject areas involved teach the same basic objectives at each level. A standardized criterion-referenced testing program helps teachers determine the progress of their students in learning these objectives.

7. PRISM is a staff development effort designed to improve the instructional leadership of administrators, the effectiveness of teachers, and the learning of students. PRISM is an adaptation of Dr. Madeline Hunter's Effective Teaching Model. This includes: the four elements of effective instruction, the lesson design for effective instruction, supervisory skills for instructional growth, and adult learning theory for effective in-service. PRISM was initiated during the 1981-82 school year in Pittsburgh.

8. The Schenley High School Teachers' Center was implemented to provide staff development for all of the high school teachers in the school district. Teachers spend nine weeks at Schenley while substitute teachers take their places at their home schools. At Schenley, they learn from master teachers. The author's argument with SHSTC planners was their failure to build in a mechanism for evaluating the effect the Center would have on student achievement. Center planners said this could not be done; therefore, there is no explanation why achievement has not accelerated at the predominantly African-American Westinghouse High School.

9. The BESTC has as its central focus the improvement of the quality of instruction and leadership in the 53 elementary schools in the district. This goal is to be reached through several complimentary staff development strategies. The three main objectives are: (1) to demonstrate state-of-the-art instructional, curriculum, and school organizational practices; (2) to revitalize teachers in the areas of subject knowledge, instructional skills, and professional attitudes; and (3) to develop effective instructional leaders. Every elementary teacher and administrator will be rotated through the BESTC set of experiences. Under the direction of an especially selected faculty and administration at the model school, teachers and principals will have the opportunity to learn new techniques and to practice existing and newly developed skills in an atmosphere of collegial interaction.

10. Some Madison teachers transferred out to join magnet schools created by the desegregation plan; others left to join the faculties of schools closer to their homes. One was promoted.

11. The Early Learning Skills room was created for children who needed a period of time longer than kindergarten to master reading and mathematics skills necessary for success in first grade. These children attend school all day in a first grade classroom and join the other first graders in special subject activities. They have intense instruction in skill development with the goal being to permit their entry into first grade in the advanced reading groups. Project Pass was designed for children who were falling behind in the third grade. This program was later abandoned because it failed to achieve its goals and became predominantly African-American, thereby segregating classes in the schools.

12. The PPS changed from the Metropolitan Achievement Tests to the California Achievement Tests in 1981.

13. The principal was observed in her office for two school weeks (ten days) and each classroom teacher was observed five days (Monday through Friday) by two different observers from January 1986, through the second week in June 1986. Semistructured interviews were conducted with the principal and each teacher. The structure of the school was studied: the roles, informal and formal organization, routines, programs, and priorities. In addition, goals stated by the principal in her interview were codified.

14. The struggle for a phonics-based reading series was a long one. In 1972, the principal of the Vann Elementary School sought and received permission to use the Lippincott series with her advanced readers when the PPS changed from Lippincott to Ginn. She felt that this reader better addressed the phonics needs of her students. The Vann Lippincott readers became known throughout the community for their ability to read so well. Later, a school board member took up the fight. As a result, *Open Court* was chosen.

15. For more information about these routines, contact Dr. Louis A. Venson, Director, School Improvement Project, Pittsburgh Public Schools, Pittsburgh, PA, 15213.

11 Qualities Shared by African-American Principals in Effective Schools: A Preliminary Analysis

KOFI LOMOTEY

Introduction

Research on effective schools shows consistently that their principals are instructional leaders who are involved in curriculum planning, teacher supervision, and student achievement evaluation (DeGuire, 1980; Wilson, 1982). In an earlier study (Lomotey, 1989), I attempted to determine how the leadership of African-American principals in effective predominantly African-American elementary schools compares with the leadership qualities generally attributed to principals in effective schools. The findings were inconclusive; some African-American principals appeared to follow the expected pattern and some did not. In this chapter, I address a second question that I asked in the study: what leadership qualities, if any, do African-American principals in effective schools hold in common with each other?

The study consisted of case studies of three African-American principals in three effective, predominantly African-American elementary schools in California (Lomotey, 1989). Three qualities were characteristic of all three principals. Each principal, in their own way, demonstrated: (1) a commitment to the education African-American children; (2) a compassion for, and understanding of, their students and of the communities in which they worked; and (3) a confidence in the ability of all African-American children to learn.

The fact that these qualities were shared by all three principals is important because it raises the question of the significance, for African-American principals in general, of these qualities in relation to the quality of instructional leadership. It is possible that, given the characteristics of these African-American schools, (e.g., economic, academic, cultural, and social), these qualities supersede all others in importance in bringing about success. In this chapter, I illustrate the three qualities through vignettes about the principals recorded in the case studies. The actual names have been changed.

The Variables

For involvement in currriculum planning, I focused on how deeply the principals were involved in curriculum planning, whether they attended curriculum planning meetings, and whether they tended to stay abreast of new curriculum developments. In assessing involvement in the evaluation of student achievement, my concern was whether the principals monitored school-wide tests, and what follow-up occurred after the results were received by the school. In seeking information regarding the principals' supervision of staff, I focused on the amount of time spent observing teachers and the amount and quality of feedback given to teachers as a follow-up to classroom observations. While I focused on these three variables in my research strategy, the results of the interviews and observations provided me with ample information to explore the question considered in this chapter: What qualities, if any, do African-American principals in effective schools hold in common with each other?

Methodology

The Sample

I began in the state of California with a population of 26 predominantly African-American elementary schools which had African-American principals who had been in their positions for at least seven years. Based upon California Assessment Program Test scores in math and reading, I ranked the schools and selected the top three for inclusion in the study.

Instruments

I used four primary data-gathering techniques: teacher questionnaires, principal observations, principal interviews, and teacher interviews. I gave the questionnaire to all of the teachers in all of the schools and received 73 percent of the forms back. I observed and interviewed all three of the principals. I interviewed a sample of five teachers in each school. The interviews and the questionnaire were constructed by me for the study and were tested in a pilot study.

Observations

Observations of each principal were direct and structured and were conducted for two days in the fall of 1984 and for two days in the spring of 1985. Observations of a four-day duration are unusually short. However, some researchers have conducted studies with observations of similar duration (Lightfoot, 1983; Mintzberg, 1973). In addition, having three additional instruments and repeating the observations helped to compensate for the brief observations.

The sampling frame for the observations included settings, actors, events, and processes. The settings were everywhere the principal went during the course of the day. The actors included the principals and everyone with whom they came into contact during the day in the course of their work. Events were those which the principal participated in their capacity as the school leader. Processes were all the things the principals did in their capacity as the school leader.

After looking at my first day's observation notes, I established the following categories of activities:

1. talking with someone outside of the school community
2. dealing with curriculum (e.g., book selection, course evaluation)
3. classroom observations
4. dealing with discipline
5. doing desk work (e.g., opening mail, signing letters)
6. in the school yard
7. having social discussions with staff person(s)
8. talking with the researcher
9. instructional time
10. talking with a teacher or administrator

The information obtained from the principal interviews and the teacher interviews was used, along with the information from the teacher questionnaires, to supplement the observation data.

The Principals and Their Schools

In a few ways, these principals and their schools were similar. The average length of teacher total experience was similar in each school. Total teacher experience in each school averaged about 15 years. Also, all of the principals had ten or more years of teaching experience and nine or more years of administrative experience. The length of the principal's day in each school was also similar. Mr. Brooks and Ms. Marshall spent about nine hours at their school each day while Mr. Charles spent about eight hours. With regard to students, all of the schools had 80 percent or more of their children receiving free lunches.

Several differences in these principals and their schools were also apparent. While Collins and Woodson are both in large, urban areas, Foster is located in a much smaller city. Different housing patterns are found surrounding each school also—Collins, private homes; Woodson, apartments; and Foster, homes and apartments.

In each school, the average teacher had served at least three years. The highest level of faculty stability was at Foster with an average of six years, and the lowest level was at Collins with an average of three years. Woodson was the only school in which the staff chose to sit in the lounge without regard to race.

Woodson is the only school of the three with a primarily African-American teaching staff; its staff was 60 percent African-American. in both Collins and Foster, most teachers were white. In Collins, whites made up 75 percent and, at Foster, they comprised 67 percent of the faculty.

Collins had the highest percentage of African-American students: 85 percent African-American students at both Woodson and Foster made up about two-thirds of the student population. While half of the students in Collins and Foster lived with both parents, less than one in forty students at Woodson lived with both their mother and father.

Parent involvement was highest at Collins, where they had the highest average number of parents at PTA meetings (30), as well as the highest number of parents who volunteered (30). In addition, Collins had the highest percentage of aides who were also parents of students enrolled in the school (67 percent). All of the schools appeared to show a high level of contact between parents and teachers, while Collins was the only school without a high level of contact between parents and the principal.

Mr. Brooks, at Foster, was the only principal who lived relatively close to his school. Ms. Marshall, at Woodson, and Mr. Charles, at Collins, both commuted over forty miles.

There were some striking differences in the way each of the principals spent their time during my observations. Mr. Charles' two most time-consuming activities were talking with the researcher in the office and talking with the researcher and the Title I Coordinator in the staff lounge. Mr. Brooks was the only principal for whom classroom observations ranked number one in terms of the amount of time spent participating in the activities included in his daily routine.

How African-American Principals Lead

Commitment to the Education of African-American Children

Mr. Charles, Mr. Brooks, and Ms. Marshall all appeared to have as their number one priority the education of the children in their school. Some other principals, in Ms. Marshall's view, have other priorities—money high among them.

The commitment of these principals to the education of African-American children became evident in discussions, interviews, and direct observation of their activities. It was typified in the following comment by Mr. Brooks, "I've had chances to move to the north [white] end of town, but, I don't know, it's the feeling I think I have for the Black community."

Mr. Brooks.   One experienced teacher at Foster said of Mr. Brooks:

> I've never seen a principal who is with the kids as much as he is. He's on yard duty all the time. He's at breakfast. He talks to them. He really does talk to them. He knows their names. He keeps track of them. I have a kid that's a behavior problem. He [Mr. Brooks] noticed that . . .[Ronald] hadn't been in trouble for three days. He really is observant. He picks up the details, so you know he must care, because he picks them up, and they're little, they're minor, and they're something you'd think only a teacher would know. That's what I see and I think that goes back to the fact that his first priority is the kids.

This teacher went on to say:

> I know that the child is really important [to him]. Mr. [Brooks] has spoken to us more than once on how to make our children feel good about themselves and [about the fact that] they have rights and that we are to treat them as we want to be treated. [In addition, he stresses that] bad conduct will not be tolerated. Also, self-value is very, very important here and is stressed along with responsibility.
>
> I've been stifled in other areas because my administrator's priorities were not with the kids and that's frustrating. And that's why I'm feeling really at home here because this is a unique school. Everything that Mr. [Brooks] does, I really believe, is in the kids' best interest. And you can really tell because he goes to his teachers and finds out. He's just squared away in that area. It's what's best for the kids and then everything else is secondary.
>
> The first week of school, I had 43 kids and I just thought that was terrible for me. And he said, no, it's not for you I'm worried. It's the kids. He goes, you can't feel sorry for yourself. You gotta feel sorry

for the kids. And it's true. It was bad on me, but it was worse for them. He just really has it together in that area, as far as I can see.

Another teacher at Foster concurred: "He genuinely cares—probably more than any other man I've ever met—for the kids and their well-being and that's what makes it click. When you get people who share his concern with him, it all meshes."

Indeed, Mr. Brooks' classroom observations were not for show. It was clear from the teacher interviews and teacher questionnaires that classroom observation was part of his daily routine. Also, he seemed, during these observations, genuinely concerned with the progress of the students. He would look at the desk work of several students and challenge them to explain it.

Mr. Charles.   During one of our talks, Mr. Charles said, "we must challenge the children continuously." In discussing the uniqueness of the African-American child, he added, "[The] Black child has all of the white child's problems and his [own], and I'm not gonna add a persecution problem to that." In most, if not all, of the discipline-related discussions that Mr. Charles had with students (or with students and parents), his focus was invariably on the importance of academics for the particular child and the classroom disruption caused by the misbehavior. Regardless of the problem, he always seemed to express the primacy and probability of the student's academic success. Also, in his various discussions with teachers that I observed, Mr. Charles was always emphasizing the need for them to push the children intellectually. He seemed to feel that some of the teachers did not have confidence in the potential of some of their students.

Ms. Marshall.   I talked with Ms. Marshall about maintaining her commitment to African-American children and the commitment of her teachers (in the face of such a high level of student transiency) and she said:

> It goes back to the kind of teacher I have here. The kind of values I have articulated. We're not here just for a job. With the one child that you think you may not be helping to develop academically, you might be sparking something that later in life might change his whole academic outlook. So it's not how low or how often you're getting a change. It's doing and giving your best and your all that year 'cause that'll be the only chance you'll get and somehow that's worked.

When talking with me about what she described as the misplaced priorities of some principals, Ms. Marshall said, "Principals should ask, why am I here? It's not to hire people, but to serve children." Indeed, her relationship with her students and their families, on one level, took precedent over her responsibilities to the central office. One day, during my observations, Ms. Marshall was scheduled to leave for a principals' meeting at slightly after one o'clock. She chose instead to meet with a parent, who had unexpectedly come in, before leaving. After she met with that parent, she met with another parent who had come in and insisted on seeing her. Before leaving for the meeting, for which she was now close to one hour late, she explained to me that the situation at the school site was her key responsibility and that, as a result, she had no misgivings about being late for the principals' meeting.

Compassion for, and Understanding of, African-American Children and African-American Communities

Mr. Brooks.   During our interview, in discussing African-American principals in African-American schools, Mr. Brooks told me:

> Being Black is not enough. One needs to be sensitive to the needs of Black students and to the total Black community. I think they ought to be not only sensitive, but knowledgeable about the needs of Black children.

In expounding on those needs, Mr. Brooks added:

> I won't say that they're any different than the needs of white children, but I think there is a degree of being more sensitive, in that I feel that where we have more broken homes, more one-parent homes, and, in many instances, more low-income families and more people on AFDC, I think it calls for a kind of a person who would be knowledgeable and caring for those kinds of, not disabilities, but those kinds of things that are, well...much of it is in our Black community.

Here we have support for the contention that a class culture is as significant as a race culture. Mr. Brooks suggests that a significant factor in relating to African-American children is a knowledge of, and familiarity with, their socioeconomic status.

Mr. Brooks seemed to personify his blueprint for principals. He appeared to know all of his students' brothers, sisters, parents, and grandparents (as well as most of the people who pass by the school in the afternoon). He seemed to continually run into former students. When discussing the important factors that set Foster apart from other schools in its district, one teacher said of Mr. Brooks: "[He] knows [the] community. He's lived in this area for a long time and the sensitivity makes a big difference, I feel."

In discussing Mr. Brooks' personal relationship with his students, another teacher at Foster said:

> Some principals will not put their arms around the kids because, you know, this threat of child abuse—you better not touch 'em. Now, Mr. [Brooks] will touch the kids. Some of them [principals] keep that distance. You over there and me over here, and don't bother me. I've kinda noticed that. There's like more of a closeness with this one [Mr. Brooks].

Seemingly, it is their compassion and understanding that enables these principals to effectively choose teachers. Mr. Brooks described "good teachers," when he told me:

> I think the classroom teacher to me is the key. The leadership that the principal shows toward having the teacher to go toward the goals and objectives, I think is very paramount. But if you get good teachers, the principal's role is relatively easy. By good teachers, I mean those teachers who are very sensitive to the needs of, let's say, our Black children, who do more than just come to school and teach and go home. Teachers who show a definite interest in the total Black community—the home, the lifestyles, and all those things that enter into what I feel is a very well-rounded knowledge of the children that you're working with.

Mr. Charles.   Mr. Charles' actions regarding discipline demonstrated his compassion and understanding. He is aware of the fact that disciplinary measures must not only fit the offense, but that they must also fit the student. On more than one occasion, Mr. Charles discussed with me appropriate and inappropriate discipline for specific children. John, a student who seemed to get into trouble often, was in Mr. Charles' office one day because he had not gotten on his bus after school on the previous day. He had gone to a friend's house. After dealing with the situation and excusing John, Mr. Charles explained to me that suspensions were not an effective way of dealing with John.

During a school-wide spelling bee in the auditorium, Mr. Charles approached two children who had been told by their teacher to stand in different corners, apparently for disciplinary reasons. He quietly told them to take their seats. On the way out, when the program was over, he told the responsible teacher that she should never place children in the corner for any reason because it had negative psychological ramifications for the child. This situation demonstrates not only Mr. Charles' emphasis on consistent discipline but also his understanding of the need for appropriate disciplinary measures.

On another occasion, after talking with two students regarding their misbehavior, Mr. Charles made arrangements for them to come to school early on the next day to clean up the front yard. In a final instance, a student and teacher came into Mr. Charles' office regarding a discipline problem. The student had been repeatedly laughing and talking out loud in the classroom. After a brief discussion, the principal had arrived at a diagnosis of the problem and excused the student from the room. He went on to suggest to the teacher that the student was lacking adequate academic stimulation, and he encouraged her to provide additional work for the child.

In discussing the failure of educators to reason with African-American students, Mr. Charles said:

> You can do anything, demand anything from the kid. Be as firm and strong as you want. But what we don't do with the Black kids is we don't tell them why. We don't reason with them.

Mr. Charles also knows of the need to have teachers who are aware of the uniqueness of the African-American student. On several occasions when talking informally with me, he discussed fears of losing such conscious teachers and the need to get more teachers with the required sensitivities.

Ms. Marshall.   A teacher at Woodson best described Ms. Marshall's compasion and understanding when talking about the way that children at Woodson relate to their principal:

> They can relate to a Black principal because the principal is a mother or father figure....I think when she [Ms. Marshall] speaks... they're used to that authoritative woman at home too. [Marie Marshall] has that softness...where the kids are free to come up to her and hug her and, yet in still, they know she might paddle their butts the next day. So I think there's a nice balance between the kids and [Marie] where they'll work hard when she asks them to. They know they're gonna get some type of reward or they're gonna get praised or they know they're gonna be scolded or they're gonna be paddled—some of them. I think they've got that love 'cause she's like a mama. You know they're gonna get it.
>
> In school you're here to learn and plus she's a good role model....They feel free to run up and touch her. A lot of times, teachers don't want you to touch them. It's a nice feeling where they feel close to her and try to achieve.

Ms. Marshall shared with the other principals a unique understanding of the need to be tuned into the heartbeat of the community in which she worked. She told me, "The particularities of the culture of a community are of utmost importance for principals. A principal cannot rely simply on the norms of the society in general." She further explained her point, using assertive discipline—a systematic approach to discipline encompassing firm consistent limits for students—as an example:

> I cannot see assertive discipline in its so-called true form for the kids in inner cities. There aren't homes that provide organized manners. So, when you state your rules, you almost have to use an eclectic form, because you just don't have kids coming from the kinds of homes that—once you set up your rules, three strikes, you're out, and I mean they're out in like three minutes, because they're gonna do a number of things to just make your plan totally unworkable. So it's like going into a classroom, teaching etiquette. First teaching standards before you can even get to a discipline plan. So that's the job of the principal. Many of the teachers come in thinking they can try that, and it's failed and they have been totally crushed. So I have to stop and say many of the children who are from the inner-city areas, who have not had the kinds of backgrounds and home structure that this program would lend itself to. You have to go back and look at the program itself and take the best parts that you feel are workable.

She added that, "You can't look for two and three year gains. A lot of the children we're getting that are low are not low because they cannot attain or attend the information." She explained that many of these students, coming to Woodson for the first time, have either had a lot of substitute teachers or have had poor teachers and were never taught the prerequisite skills, or they were from highly transient families and had been moved from school to school several times.

Ms. Marshall went on to describe the "poor background" of the students at Woodson:

> When I say poor background, it's generally an unorganized home background. Mother going one way, whether it's going to work or family going one way. The family structure isn't very close. There's no father in the home. So, it looks as if, as I look at it, the Black principal has to be the one almost looking and playing God sometimes, in terms of looking at values, looking at past history. ...No matter what new innovations or methods are coming in in education you have to look at the needs of your children, the cultural background of

your children.... You have to go back and look at how we, as a people, functioned. The extended family that was once very important died out and I'm finding at a school like this we have a gang problem because we don't have extended families. We have problems of child care with kindergartenders going home at noon, or we have, for example, kindergarteners whose mothers have to work and they set a clock 'cause the kid can't tell when to go to school. The mother dresses the five year old. She sets the clock. When the clock rings, you push a little button and then you leave to go to school. That shouldn't be. With extended families, we didn't have that kind of problem. You didn't have children just walking the streets alone. You had brothers, sisters, uncles, [and] cousins, who helped with school work and whatever. Now you have a totally different problem existing because we are saying that was something that was no good or whatever we say. So I think you first have to look at culture. That's most important. You have to look at what functions for the culture.

She added:

In this school environment parents believe in corporal punishment, but I had new teachers who don't come from this culture [and] who did not believe in corporal punishment. No one uses corporal punishment here but me, when it's used. You have to look at those values that the people hold dear and build on those. You can't just look at what society's asking as a whole and say, "I'm gonna run my school according to what is happening now." A good example [is] individualization of instruction, the learning center approach, and all the kinds of things that came out several years ago. That would not work in a Black school because the children could not handle the freedom of scheduling and whatever. You'd have to start with a very structured background with the youngsters and then build into teaching children how to schedule because that was just too much. So you have to look at, again, the culture, the values, those kinds of objectives you want articulated for your children. And then you have to be the one to see that they're implemented, whether it be monitoring those teachers [or] selecting those teachers.

In discussing the selection of teachers, Ms. Marshall said to me:

Selecting teachers in this kind of an environment is key. If you've got a teacher who is opposed to structure in the classroom, who does things haphazardly, [and] who doesn't plan, that teacher's gonna be less capable of doing anything in an environment like this.

When it is at all possible, Ms. Marshall hires new teachers as substitutes for a week or so, so that she can observe them in the classroom and talk with them before committing the district to a long-term contract. This is what was occurring with the three new teachers when I first visited Woodson. Only two of them survived. One of Ms. Marshall's teachers said in an interview, "She scrutinizes when she hires. Very rarely do they slip through the cracks."

Confidence in the Educability of African-American Children

The principals I observed appeared to be committed to equal educational opportunity for African-American students. They seemed confident that they could provide all African-American children with a better education.

Mr. Brooks.   Though Mr. Brooks did not say very much to me with regard to his confidence in the ability of African-American students to perform well, his interactions with teachers and students demonstrated this confidence. During classroom observations, he constantly challenged students regarding the work they had done, and he was always supportive in terms of inspiring them to do even better work and to not settle for mediocrity.

On several occasions, I overheard Mr. Brooks encouraging teachers who had become somewhat despondent over the academic performance of students. He would remind them that just by trying a little harder, they would be able to contribute to the children's increased learning. His confidence was reflected in his answer to a question I asked regarding the way that teachers deal with students who have academic deficiencies:

> I don't feel that there is enough zeroing in on the deficiencies. I think our program should be revised in order to really zero in on these particular areas where a student is most weak. I don't think enough of that is being done. Not only in this school, [but] district-wide.

The suggestion here is that, again, with just a little more pushing, additional academic success could be attained.

Mr. Charles.   In speaking about this confidence, Mr. Charles at Collins told me:

> I think we're doing an excellent job, but that doesn't mean that we're pleased. Because actually, our goal would be to have something like 70 to 75 percent of the children achieving on the CTBS and I think that is attainable.... But the point is that I believe that this can be attained with the present staff, with the present community, [and] with the present children.

The basic philosophy we try to have here with the staff and with the leadership is that we're not content or satisfied with our success. If one child is not achieving at his maximum potential, or close to that maximum potential, then we've failed.

He went on to say:

I'm aware of the bell curve, and I understand all of that, but, on the other hand, I'm sure you know, and I know, that there are schools in certain areas like Chicago and New York that are private and some very unorthodox private schools that are religious. They take people right off the street and they have remarkable achievement levels. I know they have controls that we don't have, but, nevertheless, I think that we can use some of their techniques and some of their motivation and approximate some of their results.

At another point, Mr. Charles reminded me that " the Black child is extremely intelligent, creative, perceptive, imaginative, and responsive to difficult tasks". He went on to say, "what we're saying is that the [African-American] child can respond to what we call the crisis skills—the skills that are at risk." All three principals, echoing Mr. Charles, believe that all African-American children can learn regardless of their background.

Mr. Charles told me, on several occasions, that he felt that some teachers were unnecessarily holding children back academically. More than once, I heard him encourage teachers to challenge the children with additional work. In one case, a parent came in who was concerned because her perception was that her daughter, Shawn, had not been sufficiently challenged academically. After a lengthy discussion with the parent, the school psychologist, and the teacher, and a review of the child's permanent record, it appeared as though Mr. Charles agreed with the parent. (He later told me tht he did and that he was not confident that the teacher was likely to begin to challenge Shawn.) Mr. Charles then called in the mentor teacher and attempted to make her feel that she was involved in the decision—that he then made—to put Shawn in *her* class, thereby improving the chances of her speedy progress.

Ms. Marshall.   Ms. Marshall's confidence in the ability of her African-American students to learn was evident in her consistent desire to analyze test scores and to see that any necessary remediation for students is done. She did not appear to think in terms of a lack of ability on the part of students. Instead, she was constantly encouraging teachers to conduct diagnoses and follow through for students. She told me that she expects teachers to efficiently and quickly diagnose and prescribe work for students. She focused many of the staff in-service programs on these instructional skills.

In one instance, I observed a teacher come in to Ms. Marshall's office three times during the day to ask about having a new student placed in a lower grade. The student, it seems, had scored poorly on placement tests. The teacher felt that the student would not be able to perform well in her class and she was anxious to move him out of her class. Ms. Marshall was very hesitant to agree to moving the child. She wanted to be sure that every effort was made to accurately assess the child's proficiencies before he was moved to a lower grade.

Even in the instance when a teacher came in to seek help with a new student who was 87 percent deaf in one ear, Ms. Marshall was genuinely concerned about what services could be offered at Woodson so that the child would be able to learn at his maximum potential.

Summary

Ms. Marshall, Mr. Brooks, and Mr. Charles all seem to have something in common; there is substantial evidence that they each have: (1) a commitment to the education of African-American children; (2) compassion for, and understanding of, their students and of the communities in which they work; and (3) confidence in the ability of all African-American children to learn. This conclusion is not surprising as aspects of it are supported in the literature. For example, researchers have suggested that effective communication and interaction come about when two people share a culture (MacLennan, 1975; Kochman, 1981). This shared culture, it seems, enables these principals to better understand their students and their communities. In the final analysis, this understanding could positively affect academic achievement.

Similarly, researchers have suggested that a belief in the educability of one's students by a principal has an indirect impact on their achievement (Edmonds, 1979; Wellisch et al., 1978). It also follows that these principals hold high expectations for their students because other researchers have shown that when educators have low expectations for student performance, the students invariably perform poorly (Rist, 1970; Beady and Hansell, 1981).

One may not, of course, generalize with any confidence from an N=3 study to a wide population. The aim of this study, however, is for comparability and translatability, not generalizability (LeCompte and Goetz, 1982). The intent was to describe the characteristics of the principals clearly so that the descriptions could serve as a basis for comparison with other principals. I wanted to provide explicitness in the descriptions, enabling confidence in future comparisons. I do offer some propositions based upon my analysis of Foster, Woodson, and Collins Elementary Schools which may guide other schools as they seek to become more successful. Also, my analysis highlights themes worthy of further study. If my descriptions of these three principals help anyone else in another elementary school, that is an appropriate form of utility.

I suspect that the leadership exhibited by African-American principals in these effective schools differs from that which would be found in African-American principals in less effective schools. That is, I would not expect African-American principals in ineffective schools to demonstrate a commitment to African-American education, a compassion and understanding of African-American students and communities, or a confidence in their students to the degree that the principals in the study demonstrated.

The exploratory nature of this study prevents further speculation as to the relative importance of these qualities vis-à-vis instructional leadership. However, these three qualities do appear to be worthy of further consideration in subsequent research.

12 African-American Achievement: A Research Agenda Emphasizing Independent Schools

JOAN DAVIS RATTERAY

Introduction

Educators, researchers, education policy makers, and the public continue to express concern over low levels of academic achievement by American students, especially among African-Americans who are attending government-operated schools.[1] As a result, many African-American families have chosen to send their children to independent schools which represent self-help strategies in education. In search of options in education that will be helpful in providing quality education for a greater number of African-American children, parents are taking from the state the primary responsibility it has acquired for educating African-American children.

The experiences of these families, teachers, and administrators point to new directions that American educators in general might consider, but they also raise new questions for future research.

A National Dilemma

A number of reports, which have been discussed widely in the media for the past several years, show that U.S. students lag significantly behind students from other industrialized countries. Prominent among these is a report comparing the performance of U.S. students with students in other countries. This study indicates that Americans ranked at the bottom seven times in 19 academic tests and never were in first or second place. Federal education officials have attempted to stem this tide of mediocrity by proposing a model curriculum that would restore a modicum of rigor to secondary education curricula.

The effects of this national dilemma have reached crisis proportions and are felt disproportionately in urban school districts, where there are high concentrations of African-American students. Not only are these pupils consistently behind the mainstream in national test results, but many of these students reportedly graduate functionally illiterate and large numbers of the remainder drop out of school each year.

It should be noted, however, that after the Civil War, approximately 90 percent of the freedmen could not read or write. By 1900, illiteracy had been reduced to 45 percent. Over eight decades later, as many as 40 percent of 17-year-old "minority" youth are considered functionally illiterate.

It is in this context that thousands of African-American families have been withdrawing their children from government-sponsored schools. Parents have been desperately trying to find learning environments that are safe, motivate children, and provide a quality education. Therefore, they have been enrolling their children in independent inner-city schools which are usually owned and operated by African-Americans, either as individuals, community organizations, or churches.

The Schools

Over 400 independent inner-city schools have been identified over a four-year period by the Institute for Independent Education. Having an average enrollment of 130 students per school, it is estimated that the known schools serve approximately 52,000 youngsters. However, researchers at the Institute for Independent Education indicate that this may be a small fraction of the total number of similiar schools that actually exist across the United States.

In a 1987 study, Ratteray and Shujaa studied more than 200 of these schools, examined their operating characteristics, and explored why parents choose them for their children. They report, in *Dare to Choose: Parental Choice at Independent Neighborhood Schools,* that over 80 percent are owned and operated by and for African-Americans. Now there is a need for further studies that demonstrate the extent of student achievement, identify the unique factors in these institutions that make them successful, and determine whether there are principles that can be applied on a wider scale to meet the needs of the masses of African-Americans.

The pursuit of self-help strategies in education is not a new phenomenon for African-Americans. Many of the schools were started in the 1970s, several are over 50 years old, and a few were started over 100 years ago. Furthermore, the concept of independent schools as a voluntary alternative to government-sponsored schools can be dated to the late eighteenth century and early nineteenth centuries.

In the Ratteray-Shujaa study, we found that one-half of the schools are owned or substantially supported by Black churches and religious organizations.[2] However, only one-half of the religious schools indicate that they emphasize specific doctrines, typically enrolling children from various denominations and from non-Christian religions. The remaining schools with a secular emphasis are owned by families, community organizations, and proprietary businesses.

The schools have five common characteristics. First, the schools are concentrated in urban areas. In fact, 70 percent are in the largest school districts of the Northeast. The sample contains scattered representation from the southwestern, southern, southeastern, and central United States, as well as the U.S. Virgin Islands.

Second, the schools tend to be racially homogeneous, each school having an overwhelming enrollment of African-Americans.

Third, these institutions respond to social conditions within the community. They are truly market-driven enterprises, even those that are nonprofit institutions or religious missions. Often led by people who are committed to social change, they promote academic excellence and respect, operate with limited resources, and charge moderate tuition in order to remain within reach of their client families. One-half of the schools have waiting lists, while 76 percent of the children on those lists in 1986 were waiting to get into religiously-affiliated schools. The average annual tuition in 1986 was $1,490 for the first child from a family attending a religious school and $2,071 for secular schools.

Fourth, the schools are neighborhood schools. They have an average enrollment of 110 in secondary schools and 49 in elementary schools, although some are in the range from 500 to 1,000 students. The student/teacher ratio for all schools is approximately 14:1, slightly higher in religious schools and slightly lower in secular schools. They also enroll children primarily from the immediate vicinity and often maintain an extended-family atmosphere.

Fifth, these institutions are operationally autonomous of the larger organizations with which some of them are affiliated, and most receive little or no support from government, corporations, or foundations.

The Families

There is no one type of parent or guardian leading the movement to independent schools. The families in the survey[3] reflect the full range of socioeconomic factors that characterize African-Americans as a whole. For example, the families tend to have four or five members, although quite a few have from two to three members. More than one-half of all the families earn less than $30,000.[4]

The families who are most committed to choice in education work in occupations that do not require a great deal of academic preparation, such as factory workers, registered nurses, and electricians. Nevertheless, 27 percent of the respondents from religious schools and 39 percent from secular shcools report having post-graduate degrees and list occupations such as accountant, attorney, physician, psychologist, and other professional careers.

Most children attending these schools live less than three miles away. Eighteen percent of the children at secular schools and 8 percent at religious schools, from both affluent and poor families, travel over 21 miles daily to school.

News about these "islands" of hope usually spreads by word of mouth, rather than by media advertising. In fact, 81 percent of the families whose children are enrolled learned about their school from other families whose children were previously enrolled.

Families chose these independent schools after they first decide to remove their children from public schools and look for "a good school." Respondents indicate they first searched for a suitable learning environment, but their next greatest concern was for the academic aspects of their child's new school. Parents are much less concerned about their children having a religious education, or even one that explictly affirms their own cultural background. Cost was ranked lowest among parental concerns.

As families experience the new institution, they decide to stay, citing their high expectations for academic achievement. They stay even if it became financially difficult to do so.

African-American Culture

An important component of this study was an effort to determine the role of African-American culture in achievement at these independent schools. In other words, did administrators and families recognize a child's need to be aware of his or her identity, the successes of other African-Americans, and the values they traditionally espouse? The investigators knew intuitively—based on their training, personal lives, and experience as teachers —that sensitivity to and an appreciation for African-American culture seems to be a motivating factor when African-American students have high levels of academic achievement.

The initial written surveys yielded responses to open-ended questions that are not consistent with some of the structured-response data, and this prompted even closer scrutiny during interviews with both administrators and parents.

Most administrators responded in writing to a Yes/No question, indicating that their school was not designed specifically to address the needs of any particular racial, ethnic, or cultural group. This applies to 46 percent of the secular schools and 63 percent of the religious schools. The open-ended questions, on the other hand, reflect many curriculum components that emphasize African-American culture, from general Black history elements to specific Pan-African concepts.

Responses such as these may be due to inhibitions in answering printed survey forms. A few administrators indicated they did not want to give the appearance of being "too Black" because they are equally concerned with offering quality academic programs.

The families, however, express a range of reactions to the question of culture. Some of them are explicit about the importance of having curriculum elements on the Black experience, the presence of Black teachers in the school, and a predominantly Black environment. Other parents stress the need for academic studies. They recognize that culture is important, although on a lesser level. One parent even wished that her child's African-American school was more integrated, while another admitted his own lack of knowledge about the history of the Black experience. Even when families deny the overt influence of culture, the verbal imagery they use often reflected its influence on their own value system.

There also is evidence of the dominant presence of African-American culture in the schools themselves. Looking at the pictorial images on the walls, the planned activities, and the ethnic verbal and nonverbal exchanges between teachers and students or administrators and students, there is no question in the minds of most observers who enter the institutions or the classrooms that these are proudly African-American environments.

Unanswered Questions

The Ratteray-Shujaa study is believed to be the first comprehensive look at a broad cross section of independent schools, especially schools that serve primarily African-American youth. It also highlights the need for further investigation in at least seven areas in order to clarify the role of independent schools and to assess their potential value to the larger educational system in America.

First, to understand the role that independent schools have had in

African-American achievement, it is necessary to examine historically the emergence of these schools and to consider some of the societal factors that helped propel them into existence. It is a truism that schools are designed to promote the interest of their creators. Therefore, in studying the effectiveness of schools for African-Americans and levels of student achievement, it is equally important to consider who created these institutions and why.

Second, school administrators, teachers, and parents in the Ratteray-Shujaa study reported that students in these schools are consistently ahead of their peers in government-operated schools. A number of independent schools measure student performance by tests such as the California Achievement Test because this is the test used by the government-operated schools in their area. Others rely on the Stanford Achievement Test, which is frequently utilized by traditional private schools. In addition, school personnel and families testify that children who are enrolled in these independent schools show dramatic improvements in their personal motivation toward achievement and the discipline of learning.

Their claims should be tested empirically, but some words of caution are appropriate. It is inevitable that African-American children will be compared to European-American children, for the pursuit of normative data is part of the formal language of our current educational system. However, the recent controversy that arose when many schools reported that their students are "above average" has put test makers on notice that the national sample of student might be out-of-date, perhaps by as many as seven years. Some critics also indicate that many students receive special preparation to which students in the Ratteray/Shujaa sample have not been exposed.

Furthermore, it is important to compare African-American children with themselves. Their benchmark or the nadir of their achievement should not focus entirely on European-American criteria, for African-Americans may have inherently higher standards themselves, and some may prefer to measure success with completely different instruments and perhaps even a different value system.

African-Americans have not yet developed for themselves normative standards that exist apart from traditional American standards. Nor has education research enabled mainstream education policy makers to study African-Americans from their own set of normative behavior, let alone separate benchmarks for different groups of African-Americans functioning in different settings. Instead, education research has been preoccupied with the "catch-up" model, which emphasizes that African-Americans lag behind the mainstream.

For example, educational programs for so-called "disadvantaged" youth, such as Head Start and Title I (now Chapter 1), have indeed fostered achievement trends. However, in spite of the billions of dollars spent on such programs and the short-term political gains that result from managing a program with seemingly immediate positive effects, no long-term achievement has ever been demonstrated for African-Americans or for children from any other ethnic group enrolled in these programs. An important reason for this is that little effort has been made to conduct research that would compare relationships within African-American achievement patterns before proceeding to cross-group analysis.

This appears to be more than mere oversight by researchers because there have been so many opportunities to evaluate these students in a homogeneous setting. For example, schools with enrollments of over 50 percent "minorities" declined from 77 percent in 1968 to 64 percent in 1972. In addition, schools reporting African-American enrollments of 90 percent or more declined from 64 percent in 1968 to 39 percent in 1972 and 33 percent in 1980. Therefore, the stability in the 1972-1980 data indicates that there still are large cohorts of African-American students in segregated environments, in spite of the substantial desegregation that has occurred since the late 1960s.

The third issue raised by the Ratteray-Shujaa study is the need to identify and describe the curriculum, materials, and techniques used by schools and teachers who have the most successful students; to compare them to the curricula, materials, and techniques used in schools where there is a high percentage of unsuccessful students. Then we need to determine the extent to which these elements contribute to student success.

The study indicates that many teachers rely heavily on teacher-made materials. They choose not to utilize commercially available classroom materials because they believe that most of these materials do not adequately represent African-Americans. The question to be answered is, "What contribution do these teacher-made materials make to any reported success of students?"

The fourth question is whether independent schools are capable of catering to the masses, or only to the talented few, or to both. During informal discussions, when African-American educators are presented with data from the Ratteray-Shujaa study, they usually insist that their first priority is to be concerned with the so-called "public" schools and say, "That's where most of our children are." Nevertheless, the study demonstrates that at independent schools, children acquire the basics and conquer the fundamental barriers to literacy. They also are motivated to have a sustained interest in a school setting.

Therefore, it may be worthwhile for educators to consider the possibility that independent schools are where the masses *should* be. If low-income African-American families send their children to government-operated schools only because they do not believe they can afford independent schools, the solution is not to continue pouring money into a failing system that destroys young minds in inner-city areas. Instead, educators should consider restructuring the flow of tax-generated income so that families can use it to choose the environment that best educates their children, even if it is an independent one.

It certainly will be unfortunate if African-Americans get caught in the same vice that gripped educators at the beginning of the twentieth century, when there was a national debate over the philosophies of Booker T. Washington and W. E. B. DuBois. The question then was whether the nation's resources should be focused on strategies that educate the masses of African-Americans, as opposed to concentrating on what DuBois called the "talented tenth." The debate was framed in the restrictive paradigm of dichotic thinking; it was all or nothing, with no consideration for a combination of the two.

The data are clear that American education today is not meeting the needs of the masses, especially since large numbers of 17-year-old "minority" youth are functionally illiterate. Furthermore, up to half of all students entering the ninth grade in urban school districts drop out within four years, presumably even before their illiteracy rate can be recorded. On the other hand, there is a paucity of data about the talented few. Who are they? In what types of academic environments do they flourish? What careers do they choose? We know that a tiny percentage continue their education in the more élite private schools, but what of the rest who are truly talented?

The fifth issue from the Ratteray-Shujaa study is the possibility of adaptation and replication. Can independent schools become part of a new approach to research on African-American children and influence the data set that is currently being generated from the larger bureaucratic settings?

In the past, African-Americans have been the target in countless achievement studies, but, more often than not, the perspective of African-Americans has not been the controlling factor in the design of this research. These studies have consumed millions of dollars defining why the African-American child is *not* achieving, rather than focusing on the strengths of these children and describing areas in which they do extremely well. Pivoting these studies to consider a broader universe of options and to focus on strengths might liberate educators in their thinking and allow them to build on the potential of African-American students.

Romanticizing about the virtues of limiting tax support to government schools is counterproductive, because we then fail to see the heights to which African-American learning can rise and at which it can be maintained. Both traditional private schools and inner-city government-operated schools create artificial environments that generate skewed data. The former tend to cater to the so-called "cream of the crop," while the latter serve large numbers of children with lower levels of achievement and also many who are labeled "underachieving."

Independent schools, however, are ideal laboratories in which African-American scholars can measure cohorts of children over time and in a variety of settings, not only because they are small in size but also because there is a broad mix of socioeconomic groups among the families and a wider range of achievement levels among the students. In addition, since the independent schools in our study are academic environments initiated by African-Americans themselves, yet another question becomes important: "Does a shift in the locus of control in education management have a positive impact on achievement levels?" Expanding achievement research to include students from these environments would provide some of the missing data that education policy makers so desperately need.

The sixth issue is the long-term effect of education in an independent school. Ethnographic interviews in the Ratteray-Shujaa study reveal that some children spend their entire academic careers in independent schools, some attend for fixed periods, while others move back and forth between public and private schools as family finances allow. One question that arises is: "How well do students who are trained in independent schools perform when they later transfer to public institutions?"

In addition, many African-Americans who now have highly successful public- and private-sector careers—at local, national, and international levels—are known to have attended independent schools. To what extent do alumni of these schools experience high achievement later in life? Is there any relationship between their success and unique elements in their training? Is success affected most by family and personal factors rather than by type of schooling?

The seventh unanswered question relates to the ultimate purpose of education for African-Americans. Families gave diverse reasons in their interviews, and there was no consensus among independent school educators. This issue of utility in education also plagues American education in general and in fact may be partly responsible for the national demise of achievement. The absence of goals for acquiring specific bits of knowledge deeply affects how a teacher can motivate children to achieve. Researchers, teachers of pedagogy, and classroom practitioners have been remiss in not speaking directly to concepts that interest African-American children. The child is told that education is important, but educators have failed miserably in providing a rationale that demonstrates why it is important.

For example, children are introduced to little analysis of how they can make a contribution to their own communities. Superficially, they may surmise that the community needs more garbage trucks to keep it clean, but how it gets clean remains part of the "magic" of government. Someone else, usually the equivalent of a white knight on a white charger, must show up to make the environment clean.

To carry the example one step further, our educational system has not focused, in recent years, on teaching children how to analyze the mathematical concepts involved in designing a machine that will collect trash. Nor is it likely to tell the child much about logistical issues in managing a city department that employs hundreds of trash collectors and support personnel. School systems certainly have few teachers qualified to discuss entrepreneurial strategies for financing, marketing, and sustaining a private trash collection service. Even fewer teachers can speak with the fervor, animation, and motivating spirit that comes from having operated any institution competitively, whether for individual profit *or* for the collective profit of a group.

Our educational system has created such a void between theoretical curricula and the practical effects of knowledge that most children do not understand why they need to learn certain concepts. Therefore, they often lose interest in the entire exercise and, as a result, achievement declines.

African-American children should be given a robust intellectual agenda. They need to be challenged not only to develop new ideas but also to understand how they can be utilized, what steps are needed to make those ideas operational, and their specific obligations as students to prepare themselves to accomplish their dreams in spite of socioeconomic obstacles.

Conclusion

African-American pursuit of independent education has very deep roots. For hundreds of years, each generation has found new resolve to break away from government-sponsored education and to continue the struggle for an independent African-American mind. Whether in tutorials or in five-day programs, whether operated by community centers, churches, or for-profit businesses, achievement always has been the goal.

Children and their parents should be told the story of how independent schools have survived in spite of the odds against them. They need to learn that African-Americans have successfully built their own institutions and that all learning does not emanate from a European value system. Educators and policy makers, too, should learn to appreciate the story of independent schools. These institutions can lead educators to understand more fully the relationship between theory and practice and to identify some of the unique factors that motivate the African-American child.

Finally, African-American children must learn very early in their schooling that the purpose of education is not just to *get* a job but to *make* a job. They must learn that developing the intellect is important not only for survival but for *independence* as well.

In order to take their rightful place in American education, these schools should be sustained as a national resource. The productivity of their teachers and administrators and the performance of their students should be enhanced. Efforts at education reform should ensure that independent schools are allowed to speak to the issue of African-American achievement. By being so recognized, independent schools can make a significant contribution to the productivity of the United States and to our global economy in the twenty-first century.

Notes

1. These institutions are commonly referred to as "public" schools, although this label denies the legitimacy of independent schools that also serve the public and therefore merit public support.

2. Operating data on the schools were obtained in telephone interviews with administrators from 211 schools, and, in addition, a representative sample of 75 schools responded to a detailed written survey.

3. Administrators from 38 schools agreed to participate in a study of their families. Written surveys were received from 399 randomly selected families, and 35 families whose children attended 10 schools gave in-depth interviews.

4. The data show that 24 percent of the families earn less than $15,000. There are 33 percent between $15,000 and $29,000; 30 percent between $30,000 and $49,000; and 13 percent earn more than $50,000.

13 Visions for Children: Educating Black Children in the Context of Their Culture

JANICE HALE-BENSON

The Corners of My Mind Remember

I look across the waters at a strange new
    land
Yet, the corners of my mind remember
It remembers me standing on its shores
A child of its soil
A child of its culture
Oh—to experience its magnificence once
    again
To know Africa as one of its beings
Let me dance in the African air
Let me feel the strength of a culture rich
For I am its child
A seed
Pulled from its soil.

Jeannette Curtis in
I Speak to You

Pulitzer award-winning playwright August Wilson warns Afro-Americans about the danger of separating ourselves from our African heritage. An *Ebony Magazine* (1987) interview quotes, "Woe to the fellow who can only sing other peoples' songs and has none of his own." "He a man done forgot his song," warns Wilson's rootworker in "Joe Turner's Come and Gone." "He a man done forgot his song. Forgot how to sing it. A fellow forget that and he forget who he is. Forget how he's supposed to mark down life."

209

Wilson uses the song as a metaphor for the cultural heritage that Blacks should retain and celebrate:

> There is an Africa in each of us that we have to get in touch with to understand our relationship to this society. When white folks look at us, they see everything that they are not. If they can make everything we are bad, that makes everything they are good. If they look at us and see "dumb," that means they must be intelligent. If we accept that, then we look at them as being intelligent and conclude that we are dumb. When we do that we have no identity, no self-determination, no self-respect.
>
> But all we have to do is to claim that part of ourselves which I think is the strongest part—our Africanism. It has nothing to do with putting on beads or dashiki's. It's simply understanding who we are in the world, understanding our relationship to this society and claiming a responsibility for ourselves and our salvation instead of letting other people claim that for us.

Wilson's words echo a question that is being raised by Black scholars. It is the question of whether we can bring about an improvement in educational outcomes for Black children without recognizing their culture. Since the 1950s, desegregation has been a focal point for educational reform that is designed to benefit Black children.

The critical issue that is being raised by Black scholars is how can we create schools that educate Black children effectively wherever they are found. Early childhood is the time to begin examining learning and care-giving settings.

The education of white children is relatively more successful than that of Black children because the schools were designed for white children. As Hakim Rashid (1981) has stated:

> Children from non-European, lower socioeconomic-status cultural groups are at a disadvantage in the schools because the American educational system has evolved out of a European philosophical, theoretical, and pedagogical context (p. 57).

Moreover, the education of white children proceeds relatively more smoothly than that of Black children because they are involved in an interrelated learning experience that complements their culture. To achieve equal educational outcomes for Black children, it will be necessary to design an educational system that complements rather than opposes Black culture.

W. E. B. DuBois (1903) described the Black person in America as having two warring souls. On one hand, Black people are the product of their African heritage and culture. On the other hand, they are shaped by the demands of Euro-American culture. Unfortunately, the Euro-American influence has always been emphasized to the exclusion of the African influence. Said another way, despite the pressure of 400 years in America, African-Americans have not melted into the pot. Rashid (1981) has pointed out that:

> The cultural and biological history of African-Americans has resulted in an "essentially African" group of people who must function in "essentially European" schools (p. 58).

Educational change will not occur until we conceptualize Black children within the context of their culture in early childhood educational and care-giving settings. We must devise educational strategies that are appropriate for them. Interrelated learning environments must be created wherein African-American culture in all of its diversity is integrated throughout the curriculum and the politics of the classroom.

It is important to acknowledge the dual socialization that is required for Black children because early childhood education can play an important role in fostering biculturalism in African-American children, thereby reducing the internal conflict that these children experience which depletes their energy and clouds their perceptions.

The "intervention" strategies of the 1960s are passé. Recent research by Black scholars (Rashid, 1981; Hale-Benson, 1986) has rejected this notion that Black children are culturally or cognitively deprived. They are members of a culture endowed with specific modes of cognition.

Early childhood educational and care-giving settings must search for cultural continuity—not intervention. Rashid (1981) states that:

> The preschool experience must therefore provide a dynamic blend of African-American culture and that culture which is reflected in the Euro-American educational setting. . . . The African-American child who only sees the Euro-American cultural tradition manifested in the preschool environment can only conclude that the absence of visual representation of his culture connotes his essential worthlessness (p. 60).

Visions For Children

Visions for Children is a program which emphasizes the special characteristics of Afro-American children, offering a teaching method and curriculum which encourages children to learn the information and skills necessary for upward mobility, career achievement, and financial independence in the American mainstream. At the same time, they feel pride in their own ethnic culture and are able to identify with and contribute to the development of their people.

This program is based on the model described in *Black Children: Their Roots, Culture and Learning Styles* (Hale-Benson, 1986). It is funded by the Cleveland Foundation. A distinctive feature is the emphasis on teaching young children cognitive skills while strengthening their self-esteem and identity as Afro-Americans.

The teaching method emphasizes Afro-American culture and integrates it in all of its diversity throughout the curriculum. The children learn about Africa and their rich cultural heritage; they learn about Afro-American and African arts and crafts; they listen to folktales and stories written by Afro-American writers; they listen to music and learn about musicians that emerge from Black culture; they learn about heroes in Black history such as Dr. Martin Luther King, Jr.

In sum, the children in this program are surrounded with messages that get them started on the right track in realizing that there is pride in being beautiful Black children who can hold their own in a competitive society.

Visions for Children emphasizes the development of cognitive skills, such as reasoning, memory, problem-solving, creativity, and language skills. Progress is assessed using both teacher-made and standardized instruments. Even though standardized instruments can contain inherent biases toward minority children, a goal of this program is to demystify these tests for parents and to help the children perform well on such measures.

There is a strong correlation between language facility and performing well on standardized measures in the professional work world. Therefore, Visions for Children's focus is on language skills. This includes expressive as well as receptive language. Too often children receive language through listening, but do not have enough opportunities to engage in expressive language. Expressive language includes holding conversations with adults, telling stories from pictures, engaging in socio-dramatic play, and responding to questions in complete sentences.

Visions for Children Curriculum

Language/communication skills.   Language-related skills are critical in the education of children. A high correlation exists between elementary school reading achievement test scores and standardized college admissions tests. The correlation suggests that a huge proportion of what is being measured in "intelligence" and "achievement" tests are language/communication skills.

Black children are very expressive in the use of oral language. However, there is a need to broaden their skills to include those that are called for as a precursor to reading and writing proficiency. Therefore, speaking, listening, labeling, storytelling, chanting, imitating, and reciting are encouraged.

The children are engaged in literacy activities that foster higher order thinking skills. Computers are used in combination with the Language Experience Approach in which the children compose stories and learn to read words that occur naturally in their vocabulary. Emphasis is placed on idea generation as a precursor to writing skills.

Cognitive skills. There are cognitive skills that lay the foundation for more advanced intellectual activity that should be strengthened in the early years. There are age-appropriate activities that are designed to strengthen the child's abilities in the areas of memory, reasoning, problem-solving, creativity, and play.

Mathematical concepts. Black children are able to master a wide range of mathematical skills in their everyday lives (like computing baseball batting averages), but they have difficulty demonstrating their skills in the classroom. Therefore, emphasis is placed on developing mathematical proficiency in this model program. The children learn about sets, seriation, time, measurements, and other mathematical concepts.

Positive self-concept and positive attitude toward learning and school. This affective goal is included as an overall curricular emphasis because children should not be imbued with cognitive skills at the expense of a consideration for the way they feel about themselves, the teacher, learning, and school. Educators must be sensitive to the many, as yet unidentified, ways in which Black children are "turned off" and "pushed out" of school.

Providing children with successful experiences, enabling them to be self-motivating, and establishing a life-long love of learning is equally as important as helping them perform well on achievement tests. It is also important to help children develop social skills which include manners, courtesy, positive personal relationships, and the ability to resolve conflicts nonviolently.

Disciplinary practices are designed to teach the children how to reason. Too often children are told what not to do, but they are not taught how to determine the proper behavior for themselves. Disciplinary situations are opportunities for teaching. The purpose of discipline is to achieve self-management.

Afro-American studies. Afro-American studies is a focal point and is also integrated throughout the curriculum of this model. Every opportunity is used to acquaint the children with the culture, cosmology, and history of Africans of the diaspora. As a result of this exposure, the children have more information about Black culture and increased pride in their racial heritage.

A purpose of this curriculum is to widen the world of the children and provide them with a variety of experiences. The curriculum includes countless topics and information drawn from numerous disciplines that are presented on the level of the child. The curriculum includes science, art, music, creative movement, geography, nutrition, history, social studies, economics, literature, and philosophy. However, these areas of the curriculum are taught in an integrated manner through field trips, speakers, movies, units, and incidental learning.

African studies.   The children are exposed to aspects of African culture appropriate to their level of understanding—foods, geography, fashions, music, instruments, songs, poetry, names, history, and art. An important part of fostering a positive self-identity is creating pride in the homeland of Black children's ancestors—Africa. There is a need to counteract the myths and stereotypes perpetuated by the mass media about Africa. The emphasis in African studies is West Africa. However, a monthly theme is devoted to Egypt. Afro-Caribbean culture is explored through monthly themes on Jamaica and Haiti.

Literacy.   Reading readiness is an important part of Visions for Children. The children are constantly surrounded by opportunities to learn to read. Items in the environment that have meaning for them are labeled. Words are written on bulletin boards, papers, and walls so that they will learn to recognize words in an incidental, meaningful day.

Psychomotor skills.   An important feature of the program is the development of gross and fine motor skills. Frequent opportunities are provided for physical release and for the children to teach themselves through play. Movement activities are used frequently in the learning process. The classroom is organized to permit maximum child movement with as much self-direction as is practical. An indoor exercise and play area is provided as well as an outdoor playground. The children are also taught creative movement, African dance, and drumming.

Computer skills.   The children are taught how to operate computers. Software is selected that emphasizes the interactive capabilities of computers. They also practice basic skills and produce artwork.

Cultural arts.   An important feature of the program is an emphasis on the cultural arts including music, creative movement, sculpture, painting, arts and crafts, woodworking, dramatics, and poetry. The children take monthly field trips to places such as the Art Museum to see exhibits of

African masks, the Afro-American Museum to see photographic exhibits, and plays in the community. They are also exposed to Afro-American and Anglo-American cultural events.

Features of the Model

High affective support. The classrooms have a high adult-child ratio, small-group learning, peer tutoring, and heterogeneous grouping (family style). All of the teachers teach all of the children in a kind of extended family system. The children are grouped into African ethnic groups and rotate among the teachers. This permits the teachers to collectively evaluate the children. Frequent touching, lap-sitting, holding hands, and hugging are encouraged.

Self-concept development. Children's self-confidence is fostered through frequent compliments, praise, displays of work, performances, open houses, and regular successful experiences. Care is given that children's work is often displayed.

Creative expression. Opportunities for all types of creative expression permeate the curriculum. The visual, dramatic, and musical arts are encouraged.

Enrichment experiences. Monthly field trips are planned that correlate with the theme for the month. However, a variety of "teachers" from the community are regularly brought into the classroom to teach special skills.

Holidays. Attention is given to the politics of holidays, particularly as they affect the history of Black and other oppressed people in America. For example, Thanksgiving is not a purely religious holiday. Most discussions of Thanksgiving convey the point of view of the "pilgrims." The perspectives of Native Americans and Afro-Americans are generally ignored. The focus of holidays is to be celebrations, commemorations, and role models who revolve around events and historical figures pivotal in Afro-American history. Among the events celebrated are:

Emancipation Proclamation
Dr. Martin Luther King, Jr., Day
Juneteenth
Malcolm X's Birthday
Kwanzaa
14th Amendment to the Constitution

Visions for Children Teaching Strategies

Body language.   Black children are proficient in nonverbal communication. Our teachers are sensitive in their use of gesture, eye-contact, and other nonverbal cues.

Standard English.   Standard English is modeled, and children's speech is informally (in a low-key, nonpunitive manner) corrected. This modeling and correcting are very important in early childhood because if a child does not "hear" certain sounds and develop the ability to reproduce them early in life, it becomes more difficult to change speech patterns later. More research is needed into the instructional needs of Black English speakers; however, one fact is clear: speaking standard English is a skill needed by Black children for upward mobility in American society and it should be taught in early childhood. At no time is baby talk spoken. The teachers speak in complete sentences and encourage the children to do so.

Equal talking time.   Teacher "talk" is regulated to the approximate amount of child talk. Laura Lein (1975) found in her study of Black migrant children that the children spoke more frequently and used more complex sentences outside of school with peers and parents. This phenomenon occurred because the peers and parents talked about the same amount as the children, who spoke least to the teacher in school, seemingly because the teacher talked a greater proportion of the time.

The teacher encourages the children to talk conversationally, in recitation, and creatively.

Enriching interactions with adults and peers.   An emphasis is given to small-group learning and hands-on contact with the teacher. Black children benefit from enriched interactions with adults and peers.

A variety of learning activities.   Children are taught with a varied format for learning activities—movement, games, music, prose, poetry.

Music in the classroom.   Afro-American music permeates the curriculum. Jazz, rhythm and blues, spirituals, and folk music is played throughout the day (whenever it is practical). Black children are exposed to music in their homes, and it is relaxing to them. Some teachers have reported that discipline problems decreased and productivity increased when music was played in classrooms with Black children (Personal conversations with teachers in Storrs, Connecticut). The children are also taught about the recording artists.

Visions for Children Equipment and Materials

Play equipment.   Many studies have found that Black children are more kinesthetic than white children, have a broader range of movements, and need to expend energy more constantly (Hale-Benson, 1986). Also, physical activity and sports are encouraged in Afro-American culture. Therefore, the children are encouraged to develop their large muscles utilizing the indoor and outdoor play equipment in the center.

Learning materials.   Open-ended learning materials are utilized: clay, water play, sandboxes, manipulatives, socio-dramatic play props (dress-up clothes, fabric for creative wrapping). Learning games are chosen that emphasize challenge, not competition.

Research Design

The research component of Visions for Children was funded for two years by the Council for Economic Opportunities of Greater Cleveland. It is presently funded by the Cleveland Foundation.

All children enrolled in Visions for Children are tested each year on the child development measures described below. A control group of children is also tested. All children in the study will be tested each year as they matriculate in the primary grades. These data will be analyzed longitudinally to establish the long-term effects of the program and to revise the curriculum based on these outcomes.

The data below are for the first two years of testing. Kindergarten scores for the first cohort are reported in this chapter. These scores provide information on the cognitive abilities of the children at the initiation of the study. These data will be useful as we measure changes in test scores as the children progress through the program and elementary school.

Research Questions of the Study and Relationship to Visions for Children Child Development Measures

Listed below are the research questions and the measures of the study based upon a review of the tests and measurements literature and a national consultation with experts in the field.

1. Does exposure to the Visions for Children program result in measurable gains in the cognitive abilities of Afro-American children?

The McCarthy Scales of Children's Abilities (MSCA).   This is a measure of children's overall cognitive skills. It is an individually administered test of general cognitive abilities which can be used with children from 2½ to 8 years of age; administration time for children under 5 years of age is approximately 45-50 minutes. The test consists of 18 individual subtests which form six scales: verbal, perceptual-performance, quantitative, memory, motor, and an overall general cognitive index (GCI—made up of the verbal, quantitative, and perceptual-performance scales). While there is considerable, ongoing debate about bias in IQ measures with Black children, the test still provides useful information about children's overall cognitive abilities.

The MSCA has many assets which counterbalance some of the liabilities of using IQ measures with Black children. (The majority of my reviewers do not call it an IQ measure.) In general, the psychometric properties of the MSCA are good. The standardization sample for the test is excellent and fairly recent. In addition, validity and reliability are acceptable. Another strength of the MSCA is that it is appealing to children. Materials are colorful and stimulating, and the individual subtests are relatively short so that the children do not tend to have difficulties attending to task. Also, unlike other measures, the MSCA contains a motor component, with both gross and fine motor tasks.

2. Does attendance at the Visions for Children program result in Afro-American children becoming more in-group oriented? There is a tendency for Black children to prefer white physical traits and to attribute more positive characteristics to white people than to Black people. A major question of the study is whether participating in an early childhood education program with an Afro-American cultural component reverses that trend.

Preschool Racial Attitudes Measure (PRAM II).   This is a picture test that is designed to assess racial bias among pre-literate children. It has excellent reliability and validity.

3. Are there distinctive styles that characterize the behavior of Afro-American children in classrooms? There is evidence in the literature that there is cultural dissonance between Afro-American culture and the culture of the schools (Rashid, 1981). This measure will be administered as a first step to examining relevant dimensions of classroom behavior.

Report of Child Behavior, by Earl Schaeffer.   This is a very recently developed instrument that has the virtue of evaluating more normal and less pathological behavior than many of the other instruments that are available. Many of the others are seeking to identify juvenile delinquency rather than normal classroom adjustment. They result in being biased against Black male children.

4. Does participation in the Visions for Children program empower Afro-American children and enhance their self-esteem?

Pictorial scale of perceived competence and social accep-tance.   This is a self-concept measure that examines perceived compe-tence and social acceptance. It has four subscales: cognitive competence, physical competence, peer acceptance, and maternal acceptance. Susan Harter, the author, has done some excellent work in the area of self-concept for older children, and this is a recently developed scale for preschool and kindergarten children.

5. Does participation in the visions for Children program enhance the ability of Afro-American children to engage in sustained effort for delayed rewards?

Delay of gratification.   A technique developed by Conrad Schwarz is used. Teachers rate the children on their ability to defer gratification, an important skill needed for achievement.

6. Does participation in the Visions for Children program result in measurable gains in reading readiness skills useful for success in kindergarten?

Achievement—Metropolitan Reading Readiness Test.   This will be an outcome measure for the children entering kindergarten. The test is a group administered, multiple-skill battery which takes approximately 80-90 minutes for children to complete. There are two levels available, with Level 1 being appropriate for the children beginning kindergarten. The kindergarten version of this test was recommended over the kindergarten version of the Stanford Achievement test. The Metropolitan is more appealing and takes less time to administer.

The test is used extensively and has good organization and clarity. In addition, a great deal of psychometric work has been carried out which demonstrates substantial reliability and validity of the test. In general, the test can provide useful screening information pertaining to achievement-oriented skills useful upon school entrance.

7. Does participation in the Visions for Children program result in measurable gains in achievement-oriented skills?

Achievement—Stanford Achievement Test.   This is an outcome measure for the children entering first grade and at the completion of each year of the primary grades. The test is a group-administered, multiple-skill battery. There are two levels available. Stanford Early School Achievement Test (SESAT) 1 is generally used for kindergarten, and SESAT 2 is generally used for first grade.

The test takes approximately 1½ to 2½ hours for children to complete. It is recommended that it be given in two to three sittings. The test is used extensively and has good organization and clarity. In addition, a great deal of psychometric work has been carried out which demonstrates substantial reliability and validity of the test. In general, the test can provide useful information pertaining to achievement-oriented skills.

Description of the Control Group

The control group for the study is a day care center located in Cleveland, OH. This center has provided child care services in the Cleveland Clinic area for 17 years. The hours of operation are 6:30 a.m.-5:30 p.m., Monday through Friday, year round. The center serves families with children ages 18 months-8 years, including full-day kindergarten, after-school, and holiday care for school-age children, and a toddler program for children still in diapers.

Characteristics of the children. An important consideration in selecting a control group was matching Visions children on the dimension of socioeconomic status. This is an important variable for Black children. Without such controls, it could be argued that any differences in the achievement of the children was due to socioeconomic characteristics of the families.

We used the Hollingshead Four Factor Index of Social Status which creates a score based upon parent education, parent occupation, sex, and marital status.

An overall T-test was conducted on age of the subjects in both groups and the Hollingshead scores to determine whether the two groups of children were comparable.

The overall average age of the Visions children was 47.13 months and the average age of the control group children was 45.00 months. (Only children who fell within the age groups served at Visions were selected for the control group.) There was no significant difference in age. The data are summarized in Table 13.1.

Table 13.1

Age

LOCATION	N	AVERAGE AGE IN MONTHS	STD DEV	T
Control	40	45.00	11.15	
Visions	51	47.13	7.90	-1.03 ns

The overall Hollingshead score for the Visions children was 42.05. The overall Hollingshead score for the control group children was 41.95. There was no significant difference in the scores between the two groups. The data are summarized in Table 13.2.

Table 13.2

Hollingshead Social Class Measure

LOCATION	N	AVERAGE SCORE	STD DEV	T
Control	40	41.95	10.09	
Visions	51	42.05	14.98	-0.04 ns

Summary of Data Analysis

A summary of the measures administered during phases 1 and 2 reveals that the Visions children scored higher on six tests during phase 1 and the control group children scored higher on two. There were nine tests on which there was no significant difference in the scores. During phase 2, neither the Visions children nor the control children scored higher on any tests. There were nonsignificant differences between the groups on all seventeen of the tests administered.

Gain scores refer to the tests on which the children who were tested in both phases 1 and 2 achieved gains in their scores in the second testing. The Visions children had higher gains scores on two tests, the control group children had higher gains scores on four, and there was a nonsignificant difference between the two groups on 11 of the tests administered.

On the Metropolitan Reading Readiness Test, there were no tests on which the Visions children scored higher. The control group children scored higher on three tests. There was a nonsignificant difference between the groups on six tests.

The first two rounds of testing are considered to be baseline measures because the program was in the initial developmental phases. Future gains will be evaluated against these scores. The control group was selected because it is a quality early childhood education center. It was felt that any gains demonstrated by the Visions for Children project would only be noteworthy if it was compared to an established, quality program. The control group program has been in operation for 17 years. The staff in the control group also has a higher level of training than the Visions staff. Therefore, the high number of test scores with a nonsignificant difference is a very good beginning.

Project Outcome

Visions for Children is designed to be a demonstration program that can serve as an early childhood education model for Afro-American children. A product will be a published curriculum that has been field tested. It will contain a bibliography of materials that can serve as a resource for programs based on this model.

Plans are underway for the development of a companion component that can be used for parent education to complement the preschool curriculum.

Visions for Children is a first step toward achieving an educational process described by Dr. Benjamin E. Mays, the late President-Emeritus of Morehouse College:

> To be unshackled,
> to improve the mind,
> to mold the character,
> to dream dreams,
> to develop the body,
> to aspire for greatness,
> or to strive for excellence
> is the birthright of every child
> born into the world.
> And no society has the right
> to smother ambition,
> to curb motivation,
> and to circumscribe the mind.

Bibliography

Introduction

Bowles, S., & Gintis, H. (1976). *Schooling in capitalist America: Educational reform and the contradictions of economic life.* New York: Basic.

Coleman, J. et al. (1965). *Equality of educational opportunity.* Washington, DC: U.S. Printing Office.

The Council of the Great City Schools. (1987). *Challenge to urban education: Results in the making: A report of the Council of the Great City Schools.* Washington, DC: Author.

Edmonds, R. (1979). Effective schools for the urban poor. *Educational Leadership, 37,* 15-24.

Hale-Benson, J. (1986). *Black children: Their roots, culture, and learning styles (rev. ed.).* Baltimore: The Johns Hopkins University.

Jencks, C., Smith, M., Acland, H., Bane, M.J., Cohen, D., Gintis, H., Heyns, B., & Michaelson, S. (1972). *Inequality: A reassessment of the effect of family and schooling in America.* New York: Basic.

Jensen, A. (1969). How much can we boost IQ and scholastic achievement? *Harvard Educational Review, 39*(1), 1-123.

Karenga, M. (1984). *Introduction to Black studies.* Los Angeles: Kawaida.

Lomotey, K. (1989). Cultural diversity in the urban school: Implications for principals. *NASSP Bulletin. 73*(521), 81-88.

The New York Times. (1986, February 11). p. 6.

Ogbu, J. (1978). *Minority education and caste: The American system in cross-cultural perspective.* New York: Academic.

Purkey, S. C., & Smith, M. S. (1982). *Effective schools—A review.* Madison: Wisconsin Center for Education Research.

Shockley, W., (1972). A debate challenge: Geneticity is 80% for white identical twins' I.Q.'s. *Phi Delta Kappan, 53*(6), 415-419.

Suzuki, B. H. (1977). Education and the socialization of Asian Americans: A revisionist analysis of the "model minority" thesis. *Amerasia, 4*(2), 23-51.

Willie, C. V. (1987). *Effective education: A minority policy perspective.* New York: Greenwood.

Wilson, A. (1987). *The developmental psychology of the Black child.* New York: Africana Research.
Wilson, R., & Melendez, S.E., (1985). *Fourth annual status report on minorities in higher education, 1985.* Washington, DC: American Council on Education.

Chapter 2

Adler, M. J. (1982). *The paideia proposal: An educational manifesto.* New York: Macmillan.
Adler, M. J. (1983a). *Paideia problems and possibilities.* New York: Macmillan.
Adler, M. J. (1983b). The paideia proposal: A symposium. *Harvard Educational Review, 53,* 377-411.
Boyer, E. L. (1983). *High school: A report on secondary education in America.* New York: Harper & Row.
Brookover, W. B., & Lezotte, L. W. (1979). *Changes in school characteristics coincident with changes in student achievement.* East Lansing, MI: Institute for Research on Teaching.
Brookover, W. B. et al. (1979). *School social systems and student achievement: Schools can make a difference.* New York: Praeger.
Brookover, W. B. et al. (1983). *Creating effective schools.* Holmes Beach: Learning Publications.
Butts, R. F. (1982). The revival of civic learning requires a prescribed curriculum. *Liberal Education,* 377-401.
Coleman, J. (1966). "Equality of educational opportunity." Washington, DC: U.S. Printing Office.
Coleman, M. (1983, November 21). Education rights policy decried by key groups. *The Washington Post,* p. A-4.
The College Board. (1983). *Academic preparation for college: What students need to know and be able to do.* New York: Author.
Cummings, J. (1983). Breakup of black family imperils gains of decades. *The New York Times,* pp. 1, 56.
Daedalus, 112, (1983, Summer). "The Arts and Humanities in America's Schools."
Daniel, W. G. (1964). Problems of disadvantaged youth, urban and rural. *The Journal of Negro Eduction, 33,* 218-224.
DiLorenzo, A. (1983). *Tuition tax credits.* Washington, DC: NEA Government Relations.
Docksai, R. F. (1981). Education. In C. L. Heatherly (Ed.), *Mandate for leadership* (pp. 163-211). Washington, DC: The Heritage Foundation.
Edmonds, R. R. (1979a). Effective schools for the urban poor. *Educational Leadership, 37,* 15-27.
Edmonds, R. R. (1979b). Some schools work and more can. *Social Policy, 9,* 28-32.
Edmonds, R. R. (1979c). *A discussion of the literature and issues related to effective schooling.* Cambridge, MA: Center for Urban Studies, Harvard Graduate School of Education.

Education Commission of the States, Task Force on Education for Economic Growth. (1983). *Action for excellence: A comprehensive plan to improve our nation's schools.* Denver: Author.

Educational Researcher, 12, (1983, April).

Educational Research Service, Inc. (1983). *Merit pay plans for teachers: Status and descriptions.* Arlington, VA: Educational Research Service.

Elam, S. M. (1983). The Gallup Education Survey. *Phi Delta Kappan,* pp. 26-32.

Featherstone, J. (1971). *Schools where children learn.* New York: Liveright.

Featherstone, J. (1976). *What schools can do.* New York: Liveright.

Fiske, E. B. (1983). High schools stiffen diploma requirements. *The New York Times,* pp. 1, 68.

Glick, P. C. (1981). A demographic picture of black families. In H. P. McAdoo (Ed.), *Black Families* (p. 107). Beverly Hills: Sage Publications.

Goodlad, J. I. (1983). *A place called school: Prospects for the future.* New York: McGraw-Hill.

Hanrahan, J., & Kosterlitz, J. (1983). School for scandal. *Common Cause Magazine, 9*(5), 16-25.

Heatherly, C. L. (Ed.), (1981). *Mandate for leadership: Policy management in a conservative administration.* Washington, DC: The Heritage Foundation.

Howe, Harold, II. (1983). Education moves to center stage: An overview of recent studies. *Phi Delta Kappan, 65,* 167-172.

Jencks, C., Smith, M., Acland, H., Bane, M. J., Cohen, D., Gintis, H., Heyns, B., & Michaelson, S. (1972). *Inequality: A reassessment of the effect of family and schooling in America.* New York: Basic.

Jensen, A. (1969). How much can we boost IQ and scholastic achievement? *Harvard Educational Review, 39*(19), 1-123.

Kemerer, F. R. (1983). New supreme court support for private schools. *Kappa Delta Pi Record, 20,* 4-8.

Kurtz, H. (1983). School boards tighten up requirements. *The Washington Post,* p. A4.

Lazar, I., & Darlington, R. (1978). *Lasting effects after preschool.* [Final Report, Abstract, HEW Grant 90C-1311 to the Education Commission of the States]. Ithaca, NY: Consortium for Longitudinal Studies.

Levine, D. U. (1982). Successful approaches for improving academic achievement in inner-city elementary schools. *Phi Delta Kappan, 63,* 523-526.

McKenzie, F. D. (1983, June 26). A predominantly black urban school system can—and does—work. *The Washington Post,* p. D-8.

Morris, V. C., Crowson, R. L., Porter-Gehrie, C., & Hurwitz, Jr., E. (1984). *Principals in action: The reality of managing schools.* Columbus: Charles E. Merrill.

Morris, V. C. et al. (1983). *The urban principal: Discretionary decision-making in a large educational organization.* Panel at the American Educational Studies Association's annual convention, Milwaukee.

Moynihan, D. P., & Mosteller, F. (1972). *On equality of educational opportunity.* New York: Vintage.

National Center for Education Statistics. (1980). *The American high school: A statistical overview.* Washington, DC: U.S. Government Printing Office.

National Center for Education Statistics. (1982). *Digest of Education Statistics.* Washington, DC: U.S. Government Printing Office.

National Center for Education Statistics. (1983). *The condition of education.* Washington, DC: U.S. Government Printing Office.

National Commission on Excellence in Education. (1983). *A nation at risk: The imperative for educational reform.* Washington, DC: U.S. Government Printing Office.

The National Science Board Commission on Precollege Education in Mathematics, Science and Technology. (1983). *Educating Americans for the 21st Century: A Plan of Action for Improving Mathematics, Science and Technology Education for All American Elementary and Secondary Students so that Their Achievement is the Best in the World by 1995.*

Ogbu, J. U. (1983). Schooling the inner city. *Society, 21,* pp. 75-79.

Passow, A. H. (1963a). *Education in depressed areas.* New York: Teachers College Press.

Passow, A. H., & Daniel, W. B. (1963b). Time is now: Some educational imperatives for 1964. *The Journal of Negro Education, 33,* 1-5.

Ralph, J. H., & Fennessey, J. (1983). Science or reform: Some questions about the effective school model. *Phi Delta Kappan, 65,* 689-694.

Rutter, M., et al. (1979). *Fifteen thousand hours: Secondary schools and their effects on children.* Cambridge, MA: Harvard University.

Schweinhart, L. J., & Weikart, D. P. (1980). *Young children grow up: The effects of the Perry preschool program on youths through age 15.* Ypsilanti, MI: High/Scope.

Sizemore, B. A., Brossard, C. A., & Harrigan, B. (1983). *An abashing anomaly: The high achieving predominantly black elementary school* [Mimeographed]. Pittsburgh, PA: University of Pittsburgh.

Thomas, W. F. (1979). "If minimum competency tests establish standards that your schools don't meet, you could lose a malpractice lawsuit." *The Executive Educator, 1* (8), 19-20.

The Twentieth Century Fund. (1983). *Making the grade: Report of the twentieth Century Fund task force on federal elementary and secondary education policy.* New York: Author.

U.S. Bureau of the Census. (1982). *Population profile of the United States: 1981.* Washington, DC: U.S. Government Printing Office.

Watson, B. C. (1980). Education: A matter of grave concern. In *The State of Black America 1980* (pp. 59-93). New York: National Urban League.

Watson, B. C. (1981). The quality of education for Black Americans. In *The State of Black America 1981* (pp. 61-85). New York: National Urban League, Inc.

Watson, B. C. (1982). Public education: A search for sanity and humanity. In *The State of Black America 1982* (pp. 141-170). New York: National Urban League, Inc.

Weber, G. (1971). *Inner-city children can be taught to read: Four successful schools.* Washington, DC: Council for Basic Education.

Weinberg, M. (1983). Great expectations typify honored schools. *The Washington Post,* p. C4.

Wise, A. E., & Darling-Hammond, L. (1983). Educational vouchers regulating their efficiency and effectiveness. *Educational Researcher, 12*(9), 9-12, 17-18.

Chapter 3

Bardach, E. (1977). *The implementation game.* Cambridge, MA: MIT Press.

Berman, P. (1986). From compliance to learning: Implementing legally-induced reform. In D. L. Kirp, & D. N. Jensen (Eds.), *School days, rule days: The legalization and regulation of education.* Philadelphia: The Falmer Press.

Berman, P., & McLaughlin, M. W. (1976). Implementation of educational innovation. *Educational Forum, 40,* 345-370.

Bliss, J. (1988). Public school administrators in the United States: An analysis of supply and demand. In D. E. Griffiths, R. T. Stout, & P. B. Forsyth (Eds.), *Leaders for America's schools.* Berkeley, CA: McCutchan.

Chubb, J. E., & Moe, T. M. (1986, Fall). No school is an island. *The Bookings Review, 4*(4), 21-36.

Cuban, L. (1984, November). School reform by remote control: SB813 in California. *Phi Delta Kappan, 66*(3), 213-217.

Cuban, L. (1986). *Teachers and machines.* New York: Teachers College Press.

Deal, T. E., & Kennedy, A. A. (1982). *Corporate cultures: The rites and rituals of corporate life.* Reading, MA: Addison-Wesley Publishing Company.

Doyle, D. P., & Finn, C. E., Jr. (1984, Fall). American schools and the future of local control. *The Public Interest, 77,* 77-95.

Edmonds, R. (1979). Effective schools for the urban poor. *Educational Leadership.* 37(1), 15-23.

Elmore, R. F. (1978). Organizational models of program implementation. In D. Mann (Ed.), *Making change happen?* New York: Teachers College Press.

Elmore, R. F. (1983). Complexity and control: What public policy. In L. S. Shulman & G. Sykes (Eds.), *Handbook of teaching and policy.* New York: Longman.

Emery, F. E., & Trist, E. L. (1965). The causal texture of organizational environments. *Human Relations, 19,* 21-32.

Epstein, J. (1984, Winter). School policy and parent involvement: Research results. *Educational Horizons, 62*(2), 70-72.

Fullan, M. (1985). Change processes and strategies at the local level. *Elementary School Journal, 85*(3), 391-421.

Gormley, W. T., Jr. (1987). A critical review. *Journal of Policy Analysis and Management, 6*(2), 153-169.

Guthrie, J. W. (1986, December). School-based management: The next needed education reform. *Phi Delta Kappan, 64*(4), 305-309.

Johnson, S. M. (1986). Incentives for teachers: What motivates, what matters. *Educational Administration Quarterly, 22*(3), 54-79.

Kirst, M. W. (1987, April). Curricular leadership at the state level: What is the new focus? *NASSP Bulletin, 71*(498), 8-14.

Landau, M., & Stout, R., Jr. (1979). To manage is not to control. *Public Administration Review, 39,* 148-156.

McDonnell, L. M. & Elmore, R. F. (1987). Getting the job done: Alternative policy instruments. *Educational Evaluation and Policy Analysis, 9*(2), 133-152.

McLaughlin, M. W. (1987). Learning from experience: Lessons from policy implementation. *Educational Evaluation and Policy Analysis, 9*(2), 171-178.

March, J. G. & Olsen, J. P. (1983, June). Organizing political life: What administrative reorganization tells us about government. *American Political Science Review, 22,* 281-296.

Peterson, K. D. (1984, December). Mechanisms of administrative control over managers in educational organizations. *Administrative Science Quarterly, 29,* 573-579.

Rosenholtz, S. J. (1985, January). Political myths about education reform: Lessons from research on teaching. *Phi Delta Kappan, 66*(5), 349-355.

Sarason, S. B. (1986). The preparation of teachers revisited. In A. Lieberman (Ed.), *Rethinking school improvement: Research, craft, and concept.* New York: Teachers College Press, Columbia University.

Silver, P. G. (1986). Review of organizational environments: Ritual and rationality. *Educational Administration Quarterly, 22*(2), 140-143.

Weiss, J. A., & Gruber, J. E. (1984). Using knowledge for control in fragmented policy arenas. *Journal of Policy Analysis and Management, 3,* 225-247.

Wildavshy, A. (1979). *Speaking truth to power: The art and craft of policy analysis.* Boston: Little, Brown.

Chapter 4

American Council on Education. (1988). *One-third of a nation.* Washington, DC: Author.

Banks, J. A. (1981). *Multiethnic education: Theory and practice.* Boston: Allyn and Bacon.

Banks, J. A. (1984). *Teaching strategies for ethnic studies* (3rd ed.). Boston: Allyn and Bacon.

Boateng, F. F. (1986). Multicultural education in a monocultural classroom. *Viewpoint: Journal on Teaching and Learning, 6,* 2-4.

Coleman, J. et. al. (1966). *Equality of educational opportunity.* Washington, DC: Government Printing Office.

Coopersmith, S. (1975). Self-concept, race and education. In G. Verma & C. Bagley (Eds.), *Race and education across cultures.* London: Heineman.

Gollnick, D. & Chinn, P. (1986). *Multicultural education in a pluralistic society.* Columbus, OH: Charles E. Merrill.

Goodenough, W. (1976). Multiculturalism as the normal human experience. *Anthropology and Education Quarterly, 7,* 4-5.

Hale-Benson, J. (1986). *Black children, their roots, culture and learning styles.* Baltimore: John Hopkins University.

McAdoo, H. P. & McAdoo, J. W. (Eds.). (1985). *Black Children: Social, educational and parental environments.* Beverly Hills: Sage.

McDavid, J. C. (1969). *Equality of educational opportunity.* Washington, DC: Government Printing Office.

Maehr, M. & Stallings, W. (1975). *Culture, children and school.* Monterey, CA: Brooks/Cole.

Mitchell, B., Stueckle, A., & William, R. (1986). *The dynamic classroom: A creative planning approach to the teaching and evaluation process.* Dubuque, IA: Kendall Hunt.

National Alliance of Black School Educators, Inc. (1984). *Saving the African-American child.* (Report). Washington, DC: Author.

Oakes, J. (1985). *Keeping track: How schools structure inequality.* New Haven: Yale University.

Ramirez, M., & Castaneda, A. (1982). *Cultural democracy, bicognitive development and education.* New York: Academic.

Rosenberg, M. & Simmons, G. (1972). Black and white self-esteem: The urban school child. Washington, DC: *American Sociological Association, Rose monograph.*

Sadker, K. M. & Sadker, M. P. (1982). *Sex equity handbook for schools.* New York: Longmans.

Stoller, P. (1975). *Black American English.* New York: Dell.

U.S. Commission on Civil Rights. (1973). *Teachers and students: Report 5.* Washington, DC: U.S. Government Printing Office.

U.S. District Court, E. M. Mich. (1979). Martin Luther King, Jr., Elementary School Children et al. v. Ann Arbor School District Board, Civil Action No. 7-71861.

Chapter 5

Carnegie Foundation for the Advancement of Teaching. (1988). *An imperiled generation: Saving urban schools.* Princeton, NJ: Author.

Glaser, R. (1987). The integration of instruction and testing: Implications from the study of human cognition. In D. C. Berliner & B. K. Rosenshine (Eds.), *Talks to Teachers* (pp. 329-341). New York: Random House.

Fuhrman, S., Clune, W., & Elmore, R. (1988). Research on education reform: Lessons on the implementation of policy. *Teachers College Record, 90*(2), 237-257.

National Commission on Excellence in Education. (1983). *A nation at risk: The imperative for educational reform.* Washington, DC: U.S. Government Printing Office.

Sarason, S. B. (1971). *The culture of the school and the problem of change.* Boston: Allyn & Bacon.

Welch, W. W. (1979). Twenty years of science curriculum development: A look back. In D. C. Berliner (Ed.), *Review of research in education.* Washington, DC: American Educational Research Association.

Chapter 6

Children's Defense Fund. (1988). *A call for action to make our nation safe for children: A briefing book on the status of American children in 1988.* Washington, DC. Author.

Coleman, J. S. (1985). *Schools, families and children.* Ryerson Lecture, University of Chicago.

College Entrance Examination Board. (1985). *Equality and excellence: The educational status of Black Americans* (p. 6). New York: Author.

Comer, J. P. (1980). *School power.* New York: Free Press.

Comer, J. P. (1983). The need for a national racial policy: American in the 1980's. *Journal of Public and International Affairs, 3*(2), 137-150.

Comer, J. P. (1984). Home-school relationships as they affect the academic success of children. *Education and Urban Society, 6*(3), 323-327.

Committee For Economic Development. (1987). *Children in need: Investment strategies for the educationally disadvantaged.* Washington, DC. Author.

Comstock, G. (1980). *Television in America.* Beverly Hills, CA: Sage.

Edelman, M. W. (1987). *Families in peril: An agenda for social change.* Cambridge: Harvard University.

Fordham, S., & Ogbu, J. U. (1986). Black students' school success: Coping with the burden of acting white. *The Urban Review, 18*(3), 176-206.

Gordon, E. (in press). *Defiers of negative prediction.* New Haven: Yale University.

Haynes, N. M., Comer, J. P. & Hamilton-Lee, M. (1988). The school development program: A model for school improvement. *The Journal of Negro Education, 57*(1), 11-21.

Hills, T. W., & David, E. P. (1986). *Classroom motivation: Helping students want to learn and achieve in school.* Trenton, NJ: New Jersey Department of Education.

Hodgkinson, H. (1985). *All in one system: Demographics of education kindergarten through graduate school.* Washington, DC: Institute for Educational Leadership.

Jones, K. M. (1986). The Black male in jeopardy: A crisis report on the status of the Black American male. *The Crisis, 93*(3), 17-47.

McLure, S. (1986). *Guide to strategic planning for educators.* Alexandria, VA: Association for Supervision and Curriculum Development.

Maslow, A. H. (1970). *Motivation and personality* (2nd ed.). New York: Harper and Row.

People Magazine. (1988, April 4). Two decades later, heirs to a dream. pp. 34-39.

Pierce, C. M. (Ed.). (1978). *Television and education.* Beverly Hills, CA: Sage.

Rainwater, L., & Yancey, W. (Eds.). (1967). *The Moynihan report and the politics of controversy.* Cambridge, MA: Massachusetts Institute of Technology.

Singer, J. L., & Singer, D. G. (1986). Family experiences and television viewing as predictors of children's imagination, restlessness and aggression. *Journal of Social Issues, 42*(3), 167-224.

Chapter 7

Abrahams, R. D. (1970). The training of the man of words in talking sweet. *Language and Society, 1,* 15-29.

Baratz, J. (1969). Teaching reading in an urban Negro school system. In J. Baratz & R. Shuy (Eds.). *Teaching Black Children to Read* (pp. 92-116). Washington, DC: Center for Applied Linguistics.

Bennett, J. W. (1969). *Northern plainsmen: Adaptative strategy and agricultural life.* Arlington Heights, IL: AHM.

Berreman, G. D. (1972). Race, caste, and other invidious distinctions in social stratification. *Race,* 24(4).

Bond, H. M. (1966). *The education of the Negro in the American social order.* New York: Octagon Books, Inc.

Bond, H. M. (1969). *Negro education in Alabama: A study in cotton and steel.* New York: Atheneum.

Brimmer, A. F. (1974). Economic development in the Black community. In E. Ginsberg & R. M. Solow (Eds.), *The great society: Lessons for the future* (pp. 146-63). New York: Basic Books.

Bullock, H. A. (1970). *A history of Negro education in the south: From 1619 to the present.* New York: Praeger.

Bullock, P. (1973). *Aspiration vs. opportunity: "Careers" in the inner city.* Ann Arbor: Michigan University Press.

Cole, M., & Scribner, S. (1973). Cognitive consequences of formal and informal education. *Science, 182,* 553-559.

Cook-Gumperz, J., & Gumperz, J. J. (1979). From oral to written culture: The transition to literacy. In M. F. Whitehead, (Ed.) *Variation in Writing.* New York: Erlbaum Associates.

Davis, A., Burleigh, B. & Gardner, M. R. (1965). *Deep south: A social anthropological study of caste and class,* (abridged edition). Chicago; The University of Chicago Press.

Dollard, J. (1957). *Caste and class in a southern town* (3rd ed.). Garden City: Doubleday Anchor Books.

Drake, S. Clair, & Cayton, H. (1970). *Black metropolis: A study of Negro life in a northern city.* New York: Harcourt, Brace, & World. (2 vols.).

Erickson, F. (1978). *Mere ethnography: Some problems in its use in educational practice.* (1978, November). Past Presidential Address Delivered at the Annual Meeting of the Council on Anthropology and Education, Los Angeles, CA.

Erickson, F., & Mohatt, J. (1977). *The social organization of participant structure in two classrooms of Indian students.* Unpublished manuscript.

Farmer, J. (1968). Stereotypes of the Negro and their relationship to his self-image. In H. C. Rudman & L. Fetherstone (Eds.). *Urban Schooling.* New York: Harcourt, Brace, & World.

Foster, H. L. (1974). *Rinnin', jinn', and playin' the dozens: The unrecognized dilemma of inner city schools.* Cambridge, MA: Ballinger.

Frazier, E. F. (1940). *Negro youth at the crossways: Their personality development in the middle states.* Washington, DC: American Council on Education.

Geertz, C. (1962). *Agricultural involution: The process of ecological change in Indonesia.* Berkeley: University of California Press.

Ginzberg, E., Bryan, V., Hamilton, G. T., Herma, J. L., & Yohalem, A. M. (1967) *The middle-class Negro in the white man's world.* New York: Columbia University Press.

Goldschmidt, W. (1971). Introduction: The theory of cultural adaptation. In R. B. Edgerton, *The individual in cultural adaptation: A study of four east African peoples* (pp. 1-22). Berkeley: University of California Press.

Goody, J. (1977). *The domestication of the savage mind.* Cambridge: Cambridge University Press.

Greenfield, P. M. (1966). On culture and conservation. In J. S. Bruner, et al. (Eds.). *Studies in cognitive growth* (pp. 225-56). New York: Wiley.

Gumperz, J. J. (1980). Conversational inferences and classroom learning. In J. Green & C. Wallat (Eds.), *Ethnographic approaches to face-to-face interaction.* Ablex Pub. Co.

Harrison, B. (1972). *Education, training and the urban ghetto.* Baltimore, MD: The Johns Hopkins University Press.

Heard, N. C. (1968). *Howard Street.* New York: Dial Press.

Henderson, V. W. (1967). Regions, race and jobs. In A. M. Ross & H. Hill (Eds.), (pp. 76-104). *Employment, race and poverty.* New York: Harcourt, Brace, & World.

Heyneman, S. P. (1979). Why impoverished children do well in Ugandan schools. *Comparative Education, 15,* 175-185.

Jencks, C. (1972). *Inequality.* New York: Basic Books.

Koehler, V. (1978). Classroom process research: Present and future. *The Journal of Classroom Interaction, 13,* 3-11.

Kochman, T. (1973). Orality and literacy as factors in 'Black' and 'white' communicative behavior. *International Journal of the Sociology of Language,* 91-115.

Kluger, R. (1969). The logic of nonstandard English. *Georgetown University Monographs in Language and Linguistics, 72,* 1-31.

Kluger, R. (1972). *Language in the inner city.* Philadelphia: University of Pennsylvania Press.

Kluger, R. (1977). *Simple justice.* New York: Vintage Books.

Lewis, D. K. (1979). *Schooling, literacy and sense modality.* U.S. Santa Cruz. Unpublished manuscript.

Luria, A. R. (1976). *Cognitive development: Its cultural and social foundations.* Cambridge, MA: Harvard University Press.

Milner, C. A. (1970). *Black pimps and their prostitutes.* Unpublished doctoral dissertation, Department of Anthropology, University of California, Berkeley.

Myrdal, G. (1944). *An American dilemma* (Vol. 2). New York: Harper.

The National Advisory Commission on Civil Disorders (1968). *Report.* Washington, DC: U.S. Government Printing Office.

Netting, R. M. (1968). *Hill farmers of Nigeria.* Seattle: University of Washington Press.

Newman, D. K. et al. (1978). *Protest, politics, and prosperity: Black Americans and white institutions. 1940-1975.* New York: Pantheon Books.

Norgren, P. H., & Hill, S. E. (1964). *Toward fair employment.* New York: Columbia University Press.

Ogbu, J. U. (1974). *The next generation: An ethnography of education in an urban neighborhood.* New York: Academic Press.

Ogbu, J. U. (1978). *Minority education and caste: The American system in crosscultural perspective.* New York: Academic Press.

Ogbu, J. U. (1979). *Origins of human competence: A cultural ecological perspective.* Unpublished manuscript.

Ogbu, J. U. (1980a). *An ecological approach to minority education.*

Ogbu, J. U. (1980b). *Ethnoecology of urban schooling.* Unpublished manuscript.

Pepper, S. (1971). Education and political development in Communist China. *Studies in Comparative Communism, 3,* (3, 4).

Philips, S. U. (1972). Participant structure and communicative competence: Warm Springs children in community and classrooms. In C. B. Cazden, V. P. John, & S. Hymes (Eds.), *Functions of language in the classroom.* New York: Teacher's College Press.

Powdermaker, H. (1968). *After freedom.* New York: Atheneum.

Rentel, V., & Kennedy, J. (1972). Effects of pattern drill on the phonology, syntax, and reading achievement of rural Appalachian children. *American Educational Research Journal, 9,* 87-100.

Ross, A. M., Hill, H. (Eds.). (1967). *Employment, race and poverty.* New York: Harcourt, Brace & World.

Schemer, G. (1965). Effectiveness of equal opportunity legislation. H. N. Northrup & R. L. Rowan (Eds.), *The Negro employment opportunity,* (pp. 67-107). Ann Arbor: University of Michigan Press.

Schulz, D. A. (1969). *Coming up Black.* Englewood, Cliffs, NJ: Prentice-Hall.

Scott, J. W. (1976). *The Black revolt.* Cambridge, MA: Schenkman.

Scrupski, A. (1975). The social system of the school. In K. Shimahara & A. Scrupski (Eds.). *Social Forces and Schooling.* New York: McKay.

Sharp, L. M. (1970). *Education and employment.* Baltimore, MD: Johns Hopkins University Press.

Simons, H. D. (1976). *Black dialect, reading interference and classroom interaction.* Department of Education, University of California, Berkeley. Unpublished manuscript.

Slawski, E. J. & Scherer, J. (1977). The rhetoric of concern—trust and control in an urban desegregated school. *Anthropology and Education Quarterly,* 9(1).

Snow, E. (1961). *Red star over China.* New York: Grove Press, Inc.

Stewart, W. A. (1969). On the use of Negro dialect in the teaching of reading. In J. Baratz & R. Shuy (Eds.), *Teaching Black children to read* (pp. 156-219). Washington DC: Center for Applied Linguistics.

U.S. Commission on Civil Rights. (1978). *Social indicators of equality for minorities and women.* Washington, DC: U.S. Government Printing Office.

U.S. Commission on Civil Rights. (1974). *Bilingual/bicultural education: A privilege or a right?* Washington, DC: U.S. Government Printing Office.

U.S. District Court for Northern California. (1979). *Opinion: Larry P. vs. Riles.* San Francisco, CA.

van der Berghe, P. (1979). Review: *Minority education and caste. Comparative Education Review.*

Warner, W. L.; Havighurst, R. J.; Loeb, M. B. (1945). *Who shall be educated?* New York: Harper.

Weinberg, M. (1977). *A chance to learn: A history of race and education in the United States.* New York: Cambridge University Press.

Wilcox, K. (1978). *Schooling and socialization for work roles.* Unpublished doctoral dissertation, Department of Anthropology, Harvard University.

Willie, C. V. (Ed.). (1979). *Caste and class controversy.* New York: Green Hall, Inc.

Wilson, H. C. (1973). On the evolution of education. In S. T. Kimball & J. H. Burnett (Eds.), *Learning and Culture* (pp. 211-41). Seattle: University of Washington Press.

Wilson, W. J. (1978). *The declining significance of race.* Chicago: University of Chicago Press.

Wolfe, T. (1970). *Radical chic and mau-mauing the flack catchers.* New York: Strauss and Giroux.

Chapter 8

American Psychological Association, American Educational Research Association, National Council on Measurement in Education. (1974). *Standards for Educational and Psychological Tests.* Washington, DC: American Psychological Association.

Glass, G. V. (1983). Effectiveness of special education. *Policy Studies Review,* 2,1.

Gould, S. (1981). *The mismeasure of man.* New York: Norton.

Heller, K., Holtzman, W., & Messick, S. (1982). *Placing children in special education: A strategy for equity.* Washington, DC: National Academy Press.

Hilliard, A. G., III. (1982). The sociopolitical implications of minimum competency testing. In J. Neel & S. W. Goldwasser (Eds.), *Minimum competency education: Issues, methodology and policy for local school systems* (pp. 88-106). Atlanta: Department of Educational Foundations, Georgia State University.

Hoover, M. R., Politzer, R. L., & Taylor, O. (1987). Bias in reading for Black language speakers: A sociolinguistic perspective. *The Negro Educational Review, 38*, 2-3, 81-98.

Kamin, L. (1974). *The science and politics of I.Q.* New York: John Wiley.

Kaufman, A. S., & Kaufman, N. L. (1983). *Kaufman assessment battery for children.* Circle Pines, NM: American Guidance Service.

Lomotey, K. (1989). Cultural diversity in the urban school: Implications for principals. *NASSP Bulletin, 73*(521), 81-88.

Lomotey, K., & Swanson, A. (1990). Restructuring school governance: Learning from the experiences of urban and rural schools. In S. L. Jacobson & J. A. Conway (Eds.), *Educational leadership in an age of reform* (pp. 65-82). White Plains: Longman.

Messick, S. (1980). *The effectiveness and coaching for the SAT: Review and reanalysis of research from the fifties to the FTC.* Princeton, NJ: Educational Testing Service.

Chapter 9

The College Entrance Examination Board. (1983). *Facts about the usefulness of the Scholastic Aptitude Test in the admissions process.* New York: Author.

Fleming, J. (1984). *Blacks in college.* San Francisco, CA: Jossey-Bass.

Fleming, J. (1985). *The usefulness of standardized test scores in the Black college environment.* (Report to the Southern Education Foundation, United Negro College Fund).

Miller, D. M., & O'Conner, P. (1969). Achiever personality and academic success among disadvantaged college students. *Journal of Social Issues, 25*(3), 103-116.

Morehouse College. (1984). *Computational cohort: Freshman predicted index.* Atlanta, GA: Author.

Ramist, L. (1984). [Personal communication with the Educational Testing Service].

Temp, G. (1971). Validity of the SAT for Blacks and whites in thirteen integrated institutions. *Journal of Educational Measurement, 8,* 245-251.

Willingham, W. W. & Breland, H. M. (1982). *Personal qualities and college admissions.* Eric Document 215636.

Xavier University of Louisiana. (1984). *Student success at Xavier* [Institutional Research]. New Orleans, LA: Author.

Chapter 10

Edmonds, R. R. (1979). Some schools work and more can. *Social Policy, 9,* 28-32.

Morris, M. D. (1975). *The politics of Black America.* New York: Harper & Row, pp. 70-89.

Sizemore, B. A. (1972). Social science and education for a Black identity. In J. A. Banks, & J. D. Grambs (Eds.) *Black self-concept* (pp. 141-170). New York: McGraw-Hill.

Sizemore, B. A. (1985). Pitfalls and promises of effective schools research. *Journal of Negro Education, 54,* 269-288.

Sizemore, B. A. (1987). The effective African-American elementary school. In G. W. Noblit & W. T. Pink (Eds.), *Schooling in social context: Qualitative studies* (pp. 175-202). Norwood, NJ: Ablex.

Sizemore, B. A., Brossard, C. A., & Harrigan, B. (1983). *An abashing anomaly: Three high achieving predominantly Black elementary schools* (Grant #G-80-0006). Washington, DC: National Institute of Education.

Weick, K. E. (1976). Educational organizations as loosely coupled systems. *Administrative Science Quarterly, 21,* 1-19.

Chapter 11

Beady, C. H., & Hansell, S. (1981). Teacher, race and expectation for student achievement. *American Educational Research Journal, 18,* 191-206.

DeGuire, M. R. (1980). The role of the elementary principal in influencing reading achievement. Unpublished doctoral. University of Colorado at Boulder.

Edmonds, R. (1979). Effective schools for the urban poor. *Educational Leadership, 40,* 4-11.

Kochman, T. (1981). *Black and white styles in conflict.* Chicago: University of Chicago.

LeCompte, M. D., & Goetz, J. P. (1982). Problems of reliability and validity in ethnographic research. *Review of Educational Research, 52,* 31-60.

Lightfoot, S. L. (1983). *The good high school,* New York: Basic.

Lomotey, K. (1989). *African-American principals: School leadership and success.* Westport, CT: Greenwood.

MacLennan, B. W. (1975). The personalities of group leaders: Implications for selecting and training. *International Journal of Group Psychology, 25,* 177-183.

Mintzberg, H. (1973). *The nature of managerial work.* New York: Harper and Row.

Rist, R. (1970). Student social class and teacher expectations: The self-fulfilling prophecy in ghetto education. *Harvard Educational Review, 40,* 411-451.

Wellisch, J. B., MacQueen, A. H., Carriere, R. A., & Duck, G. A. (1978). School management and organization in successful schools. *Sociology of Education, 51,* 211-226.

Wilson, K. (1982). An effective school principal. *Educational Leadership, 39,* 357-361.

Chapter 12

Bennett, W. J. (1987). *James Madison High School: A curriculum for American students*. Washington, DC: U.S. Government Printing Office.

Bond, H. M. (1976). *Education for freedom: A history of Lincoln University*. Lincoln, PA: Lincoln University, p. 6.

Congressional Budget Office. (1987). *Educational achievement: Explanation and implications of recent trends*. Washington, DC: U.S. Government Printing Office, pp. 91-95.

Fiske, E. (1988, February 17). Standardized test scores: Voodoo statistics? *The New York Times*, p. B9.

The National Commission on Excellence in Education. (1983). *A nation at risk*. Washington, DC: U.S. Government Printing Office.

Office of Educational Research and Improvement. (1987). *Dealing with dropouts: The urban superintendents' call to action*. Washington, DC: U.S. Government Printing Office.

Orfield, G. (1982). Working paper: *Desegregation of Black and Hispanic students from 1968-1980*. Washington, DC: Joint Center for Political Studies. Unpublished manuscript.

Ratteray, J. D., & Shujaa, M. (1987). *Dare to choose: Parental choice at independent neighborhood schools*. Washington, DC: Institute for Independent Education.

Thompson, C. H. (1938, May). 75 years of Negro education. *The Crisis, 45,* 203.

Wesley, C. H. (1983). *Prince Hall: Life and legacy* (2nd ed.). Chicago: Drew Sales Lodge Regalia.

Chapter 13

DuBois, W. E. (1961). *The souls of Black folk*. Greenwich, CT: Fawcett. (Originally written 1903).

Ebony Magazine. (1987, November, pp. 68-74). Interview with August Wilson.

Hale-Benson, J. (1986). *Black children: Their roots, culture and learning styles*. Baltimore, MD: The Johns Hopkins University.

Lein, L. (1975). Black American migrant children: Their speech at home and school. *Council on Anthropology and Education Quarterly, 6,* 1-11.

Rashid, H. M. (1981). Early childhood education as a cultural transition for African-American children. *Educational Research Quarterly, 6,* 55-63.

Index